Sign Language Interpreters in Court:

Understanding Best Practices

by

Carla M. Mathers

Bloomington, IN Milton Keynes, UK

authorHOUSE

AuthorHouse™
1663 Liberty Drive, Suite 200
Bloomington, IN 47403
www.authorhouse.com
Phone: 1-800-839-8640

AuthorHouse™ UK Ltd.
500 Avebury Boulevard
Central Milton Keynes, MK9 2BE
www.authorhouse.co.uk
Phone: 08001974150

First published by AuthorHouse 4/3/2007

ISBN: 1-4259-2341-0 (sc)
ISBN: 1-4259-2342-9 (hc)
Library of Congress Control Number: 2006902862

Printed in the United States of America
Bloomington, Indiana

This book is printed on acid-free paper.

Acknowledgements

To those who helped -- Julie Abbate, Keri Brewer, Jan Castleberry, Diane Fowler, Darlene Hubbard, Jackie Keizer, Kristin Lund, Pat Mathers, Bob Mathers, James McCollum, Pasch McCombs, Audrey McKinney, Nancy Riley, Roylnn Serati – my deepest appreciation. Some of you were always up to talking about the adventures of "Terp A," while others gave me the guidance, support and encouragement to be a lawyer, a person and have a life. No mean feat.

Table of Contents

Chapter 1
Introduction to Court Interpreting

Chapter 1
Introduction to Court Interpreting

I.   Legal Interpreting Defined -- Court Interpreting
     Distinguished

It is impractical to attempt to arrive at a specific definition of legal interpreting. Legal interpreting, amorphous at times, encompasses more than working in the courtroom, the law office, or the police station. Rather, legal interpreting entails a wide range of situations in which the deaf person or the non-English speaking person ("**NES**[1]") comes into contact with an enforceable set of rules governing civil conduct in this country. Often in assignments not remotely anticipated to be legal, interpreters find themselves faced with challenges presenting legal overtones. Much of the general practitioner's daily interpreting fare has legal implications. As a result, the study of principles and practices of legal and court interpreting will benefit the private practice interpreter as well as the legal specialist.

On the broadest level, legal interpreting includes work in such diverse settings as reading a will in a law office; interviewing a victim with the police at the scene of a crime; administering a rape kit with medical personnel in a hospital; witnessing the execution of a power of attorney with a case manager in a hospice; or interviewing a deaf person seeking political asylum with a human rights worker. The interpreter faces potential legal consequences while interpreting

---

[1] Terms and phrases noted in bold are defined in the Glossary at Appendix A.

an Individualized Educational Plan meeting where a deaf student's educational program is negotiated; a seminar by a Human Relations manager regarding downsizing or retirement benefits at a staff meeting; or a video relay call from a deaf tenant to a landlord to discuss an imminent eviction. Court ordered parenting classes, therapeutic programs for sex offenders and alcohol or drug treatment programs have legal overtones in the sense that the parties are compelled to be there, may not have any right to privacy with respect to disclosures made in those settings, and will face legal consequences for a failure to participate. Obviously, community interpreting includes many settings that posses inherent legal ramifications. Today's legal interpreter is truly a jack of all trades.

Court interpreting is simply one subset of the larger arena known as legal interpreting. Court interpreting is different from the wider spectrum of legal interpreting because of the setting in which court interpreting transpires and the unique set of procedural rules the court interpreter must know and follow. Court interpreting is governed by ethical rules, cases, codes and judicial decisions that are typically absent with other forms of interpreting. As a result, court interpreting presents a new paradigm for the professional interpreter to internalize and apply. The aim of this text is to present a description, analysis and synthesis of court interpreting through discussion of case law, court rules, ethics codes and statutes that have guided the practice and development of court interpreting in the United States.[1]

II. Competency: It's Not Like Sharpening a Pencil

Court interpreting may be one of the most challenging areas in which an American Sign Language ("**ASL**") interpreter can work. The density of information, the unique context with its special rules, strange language and the serious consequences hinging on the interpreter's ability to perform the job effectively make court interpreting a daunting task. Given the potential impact that the quality of interpreting can have on the deaf person's life, it is wise to enter the field with caution and circumspect.

The interpreter must master a number of knowledge and skill competencies to practice effective court interpreting. In addition to being competent ASL-English interpreters, court interpreters must have a basic understanding of the law, as it relates to interpreting, and of the substantive legal areas in which they interpret. Interpreters must be comfortable with the standard practices and protocol that derive from ethical codes written by courts for all language interpreters.

Court interpreters must be flexible, articulate, diplomatic and capable of quick thinking in sometimes stressful situations. At times, the interpreter will need to quickly and succinctly state the reasons for a specific point related to an interpreting need. Interpreters will find it helpful to be able to speak in the same register as is used in the courtroom because the message will be received more favorably if it is spoken in language familiar to the court. Court interpreters must be familiar with the way language is used in the legal system and internalize some of these strategies for verbal interaction. This might be as simple as knowing how to seek permission to approach the bench when an interpreting issue arises, or as involved as knowing how to make a statement for the record disclosing a perceived conflict of interest. In any event, many of the ways that judges, attorneys, clerks, bailiffs, social workers and other participants interact during a proceeding are extremely instructive and should be incorporated by court interpreters.

In part, interpreters must know the **legal authority** under which they have been appointed to work. Interpreters must develop the ability to make rational arguments with solid bases to justify their positions. Whether the interpreter is explaining the need to retain a deaf interpreter for a case or the reason consecutive interpreting is required for deaf witness testimony, it is helpful to have the mental agility and wherewithal to support an argument with some persuasive authority, rationale or reasoning: In other words, the interpreter must be able to articulate the **textual support** to justify their points. This skill must be arduously cultivated, yet the task is not insurmountable. Many ASL court interpreters have successfully accomplished the undertaking.

Interpreters must be prepared to meet a variety of challenges in court interpreting. When courts are left to their own devices, the working conditions can become unmanageable and not conducive to effective interpreting. It is unrealistic to expect most courts to be familiar with the ASL court interpreter's work. In October, 2005, the author contacted the Americans with Disabilities Act ("ADA") coordinator at the local trial court to request an interpreter, the person was confused, until she realized, as she put it, that the author was talking about someone to do "hand stuff and waving." If it is too much to expect one who holds a position of ADA coordinator to have even the most basic understanding, it may also be too much to expect from typical trial judges. As a result, much of the quality assurance in court interpreting must come from the integrity of the individual interpreter.

In part, courts can be forgiven for not having a working knowledge of ASL interpreting and deaf people. Sign language interpreting is a relatively rare occurrence for most judges who are much more familiar with the spoken language interpreting model. The interpreter must feel comfortable taking control, inserting himself or herself into the process, and relating a need or distinguishing a spoken language interpreting practice. When the interpreter is intimidated or hesitant to make the record, the opportunity for a successful interpretation is lost.

One federal case shows the general ignorance about language interpretation and the process. [2] In the case, the victim spoke Korean but understood some English. Defense counsel, when asked if he would consent to the use of the interpreter for the witness, stated "that he had no objection to the appointment of [the interpreter] if she was simply going to stand by and to assist, but that he would object if all questions to [the witness] and her answers thereto were to be filtered through the interpreter." [3] The prosecutor agreed to this *ad hoc* arrangement. No one asked the interpreter as to the effectiveness of permitting the interpreter to stand by and read the witness' mind as to when interpretation was needed. The author once saw a judge order the interpreter to sit in the jury box at a right angle to the deaf party who was ordered to sit in the audience. This type of conduct demonstrates a basic misunderstanding and distrust of interpreters. Additionally, it underscores the lack of control that interpreters have over their working conditions. Through preparation and through negotiating working conditions prior to accepting work, court interpreters can successfully realize terms and conditions conducive to the task of effective interpreting.

It should be obvious that a competent court interpreter must be willing to be a life-long student. Although court interpreting most likely constitutes a small proportion of many sign language interpreters' private practice, the study required to interpret effectively in court is extensive. The effort expended might, at first blush, appear to outweigh the return on the investment. However, court interpreting has always attracted the best and the brightest in the field of ASL interpreting. Court interpreting provides a fertile source of brain food for those whose stock and trade is cognitive, yet who have been afforded little opportunity for active involvement as an independent participant to the interaction.

III. Fluency: Something Less Than Murder

Recent training recognizes that an interpreter cannot expect to master this subspecialty in a short-term intensive course. Likewise, one text cannot necessarily include all areas of knowledge and skill needed by the court interpreter. A text, like a class, can help identify tools and resources for self-study and further development. In fact, much training includes providing extensive resources and tools for continued individual skill development – implicitly acknowledging the difficulty of providing adequate skills development during a "drive-by" training session.

Though traditionally most training has consisted of short intensive seminars, interpreters obtain further education themselves conferencing online and in-person in large and small groups.[4] The post-secondary establishment has only recently begun to offer longer term training through online education.[5] Interpreters have developed their skills on an individual level by identifying mentors: both more experienced sign language interpreters and deaf consultants for language development. Interpreters have formed study groups to prepare for the advanced certification evaluation. In groups or individually, interpreters have observed court proceedings and interacted with lawyers and judges to gain insight into the law and into the legal profession's perspective on interpreters and deaf people in court. Interpreters have sought out opportunities to observe local law enforcement practices in their communities. Overall, court interpreters have done remarkably well, without formal post-secondary institutional support, in educating themselves to become competent and consistent practitioners.

In the field of interpreting, it is axiomatic that to interpret, one must first understand. Accordingly, sign language interpreters realize that they must constantly strive to develop their understanding of the legal system, its discourse strategies, unique vocabulary, grammar, procedures, culture and rules. Court interpreters must also develop natural ASL constructs for talking about legal events when the dispute resolution system in the deaf community is governed by a different schema than that of the American legal system. The literature in the field has documented that many interpreters have significant difficulty comprehending and producing grammatically correct ASL.[6] The need for language fluency and generic interpreting competency cannot be over-emphasized. Interpreters who hold themselves out to the community as legal interpreters must engage in honest self-examination to assess their ASL skills and embrace the associated obligation to fully develop those skills.

To their credit, courts are beginning to understand, or at least pay lip service to, the complexity of the task assigned to an interpreter. As one court recognized "[a person] is not necessarily competent to translate legal proceedings because he or she is bilingual."[7] This court expressed an enlightened view of the interpreter's charge: "Courtroom interpretation is a sophisticated art, demanding not only a broad vocabulary, instant recall, and continuing judgment as to the speaker's intended meaning, but also the ability to reproduce tone and nuance, and a good working knowledge of both legal terminology and street slang."[8]

When interpreters do not have the requisite level of skill, or when they put ego and pride before effective interpretation, then they cause problems for the courts, for deaf consumers and for other interpreters. As pointed out earlier, many ASL interpreters are simply not that good at ASL.[9] However, courts are unaware of the skill differences and unfortunately are often soothed when told of the plethora of certifications. Sadly, the assumption persists that if one is bilingual, one can also interpret. If the person holds some credential, then the court gains a sense of confidence in their skill.[10]

Simply stated, advanced skills are required for court interpreting. Frequently, interpreters are pressured to work in courts before they have the requisite skill level or training because the courts, referral services and schedulers do not necessarily understand what is required to interpret effectively in court. The courtroom is no place for a new interpreter to develop their skills. One Oregon case demonstrated the technical expertise that a court interpreter must possess to avoid jeopardizing the defendant's right to a fundamentally fair trial.[11] The appeal was based on the interpreter's incorrect interpretation of the **mens rea** or mental element in a plea to manslaughter. Manslaughter was defined, in relevant part, as a "criminal homicide . . . committed recklessly under circumstances manifesting extreme indifference to the value of human life."[12] The mental element was "reckless" or "extreme indifference." The interpreter interpreted the mental element as "something less than murder" – obviously a gross oversimplification of a complex concept in criminal law.

The defendant prevailed on appeal with his claim that he did not knowingly enter a plea because he was uninformed of the mental state requirement because of the deficient interpretation.[13] The importance of interpreter training in the substantive areas of law in addition to the other aspects of court interpreting which make it unique cannot be overstated. Interpreters might be tempted to gloss over, omit, simplify or otherwise misinterpret difficult or incomprehensible vocabulary; however, this is done at great risk to the defendant and to the profession.

Use of an unqualified interpreter with limited ethical boundaries can also cause disastrous results for deaf litigants as demonstrated by one federal employee's discrimination case.[14] A deaf woman filed an employment case with the **EEOC** because she was disciplined allegedly for exhibiting insulting, demeaning and discourteous behavior towards a supervisor. Apparently during an interpreted conversation with the supervisor, the deaf woman used the sign for "crazy." The interpreter rendered the message as "the supervisor was crazy." The deaf woman accused the interpreter of misinterpreting.

In another incident, the same deaf woman and the same staff interpreter were involved in a physical altercation. The interpreter alleged that the deaf woman was "poking and prodding her in the arm with stiffened fingers."[15] The employer disciplined the employee. During the disciplinary interview, the employee requested an outside ASL interpreter to be provided as required by agency rules. The employer refused the request. For the meeting, the deaf woman was forced to use the same staff interpreter who had been involved in the physical alteration and who had been accused of the misinterpretation.

The EEOC found that the agency had discriminated against the deaf employee. The employer should have used an impartial outside interpreter for the interview to get the deaf woman's side of the story. In fact, the EEOC found that the employer was wrong in concluding that the employee had called her supervisor crazy:

> The supervisor refused even to entertain the possibility that the interpreter had erred, stating that she (the supervisor) knew what the "crazy" gesture meant. However, the sign for "crazy" had to be accompanied by some other sign – either "situation" or "woman" – to complete the thought. The supervisor did not profess to know either of those signs, leaving only the [deaf woman's] word against that of the interpreter as to whether [the] statement had been correctly interpreted.[16]

The interpreter's credential only qualified her to interpret in one-on-one settings and the **quality assurance** guidelines strongly suggested that an individual at this level only function under the supervision of a fully qualified interpreter.[17] Further two other deaf co-workers had criticized the interpreter as having inadequate and insufficient interpreting skills to meet their needs.[18]

Although the interpreting took place in the employment context, it sparked a legal proceeding. The disciplinary interviews with the deaf employee also constituted quasi-legal interpreting. The interpreter knew she was only rated for certain settings, and ethically had a conflict of interest in interpreting the disciplinary hearing. Why an interpreter would remain in this setting knowing that at least three consumers were not satisfied with her skills is a troubling question.

When ego and pride control the interpreter's thought processes, deaf people will bear the brunt of the poor decision-making. When it happens in a court room, the consequences are severe. Most interpreter ethics require the interpreter to remove himself or herself from a setting in which they feel their skills are inadequate or in which they have ethical conflicts. The National Center for State Courts ("**NCSC**") Code of Professional Responsibility governing court interpreters suggests that at times even highly qualified interpreters will be situationally unqualified and should feel no compunction at all about removing themselves when to do so will enhance justice and fairness in the process.[19] These ethical provisions must be adhered to with rigor.

IV. Certification: The Hallmark of a Professional

The definitive credential for a court interpreter traditionally has been the Specialist Certificate: Legal ("**SC: L**") awarded by the Registry of Interpreters for the Deaf ("**RID**"). According to the RID, "SC: L certification requires the successful completion of three steps: documentation of eligibility (prior education, training, and experience), a written (knowledge) examination, and a performance examination. Successful completion of each step is required before entering the next step."[20] The current process permits grandfathering of specialist certificate holders who obtained their certification prior to 1987; new applicants must complete the three steps mentioned. With respect to the mix of educational, training and experiential requirements, as of 2005, the RID has created four categories to define eligibility:

> Category #1 - Possess valid RID certified membership. Successful completion of BA or BS in any field or AA in interpreting. Five years general interpreting experience (post RID Certification) strongly recommended. Documentation of at least fifty hours of legal interpreting/mentoring experience, thirty hours of formal legal training.
>
> Category #2 - Possess valid RID certified membership. Successful completion of AA in any field. Five years general interpreting experience (post RID Certification) strongly recommended. Documentation of at least 75 hours of legal

interpreting/mentoring experience. Fifty hours of legal training.

Category #3 - Possess valid RID certified membership. Five years general interpreting experience (post RID Certification) strongly recommended. Documentation of at least 100 hours of legal interpreting/mentoring experience and 70 hours of legal training.

Category #4 - Possess current SC: L (Do not need to re-take the test, but are invited to do so.).[21]

According to the RID, "[t]he written examination is a one hundred question multiple choice examination focusing on four content areas: Legal language, the judicial system, team interpreting issues and professionalism."[22] The organization lists the following subsets and specific areas of examination on the written test:

I. Language

    a. Legal terms and phrases

    b. Challenges that legal language presents for accurate interpretation (e.g. double negatives, convoluted syntax, rights waiver)

    c. Powerless language forms within the judicial system and implications for the interpreting process

    d. Types of cultural and linguistic adjustments required when working with ASL and English in the judicial system

    e. Interpreting issues arising from the status of linguistic minorities in the judicial system

    f. Strategies for addressing interpreting issues associated with limited/minimal language competence

    g. Interpreting techniques used with consumers with limited/minimal language competence

h. Strategies/techniques for determining interpretation needs

i. Implications of age of consumer for the interpreting process

II. Judicial System

    a. Law enforcement procedures (e.g. interrogations, victim/witness statements)

    b. Miranda Warning

    c. Courtroom procedures and logistics

    d. Criminal judicial system features and processes, from point of initiation through the trial process

    e. Civil judicial system features and processes, from point of initiation through the trial process

    f. Judicial (e.g., juvenile/family court) and quasi-judicial (e.g., administrative hearings, parole

    g. Laws regulating the right to an interpreter in the federal, state, and local judicial systems

    h. Roles and responsibilities of judicial personnel (e.g., interpreter, district attorney, judge, public defender, bailiff, reporter)

III. Team Interpreting

    a. Principals and protocol of hearing/hearing team interpreting within the legal realm

    b. Principals and protocol of Deaf/hearing team interpreting within the legal realm

IV. Professional Issues

    a. Local, state, and federal legislation regarding interpreters

    b. Ethical issues related to the interpretation in the legal realm

    c. Liability issues related to the interpretations of judicial proceedings

    d. Models of interpreting

The test is stringent and examines a wide range of interpreter competencies for court and legal interpreting. While caution and constant self-monitoring are always advisable, the interpreter and the community cannot afford to wait until receiving a specialist certificate before entering the court room. For a variety of pragmatic reasons, waiting until an interpreter is credentialed prior to working in court or legal settings is not feasible. First, in order to sit for the test, one must demonstrate a certain number of hours of legal interpreting experience.[23] Second, though far better than in the past, the test is still not widely available. Third, many areas struggle with finding *any* certified interpreter; at press time, the RID listed only 141 interpreters nationwide holding the SC: L. If only SC: L certified interpreters could work in court, many deaf people would be left without services.

For effective interpreting, ASL interpreters should, at a minimum, hold a generalist certificate demonstrating competency in ASL interpreting and have legal interpreter education. The task of court interpreting is extremely difficult. Interpreters must be competent interpreters before entering the legal field. Even then, the challenges to providing an effective interpretation are great. An argument exists that dynamic equivalence in interpreting may not be completely possible in the courtroom due to the complexity of the discourse and the infrequency in which ASL interpreters find themselves in court. Surely, dynamic, pragmatic or legal equivalence in interpreting is not possible if the interpreter does not possess the language skills in either language to communicate fluently. The interpreter needs to have not only exemplary ASL and spoken English skills, but also the ability to discuss in both languages a wide array of topics in a culturally appropriate manner that one faces in the legal system. Foundational language skills are as essential as superior interpreting skills.

Interpreters often ask whether an interpreter can truly understand legal discourse without a law degree. The answer lies in adequate training, education, mentoring, observations, experience and self-study. Education is a life long process, which ASL interpreters are already well adapted to undertake.[24] Currently, an RID certified interpreter who holds a generalist certificate with the appropriate legal training can function effectively in court and approximate equivalence in interpreting. Once that interpreter has satisfied the RID prerequisites, he or she can sit for the specialist legal evaluation. Ultimately, the interpreter who holds the specialist certificate in legal interpreting has peer-reviewed, verified credentials and should be qualified for most legal settings.

As mentioned, this text focuses primarily on court interpreting – a subset of legal interpreting. Certain legal interpreting assignments, such as working in law enforcement settings, do not follow the general principles outlined in this text and should properly be treated at length elsewhere. Further, the principles and analyses suggested in this text, apply in the main, regardless of whether the interpreter is deaf or is hearing. Working with a certified deaf interpreter in court presents unique procedural challenges to obtain optimal working conditions. Although merited, an in-depth consideration of those issues is not included here. However, for the most part the deaf interpreter will benefit from the discussions presented in this text as much as the interpreter who can hear. With these preparatory remarks completed, the next chapter will address the development of the right to an interpreter in court. Chapters 3 through 6 will explore the fundamental legal principles that affect many of the decisions made by the court interpreter.

Chapter 2
Legal Right to an Interpreter

Chapter 2
Legal Right to an Interpreter

I. Constitutional Protections

There is no federal constitutional right to an interpreter. It should not be surprising that the Constitution is silent regarding the rights of linguistic minorities given the traditional ethnocentric character of the country. In the years since the founding fathers penned the Constitution, courts have had the opportunity to interpret it to provide various linguistic procedural protections to NES persons during criminal trials. At the same time courts have traditionally been unwilling to label those protections full-fledged constitutional rights. Though the distinction may seem technical, declaring that a constitutional process requires the provision of interpreters is not the same thing as saying there is an across-the-board constitutional right to an interpreter.

When the Constitution has been interpreted to require language access, the issue is typically framed in terms of the Sixth Amendment's requirements that one charged with a crime is present during the proceedings and able to assist counsel which would mean little without communicative access.[1] An early federal case addressing the right to an interpreter illustrates the standard rhetoric courts use to discuss the right to an interpreter:

> Clearly, the right to confront witnesses would be meaningless
> if the accused could not understand their testimony, and
> the effectiveness of cross-examination would be severely

hampered. The right to an interpreter rests most fundamentally, however, on the notion that no defendant should face the Kafkaesque spectre of an incomprehensible ritual which may terminate in punishment.[2]

Likewise, the Fourteenth Amendment's due process clause has been used to require the provision of interpreting services, though the actual Amendment does not explicitly mention language access.[3] ✷ Rather, due process requires that a criminal trial be conducted in a manner that is fundamentally fair. Due process requires more than subjecting a person to proceedings he or she cannot understand. ✷

As mentioned, federal courts have been careful to warn that they are not creating new constitutional rights in these cases. Rather, the courts speak of protections established to enforce existing constitutional rights. Two states, New Mexico and California offer more protection to NES persons at the state level than the federal Constitution provides. California and New Mexico have enacted state constitutional amendments establishing the right to an interpreter for non-English speaking persons.[4] Additionally, some states have set forth policies not rising to the level of a constitutional right but which expressly recognize the right to an interpreter. Accordingly, "the legislatures of Minnesota, Nebraska, Oregon, and Washington have declared that, as a matter of public policy, the constitutional rights of a [non-English speaking] defendant are to be protected by access to an interpreter."[5] Though public policy provides some measure of security, it does not offer the same level of protection afforded by a constitutional right.

Hence, the United States Constitution, state constitutions and both federal and state statutes and policy statements are sources of law that provide differing levels and types of language access in criminal settings. By sheer volume, most of the cases reported are spoken language interpreting cases. However; the principles set forth in spoken language cases have been cited as **precedent** in cases involving deaf litigants.[6] In the event that a specific principle has not been applied to an ASL interpreting case, the arguments are still analogous because the interpreting process undertaken by any language interpreter involves essentially the same cognitive processing. The primary difference with ASL interpreting is that there is an additional modality aspect of interpreting in a visual language that is not present in spoken language interpreting. As well, the deaf community is generally indigenous to the United States which confers certain rights not available to all NES people. The ability to analogize from spoken language interpreting cases to sign language interpreting cases is a skill that is tremendously helpful to ASL interpreters.

II. Federal Statutory Protections

The entitlement to interpreting services for deaf and hard of hearing people has traditionally been thought of as an accommodation to the physical disability of an otherwise cultural American. This paradigm has both positive and negative implications: Deaf persons are accorded interpreters in a wider array of life activities than NES people. However, deaf people are typically excluded from many of the important scholarly works and legal literature regarding the rights of language minorities.

Courts and attorneys, at times, attempt to distinguish the applicability of NES case principles to deaf cases because of the language differences. No logical basis for this distinction exists based on linguistic differences alone. However, other reasons may be asserted for the distinction since users of spoken language interpreters may not be United States citizens, and consequently, may be entitled to fewer protections than deaf citizens. Even NES citizens are commonly excluded from jury service because they do not know English. By virtue of being able to hear, NES speakers technically may be able to learn spoken English and American values and be qualified to sit in judgment of others. The legislators who draft the jury service statutes implicitly assume that because a NES person has not taken the time to learn English, the person will not share American values and mores. Because deaf people are thought of as regular Americans who simply cannot hear, they have been successful in obtaining the right to serve on juries.[7] At the same time, certain aspects of living as a deaf person in the United States suggest that the experience is similar to NES people who have faced linguistic discrimination and exclusion from the mainstream of society in many respects. In any event, a more intellectually rigorous examination of the NES cases shows that aside from these few differences, many of the same principles can be used effectively to define the context of ASL interpreting in court.

The federal and state statutes that provide communicative access in legal and other settings for deaf and hard of hearing people do not apply to NES people. For deaf people, by and large, the greatest protection has been afforded by federal disability statutes. Beginning in 1973, Section 504 of the Rehabilitation Act required that programs or activities receiving federal financial assistance must make those programs, services and benefits available to disabled persons by providing reasonable accommodations.[8] Reasonable accommodations include, but are not limited to, sign language interpreters for deaf people who use American Sign Language as their primary form of communication.

In 1990, the landmark Americans with Disabilities Act was passed which had a far broader reach than the Rehabilitation Act.[9] Title II of the ADA specifically applies to state and local governments, including the judicial system. The ADA requires state and local courts to ensure that legal proceedings are accessible by providing reasonable accommodations to deaf persons. The ADA also applies to private businesses and others who provide services to the public instead of targeting only those programs and services that received federal financial assistance as the Rehabilitation Act did.

Interestingly, the ADA, by its terms, does not apply to federal courts. However, the United States Administrative Office of the Courts ("USAOC") has recognized the irony of this circumstance. Technically, a deaf person litigating an ADA case against a defendant for failure to provide interpreters would have to pay for the interpreter for the federal trial. An *ad hoc* policy has been drafted to ensure that federal courts are accessible to deaf people. According to information from the National Association of the Deaf ("NAD"):

> The Judicial Conference of the Administrative Office of the United States Courts has adopted a policy that all federal courts will provide reasonable accommodations to persons with communications disabilities. The Judicial Conference requires courts to provide sign language interpreters or other appropriate auxiliary aids to deaf and hard of hearing

participants in court proceedings, at judiciary expense, in accordance with guidelines prepared by the Administrative Office of the United States Courts.[10]

As a result, at least for deaf persons, the court administrator's office filled the gap that Congress left in drafting the ADA.

III. The Development of the Right to an Interpreter

Prior to the current legislative enactments, court interpreter services were provided in a sporadic manner and varied from state to state depending upon whether the particular state's appeals court had decided a case outlining the scope of the right to an interpreter. In earliest reported times, deaf people were considered incompetent to participate in judicial proceedings.[11] The inability to hear left deaf people flawed in the eyes of the judiciary, and consequently, they had no rights as parties or witnesses in a case. There was no issue about providing interpreters: they were not provided.

As time went on, courts began to recognize the need to provide communicative access to deaf and NES witnesses and parties. With respect to NES witnesses, the Court has always had the inherent power to provide the necessary adjustments to the conduct of a trial to make it more efficient and effective for the court's benefit.[12] Using this inherent power, witness interpreters were provided to permit English speakers to understand the testimony of witness. This accommodation was not out of beneficence towards non-English speakers; rather, it was to enable the court and the jury to understand. In the absence of NES witnesses, a non-English speaking party, however, still had to provide their own interpreter if they wanted to understand the proceedings. The legal landscape changed dramatically in 1970 with the landmark case of *United States ex rel. Negron v. New York.*[13]

A. *Negron*

Negron's procedural history was somewhat unique and provided the impetus for Congress to pass the Federal Court Interpreting Act.[14] Mr. Negron was convicted for murder in New York state court. Once exhausting the state appellate process without success, Mr. Negron applied to the federal district court in New York using what is called a writ of habeas corpus. The purpose of this ancient writ is to seek help from the federal court when a defendant believes he or she was tried in an unconstitutional manner by the state court. Mr. Negron spoke no English, was tried without an interpreter, claimed that his state trial was fundamentally unfair and that he had been deprived of meaningful access to the proceedings and of due process of law. Two federal courts agreed that New York had violated Mr. Negron's rights.

During the federal habeas hearing, the Spanish interpreter testified that she had met with Mr. Negron and his attorney during two brief recesses in the course of the four-day murder trial. During those meetings, the interpreter would tell Mr. Negron "at least to some extent, the nature of the testimony of the English-speaking witnesses who had previously testified."[15] According to the Court on appeal:

> To Negron, most of the trial must have been a babble of voices. Twelve of the state's fourteen witnesses testified against him in English. Apart from [the interpreter's] occasional ex post facto brief resumes – the detail and accuracy of which is not revealed in any record – none of this testimony was comprehensible to Negron.[16]

In *Negron,* the court held that the Sixth Amendment required an interpreter be present for Mr. Negron to understand the proceedings, have meaningful access to counsel and to confront the witnesses against him. The court recognized that continuous interpretation services were required "not only for the sake of effective cross-examination, however, but as a matter of simple humaneness, Negron deserved more than to sit in total incomprehension as the trial proceeded."[17]

Because Mr. Negron did not understand the English testimony of the witnesses, he could not meaningfully confront them or meaningfully participate in his trial. Accordingly, the Court said "[i]n order to afford Negron his right to confrontation, it was necessary under the circumstances that he be provided with a simultaneous translation of what was being said for the purpose of communicating with his attorney to enable the latter to effectively cross-examine those English-speaking witnesses to test their credibility, their memory and their accuracy of observation in the light of Negron's version of the facts."[18] In essence, the Sixth Amendment requires three interpreting functions to be provided in the criminal context: (1) communication with counsel, (2) interpretation of the proceedings, and (3) interpretation of witness testimony.[19]

The Fourteenth Amendment's due process clause also required an interpreter to be provided during the trial of a NES person otherwise the trial would be lacking in "basic and fundamental fairness" because "under our system of justice, a procedure which offends the constitutional guaranties of the accused to a fair trial cannot be tolerated."[20]

The court on appeal agreed that the case should be analyzed on constitutional grounds and that the trial suffered more than just Sixth Amendment problems. The court observed, with feeling, that:

> the right that was denied Negron seems to us even more consequential than the right of confrontation. Considerations of fairness, the integrity of the fact-finding process, and the potency of our adversary system of justice forbid that the state should prosecute a defendant who is not present at his own trial . . . . And it is equally imperative that every criminal defendant – if the right to be present is to have meaning – possess 'sufficient present ability to consult with his lawyer with a reasonable degree of rational understanding' . . . . Otherwise, the 'adjudication loses its character as a reasoned interaction . . . and becomes an invective against an insensible object. . . .[21]

Negron placed the concept of linguistic presence squarely into the Sixth Amendment's right to be present. Mr. Negron was compared to one functioning under a disability: "Negron's language disability was obvious, not just a possibility, and it was as debilitating to his ability to participate in the trial as a mental disease or defect. But it was more readily curable than any mental disorder."[22] With a Spanish interpreter, Mr. Negron could confront witnesses in a meaningful way. Mr. Negron could understand the questions put to the witnesses, and he could advise counsel as to how a witness should be questioned. Without an interpreter, Mr. Negron's access was illusory.

In sum, both federal courts agreed with Mr. Negron that his New York state trial was fundamentally unfair and in violation of constitutional principles and processes. However, the relief the federal court could provide was limited only to Mr. Negron because of the nature of federal jurisdiction and the doctrine of the separation of powers between the state and federal judicial systems. The Court could not set interpreter policies for New York State or even for other federal trial courts outside of its geographical circuit. As a result, Congress took up the matter of language access using its power to draft legislation governing all federal trial courts.

B. *The Federal Court Interpreter Act*

The Federal Court Interpreters Act was passed in 1978 to require interpreting services in federal trial courts for certain proceedings and was amended in 1988 to include testing and record keeping duties under the auspices of the USAOC.[23] The Act requires the USAOC Director to prescribe, determine and certify the qualifications of persons who serve as certified interpreters in federal courts when the Director considers such certification to be merited for either persons who are hearing impaired (whether or not they also are speech impaired) or persons who speak only or primarily a language other than English.[24]

The Act requires the Director to maintain a master list of all certified interpreters and to provide periodic reports regarding the use of interpreters in the federal courts.[25]

Certified

Only for languages certified/approved by the Director:

- Spanish
- Navajo
- Haitian-Creole
- ASL (SC:L only)

Otherwise Qualified

Professionally Qualified	Language Skilled
Not permitted for:	ASL Interpreters holding
• Spanish	• CSC
• Navajo	• CI/CT
• Haitian-Creole	• NIC any level
• ASL (SC:L only)	

Figure 1 -- Hierarchy of Federally Recognized Qualifications

The statute spoke only of certified and "otherwise qualified interpreters." In 1989, the USAOC drafted interim regulations to clarify its charge under the statute. The interim regulations retained the category of "certified" and divided the category of "otherwise qualified" into two groups: "professionally qualified" and "language skilled" interpreters.[26] Professionally qualified interpreters cannot work in a language for which the Director has established certification (Spanish, Navajo and Hatian Creole).[27] Professionally qualified interpreters must demonstrate prior professional experience and membership in good standing in a professional interpreter's association.[28] The association's bylaws must require members to have at least fifty hours of conference interpreting experience; sponsorship of three active members who also have been in good standing for the past two years and who share the same working language; who can attest to the applicants performance as an interpreter; and who can attest to the accuracy of the applicant's application.[29]

A language skilled interpreter is one who "can demonstrate to the satisfaction of the court the ability to interpret court proceedings from English to a designated language and from that language to English. . . ."[30] There are no other requirements for a language skilled interpreter other than the court must be satisfied that the interpreter can communicate with the NES person involved in the matter.

According to the Regulations, an interpreter cannot be professionally qualified in a language that Director has either certified or approved. [31] Interpreters who cannot meet the requirements of certified or professionally qualified either use languages which have no test developed, they have not passed an approved test or they cannot meet the stringent membership requirements of the professionally qualified category. Language skilled interpreters are paid substantially less than certified or professionally qualified interpreters.

The regulations issued by the Director of the USAOC in 1989 define ASL interpreters as certified only if they hold the SC: L from the RID.[32] ASL interpreters holding the generalist RID certificates can not be considered professionally qualified because the USAOC has approved the SC: L. Nationally-certified ASL generalist interpreters who have not passed the SC:L are relegated by definition to the category of "language skilled" by the federal courts.

According to the annual report of the Director of the USAOC, "[a]t the end of fiscal year 2004, the database contained the names of 883 active certified interpreters and 1,563 otherwise qualified interpreters in close to 100 languages."[33] In 2004, there were 220,000 interpreted events in the federal courts in 106 different languages though the vast majority of interpreted events were in Spanish.[34] Courts report statistics on the numbers, usage, identity and experience of otherwise qualified interpreters. However, the Director's report does not break down the 1,563 otherwise qualified interpreters into professionally qualified and language skilled.

The Court Interpreting Act also provides for the use of electronically recorded proceedings to preserve the original source language testimony of the NES witness upon motion by any party.[35] One of the factors used to determine if an electronic recording is necessary is whether the interpreter is certified. If the interpreter is not certified in a language in which certification exists, it is more likely that there will be errors and the original testimony should be recorded in order to have the data available for comparison. The concern is similar if the interpreter is working in a language for which no certification exists because in that case there is no bench mark to assure even a minimal level of proven skill. In that case, the statute encourages the presiding official to consider the interpreter's qualifications, prior experience in court interpreting, and the complexity or length of the proceeding in making its determination.[36]

The statute permits any individual needing an interpreter to request one from the clerk of the court.[37] The statute also contains a series of procedural protections by which a NES person can waive the right to an interpreter. The waiver provision requires that:

> Such a waiver shall be effective only if approved by the presiding judicial officer and made expressly by such individual on the record after opportunity to consult with counsel and after the presiding judicial officer has explained to such individual, utilizing the services of the most available certified interpreter, or when no certified interpreter is reasonably available, as determined by the presiding judicial officer, the services of an otherwise competent interpreter, the nature and effect of the waiver.[38]

The section addresses the concern that a NES speaker will be forced to accept substandard interpreting services because of the time and expense involved in locating properly credentialed interpreters.

Finally, the statute requires consecutive interpretation for NES witness testimony:

> The interpretation provided by certified or otherwise qualified interpreters pursuant to this section shall be in the simultaneous mode for any party to a judicial proceeding instituted by the United States and in the consecutive mode for witnesses, except that the presiding judicial officer, *sua sponte* or on the motion of a party, may authorize a simultaneous, or a consecutive interpretation when such officer determines after a hearing on the record that such interpretation will aid in the efficient administration of justice.[39]

All NES witness testimony normally will be interpreted in the consecutive mode; however, the court retains the flexibility to hold a hearing and order other arrangements when indicated by the facts of the case. This is particularly useful when ASL interpreters are working with certified deaf interpreters which may require consecutive interpretation during of the bulk of the proceeding and not just during deaf witness testimony. A subsequent section of the statute gives the presiding judicial officer the latitude to retain special interpreting services when necessary. Interpreters should use this section to justify retaining deaf interpreting specialists when indicated by the facts of the case.[40]

→ The federal court interpreting law has several important limitations to full access to the courts for NES individuals: the law only applies in federal criminal cases or in civil matters brought by the government. The law does not require interpreters to be provided in the bulk of civil matters. In terms of quality control, though the statute requires courts to use the services of the "most available certified interpreter," it also permits courts to use an otherwise qualified interpreter or a language skilled interpreter if the services of a certified interpreter are not available.[41] A stronger statute would expressly require courts to take vigorous efforts to locate and retain a federally certified court interpreter.

No mechanism exists by statute to require courts to actually contact certified interpreters instead of less expensive uncertified interpreters. Anecdotal information from spoken language interpreters has indicated that certified interpreters routinely are not contacted when less expensive uncertified interpreters are available.[42]

For deaf people, the Act falls short of providing full access as well. As mentioned earlier, because the ADA does not apply to federal courts, the authority for providing ASL interpreters in federal civil cases rests on an internal administrative office memorandum. Spoken language interpreting is not even afforded this minimal measure of protection. Unless the courts have some voluntary internal policy, there is no obligation to ensure that civil proceedings are accessible to NES individuals other than deaf people.[43]

IV. State Court Interpreter Statutes

Even before Congress passed the ADA in 1990, many states had court interpreting statutes in place for deaf or hard of hearing litigants.[44] Typical statutes divide the legal interpreting responsibilities into three broad areas: court interpreting, law enforcement interpreting and executive branch interpreting.[45] In addition, the better statutes tend to describe the duties of the interpreter in court by the various functions derived from the constitutional cases such as *Negron*. As a result, those statutes discuss interpreting for deaf witnesses, for the proceedings for a deaf party and for privileged communications with counsel. The more comprehensive statutes also clearly describe law enforcement's obligations to provide qualified interpreters for suspects under questioning and make provisions for videotaping the interactions.

A. Function-Based Statute

A model statute is the District of Columbia Interpreting Act, which was passed in 1988, after input from many community stakeholders, legal organizations and law enforcement interests. The statute provides, in pertinent part:

Interpreters required.

> (a) Whenever a communication-impaired person is a party or witness, or whenever a juvenile whose parent or parents are communication impaired is brought before a court at any stage of a judicial or quasi-judicial proceeding before a division or office of a court of the District of Columbia, including, but not limited to, civil and criminal court proceedings, proceedings before a commissioner, juvenile proceedings, child support and paternity proceedings, and mental health commitment proceedings, the appointing authority may appoint a qualified interpreter to interpret the proceedings to the communication-impaired person and to interpret the communication-impaired person's testimony. The appointing authority shall appoint a qualified interpreter upon the request of the communication-impaired person.

> (b) In any criminal, delinquency, or child neglect proceeding in which counsel has been appointed to represent an indigent defendant who is communication-impaired, a qualified interpreter shall be appointed to assist

in communication with counsel in all phases of the preparation and presentation of the case.

(e) Whenever a communication-impaired person is arrested and taken into custody for an alleged violation of a criminal law, the arresting officer shall procure a qualified interpreter for any custodial interrogation, warning, notification of rights, or taking of a statement. No person who has been arrested but who is otherwise eligible for release shall be held in custody pending arrival of an interpreter. No answer, statement, or admission, written or oral, made by a communication-impaired person in reply to a question of a law-enforcement officer in any criminal or delinquency proceeding may be used against that communication-impaired person unless either the answer, statement, or admission was made or elicited through a qualified interpreter and was made knowingly, voluntarily, and intelligently or, in the case of a waiver, unless the court makes a special finding upon proof by a preponderance of the evidence that the answer, statement, or admission made by the communication-impaired person was made knowingly, voluntarily, and intelligently.[46]

In other sections, this comprehensive statute requires a court to make a preliminary determination that the deaf person can understand the interpreter; the interpreter to take an oath to interpret accurately; certain protections to be met if a deaf person wants to waive the right to an interpreter to ensure the waiver is knowingly entered; and an "intermediary" deaf specialist who is able to mediate the communication of a deaf person at a higher level of accuracy when presented with unique language challenges.[47] The statute establishes an Office of Interpreter Services which has been placed within Superior Court to screen, retain and set standards and qualifications for interpreters working in the court proper.[48]

B. Certification-Based Statute

Some states have incorporated a requirement that ASL interpreters are professionally credentialed by particular organizations, most frequently by the RID. The Tennessee statute provides a good example. The Tennessee Code defines a qualified interpreter as an interpreter certified by (1) the National Registry of Interpreters for the Deaf; or (2) the Tennessee Registry of Interpreters for the Deaf.[49] The statute requires that the court first attempt to obtain "the services of an interpreter with the Legal Skills Certificate (sic) or a Comprehensive Skills Certificate" before accepting a lesser certified interpreter.[50]

Statutes which specifically mention organizations or credentials are problematic because the RID periodically revises its testing system and changes the names of these certificates. The RID has tested interpreters since 1972, and its sophistication in the testing of interpretation competencies has evolved. RID literature describes 18 certificates while noting that 13 of them are no longer offered. The Tennessee statute specifically names the Comprehensive Skills Certificate (last given 1987) which was replaced by two independent interpreting certificates: the Certificate of Interpretation and the Certificate of Transliteration. The Certificate of Transliteration and the Certificate of Interpretation have now been replaced by one interpreting examination created by the RID and the NAD called the National Interpreting Certificate. In an interpreting statute, problems caused by changes in certification evaluation systems could be avoided by less specific language simply requiring the legal certification from a national association.

C. The National Center for State Courts Consortium

The National Center for State Courts has recognized the need in state courts for diverse language services. Through a long-standing court interpreting project, the NCSC has developed a resource-sharing consortium by which member states may take advantage of the NCSC's centralized store of language interpreting tests, interpreter and judicial education materials. As of 2006, thirty-four states had joined the consortium.[51] The consortium has developed tests in Spanish, Russian, Vietnamese, Korean, Hmong, Cantonese, Laotian, Haitian-Creole, Arabic, Mandarin, Somali, Portuguese and Serbian.[52] Like the USAOC, the NCSC has not developed a test for ASL interpreters. The NCSC recognizes the SC: L certificate as conferred by the RID for its member states' ASL interpreting needs.

The NCSC has promulgated a comprehensive code of ethics for court interpreters that it describes as a cornerstone for education of interpreters, attorneys and courts. A strong ethical foundation is critical for all court interpreters. In addition, NCSC realizes that state courts rely upon language skilled persons who may have no interpreter training and can provide no guarantee of skill or professionalism. Requiring language skilled persons to follow an ethical code reassures courts that these interpreters are functioning ethically.

Judges are trained to actively supervise the interpreting process in court to ensure that the interpreter is behaving ethically. Administrators are instructed to include questions regarding ethical situations to interpreters in employment interviews in order to ensure that the interpreter is familiar with and capable of complying with its requirements. The NCSC urges state administrators to lobby for the formal adoption of the code of conduct into the court rules or the statutes regarding interpreters.[53] The NCSC also recommends that the state administrator's office hire a professional certified interpreter to manage the state's court interpreter program. Several NCSC states and municipalities such as the District of Columbia, Cook County, Illinois, New Jersey, Arizona and Oregon have hired full-time ASL court interpreters to coordinate their services.

The current climate of providing access to judicial proceedings is a far cry better than in the days when deaf people were considered incompetent by virtue of being unable to hear. Nevertheless, once access is embraced as a right, the focus shifts to providing competent and quality linguistic access to deaf people and other non-English speakers. Training and certification has helped, though there will always be courts which, through ignorance or otherwise, choose expedience or economics over quality. The true guarantee of quality, however, will come from individual interpreters who can analyze an assignment and honestly and accurately assess their abilities to provide a successful interpretation. In order to undertake the analysis of the interpreter's fit to a specific legal assignment, the interpreter should have a grasp of several evidentiary concepts that are implicated when there are NES or deaf people involved in a legal proceeding. To those, we turn next.

Chapter 3
On Privileged Communications,
Hearsay & Relevance to Interpreting

Chapter 3
On Privileged Communications, Hearsay & Relevance to Interpreting

The task that a sign language interpreter is hired to perform in court is shaped by a number of constitutional, evidentiary and ethical doctrines. In every instance, the interpreter staffing a case should consider these factors. Because the analysis frequently begins with the question of privileged communications, the interpreter must have a thorough understanding of privilege law and associated doctrines.

I.   Privilege: The Starting Point

The law of privileged communications is a substantial and venerable body of law designed for the most altruistic of purposes – to protect the unsophisticated client from unwittingly sharing sensitive information in a way that might jeopardize his rights by forcing the disclosure of the content of that communication.[1] Privilege law is governed by state law. Every state has evidentiary privileges that exist to protect the confidential communications between two parties to specified relationships. Each privileged relationship consists of a layperson seeking advice and a professional giving advice. The layperson owns the privilege and can waive its protections intentionally or inadvertently.

II. The Purpose of the Privilege

In order for the professional to receive honest and complete information, the law provides a guarantee to the layperson that if certain prerequisites are met, the professional will not be forced to reveal the contents of their communications. In the absence of such a guarantee, the layperson might be reluctant to be fully forthcoming about embarrassing, but critical, information needed by the professional to provide advice or make recommendations. Though many relationships are protected by law, in the context of this text, the focus will be on the attorney-client relationship and its concomitant privilege.

III. Interpreting and Privileged Settings

It is important for interpreters to understand the concept of privileged communications because interpreters working in non-privileged assignments, or assignments in which the privilege has been waived or breached, can be required to divulge the details of the assignment by subpoena *regardless of professional ethical tenets mandating confidentiality.* At the same time, the interpreter who has interpreted in a setting in which a valid privilege exists cannot be compelled to divulge the contents of the communication.[2] As a result, the interpreter must understand and consider each element of the privilege test to determine (1) whether the setting in which he or she is interpreting is privileged; (2) the likelihood of being called as a witness in a later proceeding; and, (3) the most appropriate course of action.

Most generic interpreting assignments are not privileged. If subpoenaed, the interpreter must testify to the prior interpreted assignment or face sanctions. Some legal assignments are privileged, such as attorney-client conferences, and the interpreter cannot, absent waiver or breach, be compelled to testify. Many legal assignments such as interpreting for the police, for prosecutors, in depositions and during court proceedings, however, are not privileged and the interpreter can be commanded to testify.

The absence of a privilege does not require the interpreter to decline the assignment. If that were the case, deaf people would rarely have interpreting services since, by and large, interpreting assignments are not privileged. However, in staffing certain legal assignments, the privilege analysis may dictate a specific configuration of interpreters to avoid compromising the later proceedings. For example, the interpreter who interprets a non-privileged police interrogation should not be assigned to interpret the later court proceedings. A coordinator called with an interrogation assignment may choose to send a local highly qualified interpreter to the emergency assignment, knowing that if the case comes to trial, outside interpreters will need to be hired. The coordinator knows that at trial the local interpreter could be called as a witness and thereby disqualified from interpreting.[3] Yet, the coordinator can buy time by sending the most qualified interpreter to the emergency setting, and use the subsequent time to prepare the courts for the need to then bring in outsiders for a full trial.[4]

The interpreter who is coordinating the legal assignment must understand the principles associated with privilege and the interplay of the various evidentiary rules to avoid creating a conflict of interest. For any legal assignment, the staffing process should begin with the privilege analysis to which we now turn.

IV. The Elements of the Attorney-Client Privileged Relationship

A privileged communication in the attorney-client context is (1) a confidential communication (2) made by a client to an attorney (3) for the purpose of obtaining legal assistance (4) and in which the professional cannot be compelled to reveal the content unless the holder waives the privilege.[5] Each element in this definition must be met in order for the communication to be protected. If the communication is protected, the interpreter does not need to testify unless the deaf person waives the privilege. If each element is not met, the interpreter can be compelled to testify.

A. In Confidence

A confidential communication is one in which both parties expect and intend the discourse to be private. If the parties are careless and speak within earshot of others, then there should be no expectation of privacy in those conversations. Hence, in order to preserve the privilege, the discussion between attorney and client must actually be made in private or in a setting in which there is a reasonable expectation of privacy, such as when whispering to counsel at the table in court. It is well settled in law that the presence of a third party destroys the privileged nature of the communication.[6]

B. *Exception to the Well-Settled Rule*

It is equally well-established that if the third person is present because their services are necessary for communication, the privilege will not be compromised. When an interpreter is working between two parties to a communication in which the privilege would exist without the interpreter, the presence of the interpreter does not affect the privileged nature of the communication.[7] The interpreter can be described as an agent of both parties and therefore, the acts and words of the interpreter are viewed as the same as the acts and the words of the attorney and of the client.[8] Under this theory, if the attorney's words or the client's words would be privileged in the setting without an interpreter, then, the interpreter's words are also protected. A number of states have enacted statutes which formalize this exception and provide that if the interpreter is interpreting in an already privileged setting, the interpreter cannot be called to testify absent a waiver by the client.

C. *Remaining Elements*

The remaining elements of the attorney-client privilege must also be met for the interpretation to be protected from compelled disclosure, though generally they do not cause many problems. The communication must be made by the client and not by someone accompanying the client or someone speaking on the client's behalf to the attorney. If the client's mother calls the attorney, the communication is not protected by the attorney-client privilege. Further, the purpose for the communication must be to seek legal advice. This is most commonly demonstrated by communications in documents. For example, tax documents are prepared for the purpose of informing the IRS of the person's income. By giving the documents to the attorney, the written communications therein do not become privileged because they were not created for the purpose of obtaining legal advice. Finally, privileged communications enjoy protection as long as the client does not waive the privilege. A waiver is the voluntary relinquishment of a known right. Clients normally waive the privilege when it is perceived as beneficial to them to have the information become public. The first time the author testified in court about a prior interpreting assignment was because the information was helpful to the deaf person who readily waived the privilege.

V. Evidentiary Principles

In the absence of a valid privilege, the interpreter can be required to testify about a prior interpreted assignment. Naturally, interpreters are uncomfortable when asked to testify about a previous assignment. Interpreters believe that it is a **per se** violation of their professional ethics to reveal any information about an assignment. The Code of Professional Conduct promulgated by the RID prohibits the disclosure of any assignment related information by the interpreter.[9] Because of this ethical prohibition against disclosures, interpreters are cautious about breaching confidentiality. When tension exists between a professional organization's code of conduct and a court rule or statute, however, the statute or rule will always prevail.

In order to appreciate the risks involved in interpreting non-privileged settings, it is helpful for interpreters to understand the reasons that attorneys call them to testify about these settings. In court, a judge or the jury is always weighing the truth of testimony about events that occurred in the past. By design, the jury and the judge have no personal knowledge of the events in question and, therefore, must rely upon witnesses to recreate the events. Courts need to ensure that evidence obtained from these witnesses can be trusted to be a reliable and accurate recreation of actual events.

A. Understanding Hearsay Rules

Because witnesses do not always re-tell events accurately -- inadvertently or intentionally -- the rules of evidence have created certain doctrines that are designed to eliminate unreliable testimony. The hearsay rules represent a major tool to prevent untrustworthy testimony from entering into the jury's consideration.

Hearsay is defined by the Federal Rules of Evidence as a "statement, other than one made by the declarant while testifying at the trial or hearing, offered in evidence to prove the truth of the matter asserted."[10] For illustrative purposes, consider Witness A, who says to Repeater B, "I saw Mr. Smith hit Mrs. Smith." Witness A then leaves the country, and Repeater B is called to the stand to testify about Witness A's statement about Mr. Smith hitting Mrs. Smith. Repeater B is repeating an earlier out-of-court statement to the jury. If the attorney calling Repeater B wants the jury to believe that Mr. Smith actually hit Mrs. Smith, then Repeater B's statement is being introduced into evidence for the truth of the matter asserted. Generally, hearsay is not permitted to be conveyed to the jury; however, there are numerous exceptions that authorize certain hearsay statements to be introduced into court. Several of those exceptions will be discussed below as they relate to understanding interpreter hearsay issues.

B. *Cross-Examination as a Tool to Test Reliability*

Hearsay is banned in court because it is considered unreliable: "The general rule that hearsay evidence is inadmissible because it is inherently unreliable is of venerable common law pedigree."[11] Courts do not permit people, while in court, to repeat statements made outside of court, particularly when the purpose of repeating the statement is to have the jury believe that the statement is true. Out-of-court statements repeated in court are considered unreliable because the person who made the statement (Witness A in the earlier example) is not present in court to be questioned, did not take an oath to tell the truth at the time the statement was made, is not currently present for the jury to view his or her demeanor, and critically, the person repeating the out-of-court statement (Repeater B) may not necessarily have personal knowledge of the events or conditions in question.

C. The Repeater Cannot Be Impeached

If the original maker of the statement (Witness A) is in court, the attorneys can call that person to the witness stand and examine the person's ability to recall the events accurately, to perceive the events, and test any motive to skew the testimony. When the person is on the witness stand, the attorney can challenge the person's bias or interest in the outcome of the events or their relationship with one side or the other. The law places great reliance on these factors to determine whether the witness' version of events is worthy of the jury's belief. On cross-examination, these factors are scrutinized in excruciating detail. Additionally, in the criminal context, the defendant has a constitutional right to be presented with witnesses against him. The hearsay rule must forge a sometimes uncomfortable relationship with the confrontation clause of the Sixth Amendment.[12] In the case of repeated statements, when the person who made a statement is not in court, the defendant is not actually confronting his or her accusers as is required by the Constitution. In addition, the cross-examiner loses a vital opportunity to ascertain truth because the *repeater* will not able to answer important questions.

CROSS-EXAMINATION OF A REPEATER

Repeater:	Mr. Jones told me "The red car ran the light and hit the truck."
Cross-Examiner	Mr. Jones wasn't wearing his glasses at the time of the car accident, isn't that true?
Repeater:	I don't know, he didn't mention it.
Cross-Examiner:	Hasn't Mr. Jones been an eye witness to fifteen prior car accidents involving this truck driver over the past two years?
Repeater:	I have no idea. He never said a word about that .

Figure 1

The cross-examiner above cannot challenge either the witness' physical abilities to perceive the details of the incident or examine the witness' bias in the case. The *repeater* is the wrong person to be asking these important impeachment questions. If Mr. Jones' information is important, the attorney must bring Mr. Jones in to testify for himself. Without good reason to excuse the maker of the statement from being present, it is unfair to permit these repeated statements into the trial as evidence of the truth.

D. No Personal Knowledge

In addition to depriving the attorney of the ability to impeach for ability, bias or prejudice, the repeater does not necessarily have personal knowledge of the event. A basic tenet of evidence law is the requirement that all fact witnesses must have personal knowledge of the facts about which they will testify. Federal Rules of Evidence 602, in pertinent part, reads "[a] witness may not testify to a matter unless evidence is introduced sufficient to support a finding that the witness has personal knowledge of the matter."[13]

EXAMINING A REPEATER	
Mr. Alvarez	My boss makes fun of my accent.
Repeater:	Mr. Alvarez told me his boss made fun of his accent.
Cross-examiner:	Well, isn't it true that Mr. Alvarez' boss also spoke with a heavy accent?
Repeater:	I don't know

Figure 2

The repeater, having *no personal knowledge* of the facts, will be unable to respond on cross-examination to important questions that bring to light facts helpful to a clear understanding of the events. Hence, fairness requires that the maker of the statement be present in court and tested on cross-examination. If the maker is unavailable, in most cases, the hearsay rule precludes any witness from repeating the out-of-court statement to the jury.[14]

E. Un-sworn Statements Are Less Trustworthy

All witnesses are given an oath to impress upon them the solemn obligation to tell the truth. The law has the power to impose sanctions when a witness violates the oath and does not tell the truth. Statements made outside of court, without taking an oath to tell the truth, are viewed with heightened suspicion. Because out-of-court statements are missing the reminder to be truthful at the time the statement is made, they lack a guarantee of truthfulness. Most out-of-court statements are not made under oath, and thus, they present reliability issues when repeated in court.

F. Demeanor Evidence Is Not Available to the Jury

According to conventional wisdom, juries can tell if a witness is lying or telling the truth by the witness' body language, expression and manner of speaking. If the person speaks evasively or without maintaining eye contact, the thinking is (often erroneously because of cultural differences) that the person must either be lying or have something to hide. When the maker of a statement about an event it is not in front of the jury, the jury cannot gauge the person's appearance, demeanor and manner of presentation. In those circumstances, the reliability of the statement is lessened because the credibility of the person who made the statement is at issue, yet that person is not present.

VI. Exceptions to the Hearsay Rule

Though hearsay is unreliable in most instances, courts have created exceptions to permit the repetition of certain out-of-court statements under limited circumstances. The exceptions were created primarily because certain statements are highly reliable, necessary and no other way to produce the maker of the statement exists. The hearsay nature of the statement is expressly acknowledged, yet a policy decision is made to let the witness repeat the statement in court due to the twin rationales of necessity and reliability.

Over the years, evidence law has created numerous exceptions to the hearsay rule. Each exception has requirements that must be met: commonly termed elements. If the hearsay statement satisfies each of the elements of the exception, the evidence may be admitted in court. The essentials of a hearsay exception have been described as: "[t]he requisites of an exception to the hearsay rule are: (1) necessity; and (2) circumstantial guarantees of trustworthiness."[15] Hence, the hallmark of any exception to the hearsay rule is that the statement is reliable and necessary.

Some highly reliable, out-of-court statements would be excluded simply because the maker of the statement is unavailable. Without an exception created for highly reliable statements, critical evidence would be lost. For example, at common law, one exception to the hearsay rule was called the "dying declaration." If a person was injured, dying, actually died, and also made a statement which concerned the cause of the injury, under the belief of impending death, that statement could be repeated in court. The statement was necessary in court because the maker was dead and could not be called to testify. The statement was reliable because it was considered unlikely that the dying victim would be dishonest about the very cause of his demise. Meeting the two-pronged test for a hearsay exception, the dying-declaration exception permitted one who overheard the statement of a dying victim about the cause of death to repeat it in court.

There is a third category of out-of-court statements governed by Federal Rule of Evidence 801(d) that are so valuable courts simply define them as "not hearsay" and admit them without creating an exception.[16] By judicial fiat, these statements have been declared "not hearsay." As will be shown, interpreted statements fall into this final category of "not hearsay" statements which are permitted to be repeated to a jury if certain preconditions are met.

To summarize, in order for a statement to be introduced into evidence, the statement must clear the hearsay hurdle. This can be done in one of three ways: (1) the statement is not hearsay because it is *not* an out-of-court statement repeated in court for the truth of the statement, (2) the statement *is* hearsay but there is an exception that permits its introduction, or (3) the courts have declared that the statement is "not hearsay" because the need for the statement is so great that it merits special consideration. Once the statement clears any of these hurdles, the repeater may testify to the content of the statement.

VII.   Interpreters as Repeaters

The next step is to analyze how the interpreter affects the equation and the way in which interpreted statements typically fall into the category of "not hearsay." In an interpreted setting, there are generally at least three parties: the deaf person, the hearing person and an interpreter. The **reported cases** typically involve a NES criminal suspect and an interpreted interrogation. The analysis, however, applies to a far broader range of interpreted settings than simply the police station. In fact, since most interpreted assignments fall outside the scope of any privileged communications, it is fair to say that *most* interpreted assignments are susceptible to this analysis.

Since the deaf person and the hearing person do not share the same language, they do not have *personal knowledge* of each other's statement. Each only learned of the content of the other's comments because the statement was repeated by the interpreter. Although illogical to interpreters, in the eyes of the law, there are two statements in any interpreted interaction: (1) what the deaf person signed (the ASL statement) and (2) what the interpreter said the deaf person signed (the voiced interpretation). Both statements must independently clear the hearsay hurdle in order for the interpreted statement to be presented in court as evidence.

A.   Multiple Hearsay in Interpreted Statements

For purposes of illustration, consider the following scenario:

Repeating Interpreted Statements for Content

Officer:	What happened? (spoken English)
Interpreter:	What happened? (ASL)
Mr. Deaf Person	*I killed my wife.* (ASL)
Interpreter:	I killed my wife. (spoken English)
	<u>Later at court</u>
Prosecutor:	What did Mr. Deaf Person say at the station?
Interpreter:	Mr. Deaf Person said he killed his wife.

Figure 3 -- Personal Knowledge Rule

In the ASL statement – "I killed my wife" -- the interpreter is the only person who has *personal knowledge* of the deaf person's statement by virtue of knowing sign language. If the attorney wants the jury to believe this out-of-court ASL statement, the only person with personal knowledge of the statement – the interpreter -- must repeat it in court.[17]

Of course, most lawyers, at least most prosecutors, do not want *the interpreter* to repeat the deaf person's statement to the jury. Prosecutors want the *trained police officer* as a witness to repeat the interpreter's rendition of the deaf person's statement to the jury.[18] Police officers are trained to remember critical details that are needed for the prosecution to prove its case. Police officers generally have extensive experience in testifying and know how to testify in a manner that has a better chance of clearing the various evidentiary hurdles. Lay witnesses, like interpreters, generally do not. Important evidence can be lost because a lay witness cannot figure out how to answer a question without drawing an objection.

Officer:	What happened? (spoken English)
Interpreter:	What happened? (ASL)
Mr. Deaf Person	*I killed my wife.* (ASL)
Interpreter:	I killed my wife. (spoken English)
	<u>Later at court</u>
Prosecutor:	What did Mr. Deaf Person say at the station?
Officer:	Mr. Deaf Person said he killed his wife.

Figure 4 -- Professional Repeater

Hence, the prosecutor wants the officer to repeat the content of the deaf person's statement. In order for this to happen, both the interpreter's repetition of the ASL statement and the officer's repetition of the interpreter's statement (voice interpretatation) must meet an exception or be exempt from the operation of the hearsay rule.

B. The ASL Utterance

The hearsay analysis of the deaf person's ASL statement to the interpreter – "I killed my wife" proceeds as follows: In the context of the police station and interrogation of the deaf suspect, frequently the statement is some kind of an admission or implicates the deaf suspect in the criminal activity. A statement implicating the person in a crime always fits into a hearsay exception because such a confession is highly reliable and trustworthy.[19] Most innocent people simply do not falsely implicate themselves to the police during an interrogation. Hence, the statement is more than likely true and reliable.

In addition, confessions are necessary to the criminal justice system because the defendant cannot be placed on the witness stand and asked to repeat the statement. The defendant is protected by the Fifth Amendment safeguards against self-incrimination.[20] Hence, both the necessity and the reliability rationales for creating a hearsay exception are satisfied. Confessions have long been deemed admissible out-of-court statements and are admitted through the hearsay exception called the "statement against interest."

C. The Interpreter's Statement in English

If the analysis stopped here, the interpreter would be required to repeat the deaf person's confession for its content on the stand because of the personal knowledge rule. In a series of cases beginning in the late 1880s, courts refused to admit interpreted witness statements at all because of the hearsay rule.[21] The interpreter was the only one who knew the foreign language and was required to testify to the content of the foreign language statements. For example in 1874, a California court refused to permit repetition of interpreted statements and only permitted the officer-witness to testify to those comments made in the foreign language that he actually understood.[22] The officer lacked personal knowledge of the statements he could not understand in the foreign language. Only the interpreter who had personal knowledge of the content could repeat those statements in court.

The earliest cases even considered *in-court interpretation* to be an impermissible repetition of the testimony coming from the witness stand. Such a rule, of course, would not be able to exist long or non-English speakers could never serve as witnesses. In any event, in the typical criminal case, it is the officer, not the interpreter, whom the prosecutor wants to repeat the non-English speaker's statement. Therefore, the repetition of the interpreted confession by the officer to the jury must also satisfy a hearsay exception or be classified as non-hearsay because of the necessity and reliability of the statements.

Courts have vacillated over the years trying to fashion various evidentiary theories to permit the officer to testify to the interpreted statement.[23] The modern trend has been for courts to analyze of the interpreted statement under the agency analysis. When a repeated statement is admitted under the agency analysis, the statement is "not hearsay" because it is attributed to the deaf person, not the interpreter. In other words, if agency is found, it is as if the deaf person and the officer were speaking to each other directly without the aid of an interpreter.[24] If the interpreter is a joint agent of both parties, then the officer is permitted to testify because he or she would have direct personal knowledge of the deaf person's statement.

If the interpreter is not an agent of both parties, only the interpreter has personal knowledge, and only the interpreter can repeat the content of the deaf person's statement.

VIII.   Joint Agency Analysis

Agency principles have a long-standing and illustrious history in the law. Agency law serves as the basis for modern day employment law. In agency relations, there is a principal and an agent who correspond respectively to the modern-day employer and employee. The principal gives the agent the authority to act and speak for the principal. The acts of an authorized agent are the same, in the eyes of the law, as the acts of the principal. The agent can bind the principal to contracts, agreements, and even bad acts. Legally, the authorized agent and the principal become one person.

When the authorized agent repeats the principal's statement, it is as if the principal were *personally* making the statement. The law does not consider the agent's statement a repetition at all. Therefore, the logic is that there is no hearsay involved because the law has classified this particular type of statement as a personal statement of the principal and not a repetition by the agent. It is not hearsay and it exempt from the application of the hearsay rules.[25] Hence, if the interpreter is found to be an agent of *both deaf and hearing parties*, the officer can testify to the statement. The issue of whether the interpreter is the parties' agent determines whether the officer will repeat the statement or whether the interpreter will repeat the statement. In order to decide the issue, as will be shown, the interpreter must testify.

A.   The Interpreter as Agent

Many courts have taken the position that when the parties select and use an interpreter, they implicitly approve or authorize the interpreter to speak for them.[26] An early Massachusetts court employed the agency analysis to address an interpreted statement.[27] The prosecutor wanted the defendant's out-of-court statement to his wife (the interpreter) to be repeated in court. The court stated:

> When two persons who speak different languages, and who cannot understand each other, converse through an interpreter, they adopt a mode of communication in which they assume that the interpreter is trustworthy, and which makes his language presumptively their own. Each acts upon the theory that the interpretation is correct. Each impliedly agrees that his language may be received through the interpreter. *If nothing appears to show that their respective relations to the interpreter differ*, they may be said to constitute him their joint agent and to do for both that in which they have a joint interest.[28]

"[I]f nothing appears to show that their respective relations to the interpreter differ" demonstrates that, as early as 1892, the relationship between the interpreter and the parties had to be explored through testimony from the interpreter. The interpreter's *respective relations* to both parties would determine whether the interpreter should be trusted as an agent of both parties or not. If an interpreter could not be required to testify, the parties would have no way to explore the interpreter's respective relations to the parties.

Many courts have determined that by virtue of using an interpreter for communication purposes, the parties make that interpreter their joint agent. In using the interpreter, the words of the interpreter (agent) are the same as the words of *both* principals -- the deaf person and the hearing person. The landmark federal case *United States v. Nazemian,*[29] set forth the factors to consider on a case-by-case basis to determine if the parties actually constituted the interpreter as their agent.

Ms. Nazemian, who spoke Farsi, was convicted for conspiracy to possess heroin with the intent to distribute it. An undercover officer, Agent Eaton, spoke only French and was posing as a rich businessman. Agent Eaton and Ms. Nazemian used a friend of a confidential informant's to interpret their meetings. At trial, Agent Eaton was only able to identify the "friend" by her first name and to say that he believed her to be an Iranian, like Ms. Nazemian.[30]

At trial, the defense objected to Agent Eaton's testimony on the basis that the friend-interpreter was biased and skewed the interpretation, that there was no evidence to show the friend's language competence, and that the interpretations were unreliable because they were inaccurate and incomplete.[31] The court found the fact that the interpreter is procured by or aligned with one side or another, in and of itself, was not determinative. Rather, because the interpreter was used over a period of time during the conspiracy for multiple meetings, both parties must have been satisfied that the interpretation was adequate or they would not have continued using the friend. Finally, the court found that Ms. Nazemian did not point to specific misinterpretations made by the interpreter that would demonstrate incompetence.[32]

Though the court permitted Agent Eaton to testify, it established a test which has been adopted by many jurisdictions when faced with the admissibility of interpreted statements. The court set forth the general principle by stating: "Provided the interpreter has a sufficient capacity, and there is no motive to misrepresent, the interpreter is treated as the agent of the party and the statement is admitted as an admission unless circumstances are present which would negate the presumption of agency."[33] The case by case analysis must show that the interpretation is reliable, accurate and unbiased. The pertinent *Nazemian* factors, to determine if the presumption of agency should be negated, include:

• Who hired the interpreter?
• How did the interpreter arrive at the setting?
• Does the interpreter have a motive to skew the interpretation?
• Is there any reason to suspect bias?
• Is the interpreter a police officer or otherwise a aligned with the authorities?
• Is the interpreter aligned with the NES person?
• What are the interpreter's qualifications and language skills?
• What are the interpreter's credentials?

Figure 5 -- Nazemian Factors

Many jurisdictions permit the interpreter's repeated statement to be introduced into evidence if there are factors that indicate a joint agency relationship exists. The following cases illustrate how various courts have applied the joint agency factors. The analysis is always fact intensive. No court has issued a bright-line rule that where there is an interpreter, there will automatically be an agency relationship.

B. Bias, Accuracy & Alignment Factors

The Florida courts affirmed the conviction of a defendant, Mr. Chao, who shot his ex-girlfriend and then arranged to surrender by having his uncle, Pedro Mendez, interpret for him and the police.[34] At trial, Mr. Mendez testified that he did not remember exactly what his nephew had said to him but that he had translated between the officer and Mr. Chao accurately. The officer then testified that the uncle had interpreted Mr. Chao's statement as "he says he shot her because he loves her and wants no other man to have her."[35] Mr. Chao appealed on the basis that the officer's repetition of the uncle's interpretation was inadmissible hearsay.

The parties' respective relations were reviewed under the agency analysis. The uncle's repetition constituted classic hearsay under Florida's evidence rules. Florida has an exception for statements that are offered against a party, and made by one specifically authorized to make the statement concerning the subject. The court held that Mr. Mendez' interpreted statements fell under this exception for statements of an authorized agent.

Two facts proved decisive: first because Mr. Chao personally brought his uncle to interpret, Mr. Chao most likely had confidence in and could understand him. The Court considered it unlikely that Mr. Chao would have chosen someone to interpret for him whom he was unable to understand. Second, had the uncle, out of some desire to protect his nephew, skewed the interpretation, the statement most likely would not have been so damaging to Mr. Chao's case. Because the statement was incriminating, the concern regarding family bias was diminished. Based on these two factors, agency was found. The officer's testimony was properly admitted by the trial court. Notice that in order to obtain this information, the interpreter, Mr. Mendez, had to take the stand and testify that he had accurately interpreted his nephew's statement before the officer took the stand at trial. This process is called authentication and is required to be addressed by the court prior to admitting any evidence.

C. Parties' Ability to Monitor

A similar result was found in a federal case in which the defendants had used a family member to interpret an on-going conspiracy between them and a police informant.[36] The 15-year-old niece had introduced her uncle, an undercover informant, to a distributor of cocaine in Miami. Her uncle did not speak Spanish, but his niece, who did not know he was an informant, did and interpreted the conversations. At trial, defendants objected to the repetition of the statements between them and the uncle and mediated by the niece.

The court decided that if the niece had actually distorted the interpretation, the defendants who were somewhat bilingual, would have corrected her. Further, had the niece been inaccurate in her interpreting, the defendants would not have continued to use her. As a result, the niece was found to be the parties' joint agent.

The defendants' ability to monitor the niece during the interpretation was significant in determining that the interpretation was accurate. Because the defendants were bilingual and could monitor the niece, the level of reliability of the out-of-court interpretation was enhanced. Hence, the niece's statements were not hearsay, but the words of the parties to the transaction made by their joint agent.

D. No Agency

On a different set of facts, the Washington state court found that when there are clear indicators of unreliability and coercion, joint agency is unlikely and interpreted statements should not be admitted.[37] The defendant, Mr. Garcia-Trujillo, was convicted of second-degree rape of a child. Mr. Garcia-Trujillo appealed on the basis that the interpreted statements taken at the police station were hearsay and should not be admitted because he was forced to use an interpreter who was not his agent.

When Mr. Garcia-Trujillo learned that he was a suspect in the alleged crime, he went to the police station to speak with the detective in charge. Detective Moser learned that Mr. Garcia-Truillo did not speak English and was not legally in the country. Detective Moser arranged for an in-house interpreter to convey the Miranda warnings. However, for the interview, Detective Moser arranged for a border patrol agent to interpret.[38] At the hearing, the agent did not recall the details of the interpreted interview and Detective Moser was called to repeat Mr. Garcia-Trujillo's confession. Mr. Garcia-Trujillo objected to the detective's testimony on the ground that it was inadmissible hearsay.

The Washington courts have specifically rejected what they call the "conduit" theory of agency. Under the conduit theory, if an interpreter is present, the interpreter is functioning invisibly and accurately as a machine. Hearsay does not prevent an officer from repeating an interpreted statement under the conduit theory. The conduit theory includes no analysis of the *Nazemian* factors to determine if the interpreter is biased or unskilled. Through a line of several cases, Washington has rejected the conduit theory and has endorsed the full joint agency analysis which requires an inquiry into the interpreter's motive, skills and whether the defendant would have actually appointed the specific interpreter as his or her agent.[39]

The Court held that the border patrol agent was not a joint agent for several reasons. First, Detective Moser knew the defendant was an illegal immigrant. By seeking out another officer to interpret the interrogation, subtle pressure was placed on Mr. Garcia-Trujillo to cooperate. Second, the detective had access to professional interpreting services: the border patrol agent was unnecessary except as a mechanism to coerce a statement from Mr. Garcia-Trujillo. Applying joint agency principles, the Court doubted that Mr. Garcia-Trujillo would have voluntarily chosen the agent as his representative:

> That the government supplies an interpreter is not necessarily dispositive in every case. But here the interpreter was himself an agent of the United States Border Patrol and in a position adversarial to Garcia's who was an illegal immigrant. Even if Garcia had not been an illegal immigrant, his immigration status would be affected by the outcome of this case. The issue is not whether Agent Bejar had a motive to lie or to deliberately mistranslate. The issue is whether, under the circumstances, the facts support a finding that the interpreter was Garcia's agent authorized by him to speak on his behalf. Given Bejar's role as a border patrol officer and Garcia's

status as an illegal immigrant, there is simply no basis for finding that either was the case.[40]

In considering the psychological pressure intentionally brought to bear on Mr. Garcia-Trujillo, the Court acknowledged that members of minority groups who interact with the police are often placed at a disadvantage which can be manipulated by the police. Among the states which employ the joint agency analysis, Washington is on the forefront in applying the analysis in fact-driven, thoughtful manner to determine the existence or not of joint agency.[41]

E. Un-sworn & No Formal Appointment

Similarly, a federal court refused to find joint agency, without much analysis, where a prison camp guard was used to interpret.[42] The defendant had walked away from a federal prison labor camp, got drunk and was found wandering some miles from the camp. The detective who questioned him used a bilingual camp guard to interpret. The guard testified at the trial that he had interpreted accurately but he did not recall the substance of the questions or the answers.[43]

The court determined that the interpreter was not the defendant's authorized agent. The Court of Appeals tersely stated that

> [t]he guard was not appointed by a court as an interpreter and, consequently had no official standing to act in that capacity. He was not named nor appointed by the defendant to act as his agent. There was an obvious conflict of interest between them. Under these facts, the agency-language-conduit theory advocated by the government is inapplicable in this case and it cannot be used to make Marshal Hardeman's hearsay statement that of the defendant.[44]

Though the court rejected the conduit theory, it did not carefully apply the *Nazemian* factors. For example, no requirement exists that the out-of-court interpreter be formally appointed, sworn or have any official capacity to be considered an agent. For most out-of-court settings in which the interpreted conversation will eventually be repeated in court, it would be impractical to have a court appoint the interpreter prior to the interpretation. Court-appointed or official interpreters cannot realistically be on-call in the event that they are needed for an arrest or interrogation, or the myriad of other non-privileged settings that are interpreted. The court did recognize the conflict of interest of using a fellow officer; however the court did not discuss how the guard's status skewed the interpretation. The prosecution apparently had argued in the case that the hearsay statement should be introduced under either the conduit theory or the agency theory. The court pooled both analyses into one agency-language-conduit theory. The agency theory should be carefully applied. When the theory is used simply as a means to an end, its application does not make sense – it only makes bad precedent.

F. Interpreter Privilege Statutes & Repeated Statements

Texas is another state that has adopted the joint agency analysis to respond to a hearsay objection based upon statements repeated by a party to an interpretation.[45] In appropriate circumstances, Texas courts permit the repetition of interpreted statements after a finding of joint agency. Appropriate circumstances exist when a party can demonstrate that the interpretation is reliable and trustworthy– in other words, when the court is satisfied that both the NES person and the English speaker have jointly chosen the interpreter.[46] In order to be confident that the interpreter was acceptable to both parties, the interpreter must testify that an accurate and ethical interpretation was produced.

Mr. Gomez was involved in a car accident. Mr. Andrede, a bilingual witness, interpreted between Mr. Gomez and the officer. When the officer was asked to repeat Mr. Gomez' incriminating statement during trial, an objection was lodged to the double hearsay. The court was unwilling to exclude a statement that clearly would have been admissible in the absence of an interpreter. The court did not want the interpreter to shield or give extra protection to interpreted statements that would not exist for non-interpreted incriminating statements.[47] Essentially, the court did not want to place the non-English speaker in a better position than an English speaker.

On appeal, the court engaged in a standard hearsay analysis of Mr. Gomez' statement in Spanish holding it was admissible as a confession. Therefore, the Spanish statement could be repeated by a Mr. Andrede who understood it without the interpretation. However, Mr. Andrede was not present. The officer was asked to repeat the interpreted statement. The officer's repetition, without personal knowledge, constituted a second level of inadmissible hearsay. Though the first statement may have been admissible through the interpreter, it was not admissible when repeated by the officer.

Mr. Gomez argued that the testimony should have been excluded in because "(1) the interpreter had not been called to testify, (2) the interpreter spoke Spanish poorly, and (3) neither [parties] adopted the interpreter as their agent."[48] The appellate court agreed that the officer should not have been allowed to repeat the interpreted statement. Because Mr. Andrede had not first been examined as a witness, Mr. Gomez lost the opportunity to confront a witness and challenge the accuracy of the interpretation.[49] The question of agency *could not be addressed* because Mr. Andrede was never called to the stand to testify. As a result, the court erred in permitting Officer Peters to testify to the interpretation.

Texas explicitly adopted the *Nazemian* standard established in the federal system.[50] Texas is unique because of its ASL interpreter privilege statute[51] which criminalizes the disclosure of any information learned on an assignment. In the past, interpreters in Texas have refused to testify and have relied upon the statute as justification. According to Texas case law, however, the interpreter *must* be called to the stand and testify about their skills and the prior interpreting assignment (authentication) in order for the officer or other repeater to testify to the interpreted statement.

G. Other Cases Requiring Interpreters to Testify

A survey of other jurisdictions using the joint agency standard shows that the interpreter is required to take the witness stand and authenticate the prior interpretation which demonstrates that the interpretation was accurate and free from bias. For example, in Illinois, a court explained: "We must emphasize that unless the person who acts as the interpreter testifies as to the taking of the statement, the statement is inadmissible hearsay." [52] One federal appeals court stated, "[i]n light of our application of the *Nazemian* factors to the case at bar, we hold that *absent in-court testimony* by [the interpreter] that will help the court assess his reliability as a translator and [provide] an opportunity to attack the quality of the translation," the statement will be inadmissible hearsay.[53] Other jurisdictions are in accord and require the interpreter to testify to the *Nazemian* factors (authentication) to avoid having to testify as to the content of the interpreted communication.[54]

Authentication permits attorneys to inquire of the interpreter's skills, education, credentials, experience, training and knowledge to determine if the statement was accurately interpreted and the interpreter should be considered a joint agent. Neither party to the interpreted conversation can answer questions that are unique to the interpreter. The attorneys must examine the interpreter to determine if the interpretation was accurate. At times, attorneys must inquire into the actual content of the communication to determine if the interpretation was accurate. The interpreter's responses shed light on whether the agency relationship should be trusted and whether the officer should be permitted to repeat the interpreted statements. Once the interpreter has authenticated the prior interpretation, the officer can testify to the content of the hearsay statement.

The following illustration provides an example of a hypothetical cross-examination of an interpreter to authenticate a prior interpretation with respect to accuracy, bias and some content.

Cross-examination to Authenticate Using *Nazemian* Factors

Establish prior work

- You were called by the officer to interpret for Mr. X?
- How long have you known the officer?
- How many times have you worked for the police?

Bias Questions

- You were paid for your work by the police, isn't that correct?
- You were paid each time you worked for the police, isn't that true?
- Ever gone to any of their officer parties?
- Ever socialized with any of them in any manner?

Competency Questions

- You were certified in 1985, isn't that true?
- That test was revised because of reliability issues, true?
- You haven't taken the new test, isn't that correct?
- There is national legal certification, isn't that true?
- Isn't it also true that you do not hold that certification?
- Isn't it true that there are requirements to sit for that examination?
- Isn't it also true that you do not qualify even to sit for that examination?
- Isn't it true that there is specialized training in interpreting for the police?
- You have not taken that training isn't that correct?

Figure 6 – Authentication

Accuracy (Content) Questions

- You never met Mr. X before interpreting for him, isn't that correct?
- You spent only 10 minutes to establish communication prior to interpreting, isn't that correct?
- Isn't it true that there are regional variations in sign language?
- And you knew Mr. X is from Iowa, correct?
- And you are from New York, correct?
- You knew Mr. X was charged with robbery, didn't you?
- The police told you that, correct?
- You testified that Mr. X signed that he was en route to the hospital to rob it of drugs, correct?
- And he used a sign you described as an "h" on the forehead for hospital, correct?
- You have never met Mr. X's deaf brother Harry X have you?
- So if I asked you what Harry's name-sign was you wouldn't know, would you?
- So you wouldn't know if it was the same as the New York sign for hospital would you?
- And you do not recall the sign Mr. X used for "rob," isn't that correct?
- And you didn't know that Harry was a diabetic who received his medicine from the hospital's pharmacy, correct?
- Yet, you thought it was appropriate to interpret that Mr. X was on the way to *rob* a hospital?

Figure 7 – Authentication

The facts upon which to base a finding of joint agency can only be brought to light if the interpreter testifies about the interpretation. When the agency analysis is undertaken in a careful manner, the question of whether the interpreted statement is reliable is resolved either in favor of finding agency or not. The agency analysis is a valuable tool. However, the depth of the inquiry either imbues the analysis with value or makes it rote application simply to find a means to an end. When courts simply announce that the interpreter is an agent of the parties by virtue of *the fact that they used* the interpreter to communicate, a disservice is done to the parties and to the ideal of a fair trial.

IX. The Importance of the Agency Analysis for Deaf People

The bald conclusion -- interpreter therefore agent – puts form over function and damages the integrity of the entire system. In one case, the Court's entire agency analysis consisted of the following: "the record reflects that [the interpreter] was translating and was *merely a language conduit* between [the parties]. Therefore, his testimony is within the same exception to the hearsay rule as when a defendant and another are speaking the same language." [55]

There is no hearsay rule governing a defendant and another speaking the same language. The court might have meant that a defendant's confession to another is not barred as hearsay but that is not what it said. The court might have meant that the interpreter was an authorized agent but the facts must demonstrate that the agent has the authority to speak for the principal in order to gauge the reliability and trustworthiness of the interpretation. Even in the Texas case where the court required the interpreter to testify to the accuracy of the interpretation, the court reasoned that because the non-English speaker acquiesced in using the interpreter, the first prong of the agency test was satisfied. Unthinking application of the agent label is a precarious course of action for several reasons.

Primarily, the legal system simply does not recognize the traditional power imbalance that exists between non-English speakers and English speakers. There is an additional power imbalance between suspects and officers. To find joint agency simply because the deaf suspect did not object to the use of an officer to interpret is to employ insidious reasoning that ignores reality. Deaf suspects in custody are not in a powerful position and may not feel confident enough to object to an officer-interpreter who is a member of the dominant majority and whose position in that society sports a badge of power. The failure to object should not be equated to approval of an interpreter. Deaf people have long been used to making do with substandard interpretation. Complaints about the quality of interpretation in any setting have typically been unsuccessful. Requiring an interpreter to take the stand and be cross-examined about their interest, skills and training helps to adjust the power imbalance.

The reality is that in most settings, not only legal settings, true joint agency is unlikely. Normally, the parties who can hear have an obligation to hire and locate the interpreter. Those are the people who approve of the interpreter. Deaf people are rarely consulted, even though under government regulations, deference is supposed to be given to the deaf or hard of hearing person's choice of accommodation.[56] The only time a deaf suspect could be said to choose the interpreter as their agent is when the deaf person actually brings an interpreter to the police station. In that case, most courts would properly find joint agency.

As was demonstrated in Mr. Garcia-Trujillo's case, the best communicative interests of the suspect are not necessarily at the forefront of the officer's choice of interpreter. Frequently, if writing notes is not possible, the interpreter provided is a usually a member of the police force aligned with law enforcement. Under a thoughtful joint agency analysis, this will be *one* factor the court will assess to determine if agency exists. In isolation, the fact that an officer was used to interpret is rarely determinative. Courts have not made an automatic rule that officers are inherently biased and cannot be used to interpret.[57] However, coupled with other circumstances, courts have determined that an officer was not an agent of the NES suspect and should not have been used.

When agency is found without a thorough analysis, the statements are admitted without the opportunity to vigorously examine the signer's background, credentials, skills, bias, training and education. In addition, cross-examination into the signer's motive to skew the interpretation is foreclosed. Deaf people are often forced to use semi-lingual signers in a stressful environment in which all of the cards are stacked against them. As a result, the joint agency analysis, when undertaken superficially, is simply an empty doctrine.

In a jurisdiction with a so-called interpreter privilege statute, the parties are prevented from issuing a subpoena to this interpreter at all. In that case, the agency analysis could not be undertaken because it would violate the state statute. These statutes prevent the interpreter from disclosing information learned in any setting. These provisions run afoul of the court's inherent ability to try cases according to the rules of evidence. No case has yet tested such a statute's viability when pitted against the hearsay rules designed for the efficient introduction of reliable evidence. In the event of such a legal challenge, the rules of evidence should prevail over an interpreter privilege statute. In other words, the interpreter should be required to authenticate the prior interpretation by testifying.

Other interpreter privilege statutes exist to protect an interpreter from being required to disclose information learned in an *already privileged* setting.[58] These statutes simply create a statutory privilege of the traditional common law rule that a third-party necessary for communication does not breach the privilege.[59] Police interrogations are never already privileged settings. The law enforcement-interpreter can be called to testify in states with this type of interpreter privilege statute.

A potential solution to the joint agency issue, though one still vulnerable to abuse, was suggested by a thoughtful group of interpreters in Denver.[60] The group proposed creating a confirmation form for accepting law enforcement assignments. The confirmation form would include language requiring the officers to ask the deaf person if they were satisfied with the interpretation. If a later hearsay objection was lodged to the repeated interpreted statement, the form could be used to show that the officer and the deaf suspect jointly accepted the interpreter. Of course, the manner in which the deaf person's agreement to use the interpreter was obtained might still be open to legal challenge. If there was a question about the voluntariness of the deaf person's agreement to use the interpreter as an agent, the interpreter would still be called to address the circumstances surrounding the acceptance of the interpreter as an agent.

JOINT AGENCY STATEMENT

On this _____ day of _____, 20____, _____[Interpreter's name] was hired by this jurisdiction to interpret between its agents and _____[deaf person's name], a deaf or hard of hearing user of American Sign Language.

The interpreter and the deaf person have had the opportunity to converse with each other about non-investigation related topics, and the deaf person is satisfied that the interpreter can understand and interpret accurately for him/her.

The investigating officer is also satisfied that the interpreter can understand and effectively interpret for him/her.

It is hereby acknowledged that this form was interpreted to the deaf or hard of hearing person who understood it.

It is hereby acknowledged that the interpreter used was a joint agent of the parties.

_____   _____
Signature of Interpreter   Date

_____   _____
Signature of deaf or hard   Date
of hearing person

_____   _____
Signature of Officer   Date

Figure 8 -- Joint Agency Analysis

Another solution was suggested by a creative defense attorney for a deaf person charged with murdering another deaf person.[61] At the police station, a confession was taken through the interpreter. At trial, the officer testified to the substance of the confession. On appeal, the defendant challenged the officer's testimony as hearsay. The defendant suggested that the traditional agency theory be modified in cases involving language interpretation to read: [62]

The interpreter must

- be competent, and
- have no motive to misrepresent what the speaking party says; and

The speaking party [either deaf or hearing] must

- not reject the interpreter and,
- agree substantially with the translation.

Figure 9

Though this test would give the users of the interpreter far more control over the quality of the interpretation, the court rightfully noted that it would also give the defendant a veto over the use of an interpreted confession in every case by disagreeing with the accuracy of the translation.[63] Nevertheless, this solution does comport with ASL interpreters' traditional deference to the consumer's express preference in the choice of interpreter. The solution, as stated, would still require a showing that the interpreter was competent and had no motive to misrepresent. In essence, the interpreter would have to testify and be subject to cross-examination which is the traditional way to uncover competency and motive.

Once the court interpreter is reasonably comfortable with the hearsay analysis, he or she can use the analysis in the practice of legal and court interpreting. Appreciation of the risk of being called as a witness is a valuable tool for most interpreters since very few will work in already privileged settings. Therefore, the privilege analysis plays an important role both outside and inside of court. In court, there are several functions that court interpreters take and all are affected by considerations of privilege and hearsay. The next chapter will examine the definitions and specific duties of each function an interpreter can take in court.

Chapter 4
Roles of the Court Interpreter

Chapter 4
Roles of the Court Interpreter

I.   The Interpreter as Court Expert

Court interpreters, often called proceedings interpreters, are defined as officers of the court who take an oath to interpret accurately and who function as experts by virtue of their unique linguistic skills and knowledge.[1] As an expert, the court interpreter is the language specialist who assesses the assignment to assist the court in providing the appropriate level of communicative access for the deaf participants. The basis for defining the court interpreter in this manner originates in the rules of evidence, ethical conventions and case law. In this section, we will explore the underpinnings of the view of an interpreter as an officer of the court who is qualified as a expert and who is bound to ensure the integrity of the proceedings is not compromised by interpreting issues.

A.   The Evidentiary Approach

The interpreter's status as an expert is well established in the case law and by the rules of evidence.[2] Federal Rule of Evidence 604 regarding interpreters states: "An interpreter is subject to the provisions of these rules relating to qualification as an expert and the administration of an oath or affirmation that he will make a true translation." In addition, Federal Rule of Evidence 706 gives the court specific authority to retain experts for its own benefit to advise and consult with in areas in which the court is lacking information. Both prongs of this definition need to be examined to understand how the court's view of the interpreter's duties is different from the role to which community interpreters are accustomed.

B. The Interpreter's Oath

Unlike attorneys, who take an oath only once upon being admitted to practice in a specific jurisdiction, most interpreters take the oath prior to interpreting every proceeding. A typical state court interpreter's oath reads "[d]o you solemnly swear that you will interpret accurately and impartially to the best of your ability, in the case now pending before this court, so help you God?"[3] The purpose of the oath is to impress upon the interpreter the seriousness of the obligation to interpret accurately. Additionally, the oath is a critical tool because it binds the interpreter to the court. More specifically, the oath binds the interpreter to preserve the integrity of the record through a faithful interpretation.

The interpreter can rely upon the oath if he or she is placed in a position in which working conditions are untenable. For example, it would be impossible to interpret accurately and abide by one's oath if a court refused to provide a team of interpreters for a complex proceeding. When the interpreter states for the record that she or he is unable to comply with the oath due to the fatigue of working alone, the court is afforded the opportunity to modify the ruling and provide the appropriate working conditions to ensure the deaf litigant is fully present for the proceeding. If the court refuses, the issue may be noted for appeal by the attorney. Though the failure to administer the oath is not often a successful ground for reversal, it has served as the basis for appeal on many occasions.[4] Because the evidentiary rules typically define the interpreter as an expert, we will first examine the rules governing generic expert witnesses before looking specifically at interpreters as experts.

1. The Expert Witness

The expert witness typically has information that is outside of the ken of the average jury member or judge which may be helpful in deciding some of the facts in issue.[5] Prior to giving an opinion on an issue, all experts must have their qualifications examined to show that they possess information that would be helpful in the case. Generally, the expert is placed on the witness stand and questioned though a process called *voir dire* during which the expert explains his or her credentials and is subject to cross-examination. If it is shown that the expert has sufficient training and education to be helpful, he or she is permitted to testify and be examined and cross-examined with respect to the opinion. At that point, the trier of fact (judge or jury) decides whether or not to credit the expert's testimony. In other words, the expert's opinion is not binding. The trier of fact may disregard the expert's opinion if it chooses.

2. The Expert Interpreter

As experts, court interpreters must also testify with respect to their skills, education and qualifications.[6] In the case of court interpreters, the process of *voir dire* is commonly referred to as being **qualified** (as it is with expert witnesses) and once it is shown through direct and cross-examination that the interpreter holds the requisite skill, he or she is then permitted to interpret the proceedings. Unlike the expert witness whose job it is to explain an area of expertise to the trier of fact, the interpreter does not take the stand and provide further testimony.[7] Rather, once the interpreter has been qualified, the interpreter is sworn to interpret accurately. Unlike the expert's testimony, however, the jury is instructed *to accept as true* the interpreted version of the testimony as the evidence in the case. In fact, if a juror happens to be bilingual, the jury will be admonished to ignore the source language of the testimony and to accept as true only the official court interpreted rendition even if a juror notices discrepancies.[8]

Prior to being sworn in as the official court interpreter, each ASL interpreter working as a **proceedings interpreter** should be qualified pursuant to the requirements of the evidence rules or the specific state statute regarding interpreters.[9] Because interpreted cases provide fertile grounds for an appeal on the basis of the skills and qualifications of the interpreter, it is widely recommended that, as a protective measure, the interpreter suggest that he or she be qualified even if the attorneys neglect to do so.

Interpreters can rely upon statutory provisions as textual support for the request to be qualified.[10] The court interpreting statute in the District of Columbia, for example, requires that the trial court place the interpreter's qualifications on the record. The statute provides:

> Before appointing an interpreter, an appointing authority shall make a preliminary determination that the interpreter is able to accurately communicate with and translate information to and from the communication-impaired person involved. If the interpreter is not able to provide effective communication with the communication-impaired person, the appointing authority shall appoint another qualified interpreter.[11]

The statute requires the court to make a finding prior to appointing the interpreter that the interpreter is qualified. The interpreter is formally appointed only after taking the court interpreter's oath and after *voir dire*. Courts may not always fully qualify interpreters even in the face of the statutory language, particularly in jurisdictions which employ full time coordinators who are expected to retain only qualified interpreters. Nevertheless, if an interpreting problem arises during trial, the failure to *voir dire* the interpreter still can serve a basis for appeal. Hence, in the states with similar statutory language, best practices and statutory interpretation require court interpreters to be qualified.[12]

Normally, the interpreter is qualified and the oath is administered as the first order of business after the case is called and the parties are introduced.[13] In addition, at that time, the interpreter should make a statement for the record disclosing any prior contact with any of the people involved in the proceeding.[14] Disclosure is required to ensure that the interpreter is not unduly affected by any relationship with any of the parties. Disclosures should not contain confidential or privileged information. Disclosures should be concise and the interpreter should not volunteer excessive information. If the court needs more information, it will inquire. Finally, the deaf person should be warned in advance of the need to make prior contact disclosures. The interpreter should simply state:

Interpreter Disclosure

Your honor, for the record, the interpreter has had a prior professional contact with the deaf person that she does not believe will affect her ability to interpret neutrally.

Figure 1 – Sample Disclosure

Once the interpreter makes the disclosure for the record, the court can determine if an unacceptable conflict exists. If the interpreter fails to disclose the relationship, it can be later argued that the prior contact affected the objectivity of the interpretation. When the interpreter is the **sole holder** of information that could appear to affect the interpretation, it is a better practice for the interpreter to err on the side of caution and disclose the information to the court for a ruling. In this manner, the attorneys can examine the exact relationship to explore any potential conflicts of interest, and the court can determine whether to swear the interpreter. Once the interpreter is sworn and accepted, objections to the interpretation are typically overruled and challenges must wait to be resolved on appeal.

In a well-known Kansas case, *State v. Van Pham*,[15] the court asked if the Vietnamese-speaking defendants objected to the court interpreter's appointment. The defendants wanted to wait until after the interpreter started working and they got a flavor for the interpreter's skills before deciding whether or not to object. The court, however, insisted that any objections be lodged at the beginning of the proceeding stating, "[t]he competency of an interpreter should be determined prior to the time he or she discharges his or her duty."[16] The court continued, "[l]ike any [expert] witness, an interpreter must take an oath or affirmation before testifying, and as a prerequisite to testifying demonstrate his or her experience, training or education."[17]

Interpreter *voir dire* questions are modeled after the questions asked of other expert witnesses. One source suggests the following as a model to be used prior to administering the oath while qualifying the interpreter in a case:

<u>Suggested Interpreter *Voir Dire*</u>

- Do you have any particular training or credentials as an interpreter?
- What is your native language?
- How did you learn English?
- What was the highest grade you completed in school?
- Have you spent any time in the foreign country?
- Did you formally study either language in school? Extent?
- How many times have you interpreted in court?
- Have you interpreted for this type of hearing or trial before? Extent?
- Do you know the applicable legal terms in both languages?
- Are you a potential witness in this case?
- Do you have any other potential conflicts of interest?
- Have you had an opportunity to speak with the non-English speaking person?
- Were there any particular communication problems?
- Are you familiar with the dialectal or idiomatic peculiarities of the witnesses?
- Can you interpret simultaneously?
- Can you interpret consecutively?
- Do you have any teaching experience?
- Have you interpreted in any non-court settings?
- Have you ever had your interpreting skills evaluated?
- Have you ever been qualified by a judge to interpret in court?
- Have you ever been disqualified from interpreting in any court or administrative hearing?
- Have you had training in the Professional Ethics for Court Interpreters?
- Have you ever been arrested, charged, or held by federal, state, or other law enforcement authorities for violation of any federal law, state law, county or municipal law, regulation, or ordinance?

Figure 2 – Interpreter *Voir Dire*

One obvious difficulty with establishing the interpreter's qualifications prior to working is that, like any expert, interpreters may be qualified on paper but not in practice. Jurisdictions requiring post-appointment interpreting errors to be reserved for appeal harm NES people who may know very early in the proceeding that the interpreter is not skilled, but who will have no immediate recourse to replace the interpreter in order to comprehend the proceedings.[19] An unskilled expert's opinion is usually only a small part of the case. The jury is free to disregard an expert's opinion for any reason. A NES defendant, however, who is forced to use an unskilled interpreter throughout the trial has no immediate recourse.

One California case suggested a reasonable compromise solution to the problem:

> What both English-speaking and non-English-speaking defendants are entitled to is a *competent* 'witness interpreter.' The question of an interpreter's competence is a factual one for the trial court. The ideal time to question the qualifications of an interpreter is before he is permitted to act, *although if the competence of an interpreter becomes an issue after he commences his duties, it can be raised at that time.* When a showing is made at trial, that an interpreter may be biased or his skills deficient, one solution may be appointment of a 'check interpreter.' When no objection is raised to the competence of the interpreter during the trial, the issue cannot be raised on appeal.[20]

The court recommended retaining a separate 'check' interpreter to monitor the skills of the working interpreter. It should be pointed out that the purpose of the check interpreter would be to fix errors in interpretation, not to replace an interpreter who was performing ineffectively.[21] The court could have gone even further by suggesting that in the event the 'check interpreter' establishes that the court interpreter is not interpreting accurately, the court interpreter would be replaced to ensure the NES person's linguistic presence in the proceeding.[22]

C. Officer of the Court Status

The interpreter's officer of the court status is less uniformly recognized than the interpreter's expert status. As an officer of the court, the interpreter is aligned with the court and not with the parties. Traditionally, interpreters have been viewed as belonging to, and at times over-identifying with, the deaf party for whom they have been providing services.[23] This practice has created tension with the objective appearance of neutrality, which will be discussed later in this chapter. The interpreter's responsibility as a court officer runs to the integrity of the interpreted proceedings and provides the interpreter with the necessary tools to obtain working conditions conducive to providing an effective interpretation.

The officer of the court designation derives from a combination of sources but primarily from the interpreter oath and codes of professional responsibility. In the Preamble to the NCSC's Code, the interpreter's status is characterized as follows:

> As *officers of the court,* interpreters help assure that such persons may enjoy equal access to justice and that court proceedings and court support services function efficiently and effectively. Interpreters are highly skilled professionals who fulfill an essential role in the administration of justice.[24]

The Commentary to Canon 3 discussing conflicts of interest, restates the Code's contention that "[t]he interpreter serves as an officer of the court and the interpreter's duty during a proceeding is to serve the court and the public to which the court is a servant."[25] The code is available to those states that are members of the NCSC consortium, and the code is binding on court interpreters if the state has adopted the ethics into its rules of procedure.[26] The NCSC Code unambiguously places the interpreter in the role of an officer of the court whose duty of loyalty runs to protecting the integrity of the proceedings.[27]

While most interpreters and academics view the proceedings interpreter as an officer of the court, few cases have directly addressed the status of court interpreters as such. There seems to be uncertainty at times as to the precise parameters of the interpreter's designation. This may be due to the interpreter's *ad hoc* status as an independent contractor. The interpreter is not fully under the control of the court as an employee. Certainly, the interpreter has different standing than a bailiff, lawyer or judge, all of whom are defined as officers of the court.

In a 1918 Iowa case, the interpreter was described as "more than a mere witness, ... he is in a sense an officer of the court."[28] A court interpreter is "perhaps the only officer of the court who provides expert services."[29] In 1972, one court heard a challenge to both the skill and the ethics of the interpreter. [30] While insisting on qualifying the interpreter prior to administering the oath, the court stated:

By the very nature of his position, an interpreter is at once a witness and to a certain extent an officer of the court. As a witness his testimony as to what is communicated to him is open to such weight as the jury may deem fit to accord it. As an officer of the court it is his duty to be the medium and conduit of an accurate and colorless transmission of testimony from the witness to the court, the parties and the jury. An interpreter who functions with the sanction of the court necessarily enjoys a preferred position, especially where, as here, his interpretations are not subject to refutation. The most competent and least biased person available should be appointed. *In order for the trial court to make this selection it necessarily follows that either party must be allowed to show that the interpreter is competent or that he is not impartial.* Since such a proceeding to determine competency may well involve matters irrelevant to the issues in the case, it also follows that such a hearing should be held in the jury's absence. Failure of the trial court to conduct such a hearing despite defendant's request and plaintiff's acquiescence was error."[31]

The court emphasized the interpreter's officer of the court status runs to the duty to provide an accurate interpretation. The interpreter's oath to provide an accurate interpretation supplies additional support to the designation of the interpreter as an officer of the court. This particular case also set forth the right to a hearing outside of the presence of the jury to determine the competency, including the impartiality, of the interpreter.

Regardless of whether one describes the interpreter as an officer of the court or an expert witness, one of the most valuable skills that a proceedings interpreter can develop is the ability to engage in a factual analysis related to the communication needs of the case. This analysis permits the interpreter to recommend the proper number of interpreters and working conditions for the case. Both the expert designation and the officer of the court designation provide the authority for the proceedings interpreter to engage in this analysis.

II. Staffing the Case

The proceedings interpreter's expert duties begin prior to the proceeding when initially contacted by the clerk, the court administrator or the agency liaison.[32] The hiring party generally is under the impression that one interpreter is sufficient for any assignment involving deaf people. The first interpreter contacted should rectify this erroneous assumption, assess the requirements of the assignment and suggest the proper level of staffing.

A. The Administrative Contribution

The purpose of any expert is to provide informed guidance in an area in which the trier of fact lacks familiarity. The interpreter's expertise is language services which the court or the jury lacks. However, the interpreter also has information regarding the proper configuration of interpreters to ensure that the deaf person is able to participate in the proceedings in the same manner as similarly situated people who can hear. Consequently, the interpreter's skill in properly staffing the case is a critical contribution to ensure that the proceedings are conducted efficiently, effectively and are not compromised by interpreter issues.

At times, courts will solicit the interpreter's input regarding the number of interpreters to hire directly and at other times, the interpreter must take the initiative to acquire the facts necessary to adequately inform the court of the required accommodations. Though the court may understand intellectually that the interpreter is functioning as an expert, the court may not want to implement the interpreter's recommendations. Working from experience with spoken language interpreters, most court are used to hiring a single interpreter for a case. An ASL interpreter who recommends that the case requires two, four or more interpreters will be required to explain the reasons supporting this number. The court interpreter should hone his or her analytical skills in order to know which working conditions are essential and to be able to present a solid rationale for each of the recommended accommodations.

B. *Providing Effective Guidance*

When hired, the ASL interpreter should inquire as to the actual function that he or she will perform. The function is often determined by the deaf party's role in the proceeding, the number of deaf participants, and the nature of the proceeding. Additional considerations include whether deaf interpreters are needed and whether the deaf parties are represented by counsel or proceeding on their own, without an attorney (***pro se***). These details assist the proceedings interpreter determine the proper number of interpreters to hire, the function each interpreter can interpret and the existence of any conflicts of interests which may limit interpreter participation.

After engaging in a proper inquiry into the specifics of the case, the interpreter can appraise the court of the actual interpreting requirements. In order to speak authoritatively, the interpreter needs to be aware that the court typically draws its understanding of interpreting issues from spoken language interpreting practice. Because there are differences between ASL and spoken language practices, confusion can result. The source of the confusion stems from, among other things, the conflicting terminology that is used to discuss court interpreter roles.

III.   A Starting Point: Vocabulary

The vocabulary differences between ASL and spoken language interpreting practices are most pronounced when discussing the interpreter's role. Variation exists, in part, because of the different physical placement of interpreters. Simply put, interpreting in a visual language requires different placement than interpreting in an auditory language.

Confusion also results because, at times, interpreters are labeled by association with the party instead of by using a task-based or functional description. For example, the term **defense interpreter** might be used to describe the spoken language interpreter who interprets all of the proceedings for a NES defendant. ASL interpreters call the person performing this task a **proceedings interpreter** or a **court interpreter**. ASL interpreters have traditionally reserved the term defense interpreter for a very specific and limited role typically called **counsel table interpreting**.

Sign language interpreters have sought, with some success, to avoid the confusion by describing the role they perform based on (1) the physical placement of the ASL interpreter or (2) the specific task or function that the interpreter is being asked to perform. As a result, ASL interpreters may speak of the table interpreter, counsel table interpreter, law office interpreter (physical designations) or *the interpreter who interprets privileged conversations and who monitors the proceedings interpreters for accuracy* (functional designation). Though the explanation makes for a mouthful, the extra time taken to describe the function is worth the benefit that is realized by ensuring that the listener knows the task to which the ASL interpreter is referring.

Though confusing at first, the differences are not so great once the reasons for them are illustrated. All interpreters, spoken and sign language, may be required to interpret any of the following functions, though the labels ASL interpreters use differ.

Label (Spoken Language)	**Function**
Proceedings Interpreting	All remarks in open court All English speaking witness testimony
Defense Interpreting	Privileged communications in and out of court
Witness Interpreting	All non-English witness testimony

Figure 3 -- Label & Function (Spoken Language)

Label (ASL)	Function
Proceedings Interpreting	All remarks in open court All English speaking witness testimony
Table Interpreting	Privileged communications in and out of court
Proceedings Interpreting (Witness Function)	Deaf witness testimony

Figure 4 -- Label & Function (Sign Language)

The literature traditionally describes the *function* of proceedings interpreting as interpreting all of the remarks that occur in court between the attorneys, the court, the parties, the jury, the audience, and all of the English-speaking witness testimony. The *function* of defense interpreting has been understood as requiring the interpreter to sit at counsel table and assist counsel and the client by interpreting all privileged conversations and out-of-court preparation activities. The literature speaks of the *function* of witness interpreting as interpreting non-English speaking witness testimony. These functional descriptions apply equally to ASL and spoken language interpreting.

As described by the authors of a leading legal practice treatise, court interpreters perform the following tasks:

There are three different contexts in which courtroom interpreters function. First, an interpreter may translate questions posed to and answers provided by a witness during examination by counsel. An interpreter performing this function is known as a "witness interpreter." Next, an interpreter may translate communications between counsel and a party during trial. An interpreter providing this service is known as a "party interpreter" or, since such services are most commonly needed by the defendant in a criminal prosecution, a "defense interpreter." Finally, an interpreter may translate for a party statements made by the judge, opposing counsel or others during the proceedings. These interpreters are known as "proceedings interpreters.[33]

This common definition is problematic. As formulated, ostensibly, each function requires a separate interpreter. In other words, if there were one NES party present, there would be two interpreters: one performing the defense function and one performing the proceedings function. If there were both a NES witness and party present then it appears that three interpreters would be required: (1) one for the proceedings (sitting at counsel table whispering to the party), (2) one for the witness (standing at the witness stand, whispering to the witness) and (3) one more at counsel table (sitting at counsel table solely to interpret privileged conversations between counsel and client.). The final interpreter (3) would be interpreting a function that physically could easily be handled by the interpreter already positioned at counsel table interpreting the proceedings (1). The requirement of a separate interpreter to fulfill the third position is excessive. Therefore, the widely used definition does not appear to comport with a rational use of limited resources.

One federal case illustrated this common false impression that each function must be filled by a separate interpreter-body.[34] The court assumed that it must provide two spoken language interpreters to sit at counsel table: one to perform the function of interpreting private communications between counsel and client; and, a second interpreter to interpret all of the proceedings to the client. Further, if NES witnesses were involved, a third interpreter would be assigned solely for the witnesses. The Court stated "[i]n essence, the appellants' interpretation of the Court Interpreters Act would require the appointment of two interpreters for each non-English speaking defendant – one to translate the proceedings, and one to translate any communication between the defendant and his attorney."[35] Naturally, in a time of dwindling resources, the Court viewed this broad construction of the statute as wasteful.

Because of the physical placement of spoken language interpreters, however, a separate interpreter is not warranted for each of the three functions. The spoken language interpreter already seated at counsel table can easily physically interpret for both private conversations and the proceedings for a single defendant. Hence, only one spoken language interpreter needs to be retained to perform both of those functions.

Spoken language interpreters *collapse* the *function* of proceedings interpreting and the *function* of interpreting privileged communications in this manner into the duties of a single interpreter who sits at counsel table. Collapsed roles have been described as:

> A witness-interpreter is used to translate, for the benefit of the court and all in attendance, the testimony of a witness who is unable to testify in the language of the forum. A defense-interpreter, on the other hand, serves as a translator for a criminal defendant who, by reason of a physical disability or non-familiarity with the language of the forum, is otherwise inhibited in his ability *to comprehend the proceedings and communicate with counsel.* [36]

The practical description plainly anticipates that the single spoken language defense interpreter performs both the proceedings function (comprehend the proceedings) as well as the function of interpreting privileged communications during the proceedings (communicate with counsel). The witness interpreter is described as a separate individual performing a different function than that of the defense interpreter. It is only when a NES witness and party are both involved does the physical placement of the interpreter at counsel table become an obstacle to efficient interpreting.

The introduction of NES witnesses and/or NES co-defendants in the same case complicates matters because the courts then must consider providing more than one interpreter. [37] In those instances, solid arguments exist for providing more than one spoken language interpreter. In the 1980s, several jurisdictions addressed the question of the number of interpreters required to adequately ensure each function was covered. Those principles were never universally adopted because of the expense involved in providing an adequate complement of interpreters. Prior to discussing those cases in detail, it is helpful to look more closely at the physical placement of ASL and spoken language interpreters to understand which functions need separate interpreters and which can be collapsed.

IV. Collapsed Functions -- Introduction

Placement limits the types of functions that one interpreter (ASL or spoken language) can efficiently perform. The three functions (proceedings, witness and privileged conversations) can effectively be performed by two interpreters. Two of the functions are collapsed into the duties of one interpreter. The other interpreter performs only a single function. One source of the role confusion accompanying the varying vocabulary use is that spoken language interpreters and sign language interpreters collapse different functions.

Spoken language interpreters collapse the functions of proceedings and privileged communications interpreting as follows:

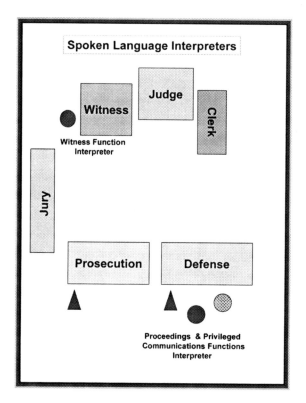

Figure 5 -- Collapsed Functions -- Spoken Language

Spoken language interpreters normally sit at counsel table and quietly interpret to the NES person.[38] ASL interpreters performing the same task are located in the middle of the courtroom facing the deaf party.[39] The ASL interpreter is also stationed near the person who is speaking in order for the deaf person to see both and gauge the speaker's demeanor visually. The spoken language proceedings interpreter needs to be close to the NES person to whisper or speak quietly to them. The spoken language interpreter does not need to be close to the speaker since the NES person can listen to the interpretation and watch the speaker at the same time for visual clues. However, the spoken language interpreter cannot easily interpret for the NES witness while sitting at counsel table. Likewise, the ASL interpreter cannot easily interpret privileged conversations while standing in the middle of the courtroom.

ASL interpreters combine the functions as follows:

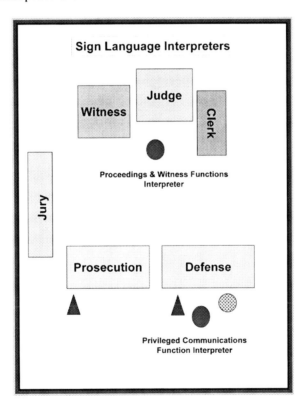

Figure 6 -- Collapsed Functions -- Sign Language

A. ASL Proceedings & Witness Interpreting Functions

In the context of American Sign Language interpreting, a proceedings interpreter is defined as an officer of the court who interprets the proceedings and all of the witness testimony for the benefit of the participants and the Court.[40] ASL interpreters do not need to differentiate between English and non-English speaking witnesses because standing in the well it is usually easy to be seen by both the deaf party and the deaf witness without significant repositioning. In fact, English-speaking witnesses do not pose problems for either ASL interpreters or spoken language interpreters with respect to placement or role issues. In both cases, the interpreter designated to interpret all of the proceedings is the one who interprets all English-speaking witness testimony.

For most cases with ASL interpreters, it would make no sense to have two interpreters standing next to each other in the well – one interpreting for the deaf witness, and another interpreting for the deaf defendant. The arrangement would unnecessarily waste scarce resources. In a few limited instances, however, this configuration is appropriate for ASL interpreters. For example, if sightlines do not permit both the deaf party and the deaf witness to view the proceedings interpreter, there is an argument for two interpreter teams in the well: two proceedings interpreters for the defendant, two proceedings interpreters for the witness. The number of interpreters may also increase if any of the parties or witnesses requires the use of certified deaf interpreters – specialists who work with a small segment of the deaf population which require a more robust interpretation than a certified interpreter who can hear is able to provide. The interpreter who must justify this type of expense to a court administrator must have mastered the concepts underlying the functions and roles of the various positions in order to persuasively argue the need for this number of interpreters to the court.

In the normal case when sightlines are adequate and all deaf participants use the same sign language, ASL interpreters collapse the function of proceedings interpreting and witness interpreting into the duties of one interpreter. It is only when the deaf person wants to speak with counsel that the positioning of the interpreter in the well of the courtroom impedes efficient interpreting. In those cases, a separate

ASL interpreter is located at counsel table to handle the function of interpreting privileged conversations. Therefore, placement in the well of the courtroom allows the ASL court interpreter to interpret for both the witness and the proceedings, but prevents easy access to interpreting privileged conversations for the client and counsel.

B. ASL – Access to Counsel Function

While in court, the ASL table interpreter sits next to the deaf client. The ASL table interpreter interprets privileged conversations prior to, during and subsequent to the proceeding and serves as a check on the accuracy of the proceedings interpreter (the monitor function) while in the court room.[41] This interpreter guarantees that the deaf person has access to counsel during the preparation and course of the trial. The interpreter handles law office meetings, investigatory interpreting work for the party and pre-trial preparation sessions between the attorney and the client. Additionally, the interpreter serves as a resource to counsel who may be inexperienced in working with deaf people and with interpreters.

Ethically, the table interpreter should not interpret the proceedings.[42] As well, the ASL interpreter who sits at counsel table cannot physically interpret the proceedings. ASL is a visual language and prolonged interpretation must take place when the individuals are facing each other, not side-by-side. The ASL interpreter who sits at counsel table only interprets the privileged conversations which are usually limited in duration and serve to assist counsel during the proceedings.[43]

The table interpreter also assists the attorney during the proceedings by assessing the performance of the working interpreters. In the event of mistranslations, the interpreter must present the errors to the attorney and may also have to present the errors to the court. Author Helen Reagan, advises attorneys that it is "very useful to have the law office interpreter attend the [proceedings] and to monitor the translation that will go into the [record]."[44] Reagan also cautions that "the client should have no communications or discussions with [the proceedings] interpreter that he or she would not want broadcast to the opponent. . . . The attorney-client privilege does not apply [to the proceedings interpreter]. This is a distinctly different interpreter role."[45]

The table interpreter is a part of the litigation team; whereas the proceedings interpreter swears an oath to the court and is duty-bound to protect the integrity of the interpreted proceedings. The ASL table interpreter should not move to the well of the courtroom and should not interpret any of the proceedings for a variety of reasons. Ethically, the *per se* conflict of interest exists when an interpreter works privately for a party and then interprets the proceedings. As a practical matter, the table interpreter will be monitoring the proceedings interpreters and needs to be available to testify if necessary. This conflict analysis comports with many of the cases stating that when an interpreter prepares a witness in private, it is inappropriate for the interpreter then to interpret the proceedings.[46] The potential bias in rehearsing testimony or the appearance of impropriety when the interpreter is seen as affiliated with one side justifies the ethical principle. Therefore, a separate ASL interpreter is assigned to sit at counsel table, to provide access to counsel interpreting and to monitor the proceedings interpreters for accuracy.

To summarize, spoken language interpreters collapse the functions of interpreting the proceedings and interpreting privileged communications because they are already seated next to the defendant. The spoken language interpreter who sits at counsel table interprets all of the proceedings, all English-speaking witnesses, and all of the privileged communications between the NES person and the attorney.[47] A separate interpreter should be brought in to interpret for NES witnesses as will be discussed in the following section.

ASL interpreters, on the other hand, collapse the functions of proceedings and witness interpreting because they are standing in the well where they can usually be seen by both the defendant and the witness. Privileged interpreting or access to counsel work is done by a separate counsel table interpreter. Collapsing those roles and providing the proper complement of interpreters best ensures that the deaf person or the NES individual is not left without access to counsel.

V. Borrowing Interpreters: The Void at Counsel Table

A number of spoken language interpreting cases have examined the issues that arise when the interpreter is borrowed to interpret for a NES witness. Borrowing means that when there is a NES witness, the spoken language interpreter at counsel table leaves the defendant's side and moves to the NES witness to interpret their testimony. When the NES defendant wants to confer with counsel during the witness' testimony, there is no longer an interpreter seated at the table for this function. The proceedings must stop and the interpreter must be called back from the witness stand to counsel table to interpret the privileged conversation.

ASL interpreters, standing in the middle of the courtroom have the same issue *in reverse* – they must stop interpreting the proceedings, leave the well of the courtroom, walk to the defendant and interpret for private counsel and client conferences in the absence of a table interpreter. ASL interpreters do not have to leave the well for deaf witnesses, only for conferences between counsel and client. Spoken language interpreters face the borrowing issue when there are both NES parties and NES witnesses present in a matter.[48] Because ASL interpreters stand in the middle of the courtroom, they face this issue *each and every time* there is a privileged conference, in any proceeding, even if there are no deaf witnesses in the case. This constitutes a critical difference between ASL and spoken language interpreters.

In the criminal context, leaving the NES defendant without access to counsel while the interpreter is otherwise occupied with a witness raises concerns of constitutional magnitude. The Sixth Amendment guarantees that one tried for a crime has a right to be present during the proceedings, to confront and cross-examine witnesses, and to have the effective assistance of counsel throughout the proceedings.[49] If the defendant is not linguistically present because the court has borrowed the proceedings interpreter to perform the witness function, then there is a valid Constitutional challenge to the fairness of the trial process.[50] With ASL interpreting, the deaf person's linguistic presence is even less secure. Absent a table interpreter, the deaf person has no access to counsel while the proceedings interpreter is carrying out the bulk of the work. The issue affects deaf litigants during the entirety of each proceeding, not just during deaf witness testimony.

To summarize, spoken language interpreters are stationed in the well of the courtroom *only* when there is a NES witness involved. If another interpreter is not provided, the NES party does not have access to counsel while the interpreter is gone. The ASL proceedings interpreter is *always* stationed in the well of the courtroom. The deaf party does not have access to counsel while the interpreter is interpreting all of the proceedings and all witness testimony.

To further complicate matters, when an ASL table interpreter is present, he or she is placed where the spoken language interpreter normally sits at counsel table. However, the ASL table interpreter is not performing the same functions as the spoken language interpreter would be performing sitting there. Considering these differences and the varying use of terminology to describe interpreters' roles, it is a wonder courts ever get it right.

While the concepts may be difficult to visualize without significant experience in a courtroom, interpreters should be able to explain the varying tasks, the vocabulary differences and the placement issues to the court and present a plan for staffing a particular case in a cogent, articulate and understandable manner.

A. The California Borrowing Cases

No uniform standard governs the number of interpreters required for the various functions, and conservative courts are unlikely to expand the right to costly protections. Nevertheless, valid lessons can be learned from the early cases that demonstrate logical and compassionate models of proper staffing of interpreted cases.

In a 1985 series of California cases, the borrowing doctrine was created. The rule was developed for California state cases in which the government proceeded against a NES person partially through the testimony of other NES witnesses. These cases established a presumption in favor of providing NES participants full access to all of the Constitutional guarantees afforded English-speaking participants. Though alternative models exist in other jurisdictions that provide less complete access to counsel, no other courts have so broadly interpreted the right to counsel to protect NES language minorities than these California cases did. The principles outlined in these cases establish the underlying justification for best working conditions in ASL court interpreting.

1. No Half Measures: One Defendant, One NES Witness

As a starting point, *People v. Aguilar* emphasized that the "NES person should be tried in a language he or she understands" and repeated the essential proposition that "[t]he right of a criminal defendant to an interpreter is based on the fundamental notion that no person should be subjected to a Kafkaesque trial which may result in the loss of freedom and liberty."[51] In *Aguilar*, the interpreter at counsel table was providing the Spanish-speaking defendant with a simultaneous rendition of the proceedings. The prosecution then enlisted the interpreter to interpret for two Spanish-speaking witnesses, and the interpreter moved to the witness stand. While the interpreter was occupied at the witness stand, Mr. Aguilar could not hear the interpreted questions nor could he speak with counsel.

One witness was the only eye witness to the crime. The other witness was the victim's son. During their testimony, Mr. Aguilar could not point out discrepancies in their version of the events to counsel. The court described the effect of the interpreter's absence during this testimony: "At moments crucial to the defense ... when damaging testimony is being introduced – the non-English speaking defendant who is denied the assistance of an interpreter, is unable to communicate with the court or with counsel and is unable to understand and participate in key proceedings which hold the key to freedom."[52] Accordingly, the prosecution may not borrow the defendant's interpreter; rather, a separate interpreter should be provided specifically for the witness function. The spoken language interpreter remains at the table with the defendant to ensure access to counsel and to the proceedings.

In creating the right, the court relied on the fact that the California Constitution provided a non-English speaker the right to an interpreter *throughout the proceedings.*[53] This Constitutional provision was violated when the prosecution borrowed Mr. Aguilar's interpreter for the witness. As the Court emphasized, "California's Constitution does not provide a half measure of protection."[54]

The court went on to describe the interpreting functions as follows:

> (1) make the questioning of a non-English-speaking witness possible; (2) they facilitate the non-English-speaking defendant's understanding of the colloquy between the attorneys, the witness, and the judge; and (3) they enable the non-English-speaking attorney to communicate . . . an interpreter performing the first service will be called a 'witness interpreter,' one performing the second service, a 'proceedings interpreter,' and one performing the third service a 'defense interpreter'. . . . While the three roles are interrelated they are distinct.[55]

Although this definition suffers from the same defect as the definition discussed earlier regarding collapsed roles, *Aguilar* still stands for the proposition that separate interpreters should perform the witness interpreting function and the access to counsel function of interpreting privileged communications during a proceeding.

2. Co-defendant Cases

The California case, *People v. Rioz*,[56] was decided in 1984 after *Aguilar* and considered a related issue. In *Rioz*, four NES defendants were tried jointly for rape. Only one interpreter was provided. However, each defendant was equipped with **electronic fm interpreting equipment** through which the interpreter spoke into a transmitter with a microphone which sent a signal to the defendants' headsets. In this manner, all the defendants heard the same interpretation at the same time through their headsets.[57]

The Court explained the difficulties this arrangement posed:

> Since the one interpreter could not act even as a proceedings interpreter and as a defense interpreter for all defendants, the conclusion is inescapable that each of the defendants did not know at all times what was going on in the proceedings, or they had no effective means of communicating with their

respective attorneys at critical points of the trial, or both. These critical points of the trial necessarily occurred during the victim's testimony and the testimony of other witnesses in the case.[58]

In other words, sharing an interpreter deprived each defendant of the ability to confer with counsel at will and to follow the proceedings when the interpreter was being used by a co-defendant to confer with counsel since the interpreter was no longer interpreting into the transmitter for the benefit of the other defendants. To avoid this problem, each defendant should be provided with their own interpreter to interpret privileged conversations. The court interpreter would then interpret solely for the NES witnesses.[59]

Other jurisdictions have considered whether borrowing will be permitted. A District of Columbia case examined the level of hostility between the defendants to determine if they should be provided with separate interpreters. The court interpreting statute allowed the court to require an adequate number of interpreters to ensure each interpreting function had coverage. [60] Because the interpreter coordinator could not find an adequate number of interpreters, the NES co-defendants shared an interpreter. The coordinator assured the court that no additional interpreters were necessary because the interpreters were bound by an oath and the code of ethics required impartiality.[61] The coordinator also assured the defendants' attorneys that their conversations were protected by the attorney-client privilege. Notwithstanding these assertions, the attorneys objected that the "client's right to speak to me and my right to speak to him is chilled by the fact that we have to wait for a break in the proceedings. . . ."[62]

On appeal, the court examined the statutory purposes for providing interpreters: "One is assistance of the communication-impaired person, in understanding the proceedings and communicating with counsel. The other is assistance of the court, in interpreting the testimony of the communication-impaired person."[63] Each of the three functions of a court interpreter is included in the District of Columbia statute. The proceedings function and the access to counsel function have simply been collapsed. Though the court held that the lower court would not be reversed for failing to provide a table interpreter for the privileged communications function, it did so at least, in part, because the co-defendants did not have hostile defenses. Because the defendants were on the same side, so to speak, sharing the same interpreter for privileged conversations was less detrimental. Had the enough interpreters been available or had the defendants' trial theories been adverse, the result may well have been different.

3. *Rioz:* Establishing Limits

The California case *People v. Rioz* which set forth the principle that co-defendants should not have to share a single interpreter to communicate with counsel also is an important case to help interpreters understand which proceedings require a full compliment of interpreters and which do not. *Rioz* explained that in many proceedings, such as arraignments, changes of plea or uncontested motions, it is permissible to hire only one interpreter to function for all co-defendants because, among other reasons, their participation in those proceedings is normally sequential.[64] Since the defendants are addressed in turn by the court, the proceedings interpreter can focus on each defendant as his turn arises. A trial, however, should be handled differently: "In any proceeding at which witnesses are called and testimony taken, the fundamental rights of a defendant to understand the proceedings being taken against him and to immediately communicate with counsel when the need arises require that each non-English-speaking defendant be afforded an individual interpreter throughout the proceedings."[65] Many interpreters are unsure when they should insist upon having a table interpreter and when one proceedings team is sufficient. *Rioz* outlined those instances in which one interpreting team is sufficient because no testimony is being taken or the need to participate fully and immediately is lessened because of the nature of the proceedings.

To summarize, best practices indicate that in the case of only one NES party, spoken language interpreters will perform both of the functions of interpreting all of the proceedings and interpreting privileged communications. However, when a NES witness is testifying, a separate interpreter should be provided because the defense/proceedings interpreter cannot be physically absent from the defendant's side. This complement of interpreters is not required for all cases -- only when there are NES co-defendants and the proceeding involves sworn witness testimony. In that case, separate interpreters must be provided to avoid sharing an interpreter with a hostile co-defendant for privileged communications.[66]

4. Ineffective Alternatives: Spoken Language Interpreting

People v. Resendes,[67] was also an important California case which critically examined an alternative approach proposed by the trial judge to enable NES co-defendants to consult with counsel short of providing each defendant a separate interpreter. In *Resendes*, two NES co-defendants were tried together with one interpreter using an electronic fm interpreting system to accommodate both defendants simultaneously. At trial, the judge suggested that instead of bringing in a separate interpreter for each defendant while the interpreter was occupied with the NES witnesses at the stand, the defendants could simply interrupt the proceedings when they sought to confer with counsel.

The Court instructed the defendants "if you wish during the proceedings to communicate with your attorney, you raise your hand and get my attention and we will stop the proceedings. And the interpreter well (sic) interpret only for you and your attorney. And that's at any time during these proceedings."[68] Therefore, the defendant who wanted to speak with counsel while the interpreter was at the witness stand would need to raise his hand and get the court's attention. The proceedings would stop, and the interpreter would physically walk across the well of the courtroom from the witness box to the counsel table. Once there, the communication between client and counsel would be interpreted. When the conference was over, the interpreter would return to the witness to resume interpreting for the witness. The trial court suggested this compromise as an efficient balance between the defendants' Constitutional right to counsel and limited state resources.

The appellate court believed that this agreement would significantly inhibit the defendant's ability to confer with counsel even though a system was in place. The court believed that the procedure made the simple task of consulting with counsel overly cumbersome and disruptive to the process because of the attention that would be drawn to the defendant at any time the defendant sought to speak with counsel. The appellate court explained:

> It is not only constitutionally essential but also eminently reasonable to require the appointment of a separate interpreter to facilitate communication between a defendant and his counsel 'throughout the proceedings' and not to permit the defense interpreter to perform an additional role of interpreting witnesses' testimony for the court. The present case illustrates the point. When the Spanish-speaking victim was testifying, the interpreter was chiefly concerned with translating his testimony for the court and was not readily available to facilitate consultation between defendant and his counsel. It is true that if defense counsel and defendant wanted to consult one another, they could indicate their desire to do so and the interpreter would be made available to them, thereby interrupting the proceeding. Such an arrangement would significantly inhibit attorney-client communication. Simply put, it would require the defendant, in order to accomplish *the otherwise simple task of consulting his counsel*, to somehow make his intention known to the court and call the interpreter back to counsel table. During the attorney-client conversation, *attention undoubtedly would focus upon the scene at the counsel table*, as occurs when counsel approach the bench for private consultation with the court.

* * *

For defense counsel's part, *the risk of alienating or antagonizing the jury or bench would infuse the mere act of speaking to his client with considerations of strategy and tactics*, in contrast to the English-speaking defendant whose consultation would be unobtrusive and likely to go unnoticed. Communication between counsel and defendant should not be hampered by such concerns, nor should the exercise of a constitutional right depend upon whether the defendant is assertive enough to bring attention to himself.[69]

The court was concerned that counsel would not speak with his client as a strategy not to anger the jury and counsel's ability to effectively represent the NES client would be impaired. The court recognized that fear of causing a disruption could inhibit the defendant from choosing to speak with the attorney during the proceedings.

The prosecution in *Resendes* argued that the compromise was constitutionally adequate. The appellate court disagreed in part due to cross cultural factors it believed could inhibit a defendant interrupting the process and potentially annoying those majority group members on the jury who are then in charge of his or her fate. The court recognized that the right to speak with counsel cannot be artificially limited to a certain number of instances, and that after interrupting the process several times, it is likely that the defendant would limit his or her interaction with counsel because of the perception that the interruptions were wasting the court or jury's time. The court stated:

> *Invocation of such a right should not be held hostage to a lingering fear that a jury wholly or mainly composed of monolingual English-speaking persons may view the non-English–speaking defendant as an obstructionist or at least a minor irritant.* While a given defendant might initiate a small number of interruptions, his willingness to continue interrupting the proceedings might be expected to vary inversely with the number of occasions. Of course, it is impossible to forecast in advance of trial how many times a defendant may wish to communicate with counsel. Unlike, for example, peremptory challenges, the right to communicate is not subject to a numerical limit.[70]

These courts recognized the difficulty of being tried in an unfamiliar language and culture. These cases protected the defendant's ability to exercise his or her Constitutional rights without fear of how the jury or judge would perceive the interruption. People who rely on interpreters are typically disadvantaged by being less familiar with the majority's institutions. Many deaf people have faced a lifetime of living in a society in which the rules of the game are not easily accessible, and would not be comfortable interrupting the court. The expectation that a deaf person should simply interrupt the court each and every time he or she wants to speak with counsel not realistic.

B. The Federal Court's Position

Generally, federal courts have allowed borrowing the spoken language proceedings interpreter for NES witnesses. Nevertheless, even the federal courts have suggested that, at times, borrowing the interpreter might be inappropriate.[71] Those cases provide textual support for the position that best practices counsel against borrowing the interpreters in order for the defendant to have full access to counsel. In one case, while not requiring a separate interpreter, the court stated:

> When utilizing a single interpreter during a multi-defendant action, the district court must always be cognizant of the underlying purposes of the Act. The district court must provide each defendant the time and the ability to confer effectively with counsel throughout the proceedings. In cases where there are a significant number of defendants, this will require the district court to grant defense counsel ample time during trial to confer with an individual defendant who wishes to communicate with counsel, separate and apart from all other defendants.[72]

Ironically, the court here approved the method that the California court specifically disapproved of in *Resendes*. The court suggested, but did not require, that separate personal interpreters for hostile co-defendants would be the wiser course of action even under the Court Interpreting Act. When the parties are hostile, for example, when co-defendants blame each other for the crime, then it is more equitable to provide separate interpreters even though not required to do so by the Act.

Even before Congress passed the Court Interpreting Act, federal courts had addressed the issue of providing a separate interpreter for access to counsel when the proceedings interpreter was occupied with a NES witness at the stand.[73] In one case, the Sixth Amendment was used to challenge the borrowing of the interpreter for NES witness testimony. The court explained its concern that borrowing limited the defendant's ability to "comment to his lawyer about the witnesses' testimony, point out inconsistencies with the facts if they occurred and make suggestions as to questions to be asked."[74] The court even suggested that:

> The defendant's constitutional rights may *require* the presence of two interpreters. Such a situation might have arisen in the present case during the period when the court interpreter was translating the testimony of the Spanish-speaking witness for the benefit of the Court, at which time Navarro was unable to communicate with his lawyer. *Such situations are likely to occur in long trials where credibility is the central issue, where cross-examination of witnesses speaking in the foreign tongue is therefore critical,* but where interruption of the testimony (as in the present case) is impractical. Unless a second interpreter is somehow furnished, the defendant's incapacity to respond to specific testimony will 'inevitably hamper the capacity of his counsel to conduct effective cross–examination.'[75]

The types of cases mentioned above require a proceedings interpreter and an interpreter for access to counsel while the proceedings interpreter is interpreting at the stand for NES witnesses. This configuration mirrors the categories set forth in *Rioz* under the California line of cases. Providing the appropriate number of interpreters in cases in which credibility is at stake because of NES testimony or in which the NES party is directly involved is the common denominator in both the federal and state cases.

Rather than compromising the defendant's rights to be fully present, these two federal cases examined the nature of the proceeding in terms of the importance of accessing counsel. For interpreters who advocate separate interpreters for NES witness testimony or for ASL interpreters who advocate retaining a table interpreter for access to counsel communications, these cases provide a guideline. Interpreters still must know how to get enough information about the type of proceedings to permit an intelligent decision on staffing to be made.

The borrowing cases suggest that the defendant should have unfettered access to counsel to fully exercise his or her rights. One drawback to this argument is that the Sixth Amendment only applies in the criminal context. Therefore, in civil cases such as family law cases, this argument is at its weakest. However, states can enact, and many have enacted, greater protections than those afforded in criminal cases for deaf and NES litigants in civil cases.

VI.   *Bednarksi:* A Civil Matter

The preceding sections presented arguments for separate interpreters for the various combinations of functions in the criminal context. The criminal context has the force of the Constitution supporting it; therefore, the arguments are more compelling. However, deaf Americans enjoy some statutory rights to communication access which are not routinely afforded to NES persons. Under federal law, deaf Americans are protected under the Americans with Disabilities Act and the Rehabilitation Act of 1973, which require courts to provide reasonable accommodations in a range of legal contexts, both civil and criminal. Additionally, many states have court interpreting statutes that include broader language for providing full access even in civil cases. Michigan is a case in point.

In 1983, Vicky Bednarski lost custody of her children to their father's parents in part because they contended that her deafness made her an unfit mother.[76] On appeal, the Michigan court tackled the issue of the right to meaningful access in an interpreted custody case under the Michigan statute. Although binding only in Michigan, *Bednarski* provides a strong argument that both proceedings and table interpreters should be retained in the civil context without the reliance on the constitutional arguments reviewed earlier.

The Michigan court interpreting statute required that interpreting services be provided for (1) all of the proceedings to the deaf party, (2) the deaf witness testimony to the court and the participants, and (3) for assisting counsel in the preparation of the case.[77] The statute incorporated the familiar functional definitions as seen with the criminal cases.

At trial, only one interpreter was sworn and that interpreter alone interpreted for all of the deaf witnesses and for Mr. and Mrs.

Bednarski, both of whom are deaf. On appeal, the case was reversed because the court did not provide enough interpreters to comply with the statute. The appellate court stated that

> [s]ince the sole interpreter was occupied with interpreting testimony of the various witnesses, [the] defendant, when not on the stand herself, was unable to ask questions or otherwise communicate with others, including her counsel, during the course of the trial. Moreover, the record is completely devoid of any evidence that an interpreter was involved with defendant and her counsel in the preparation of the action.[78]

The Court described the better practice, consistent with the interpreting statute, as: "where both parties and several additional witnesses are deaf, we think that the provisions of the act require the appointment of an interpreter for each plaintiff and defendant, and a third interpreter for the court if necessary. . . . The interpreters should be appointed well in advance of trial so as to enable their full assistance in preparation of the action."[79] Hence, under the Michigan statute a deaf person has a right to a table interpreter not only for in-court proceedings, but for pre-trial preparation as well. In states which have statutes that define the interpreters' functions traditionally, *Berdnarski* is important persuasive authority.

VII. Sequencing: Privilege to Record Conflicts

At times the sequencing of interpreted functions can create conflicts of interest for the court interpreter. The function the interpreter first performs may limit the interpreter's later choices. Frequently, when an interpreter arrives at an assignment, counsel may want to speak privately with the NES client prior to the proceedings. Particularly in metropolitan areas for cases handled by busy public defender services, this may be the first time counsel has had professional access to the client. Counsel may also have NES witnesses for whom he or she would like to prepare for their testimony. In these cases, the court interpreter may be expected to interpret privileged communications before the actual proceedings begin.

Once the matter is called, the interpreter begins by interpreting the traditional proceedings function. If the case will be proven in part by the testimony of a NES witness, the interpreter may then be expected to perform the witness interpreting function. If the interpreter also prepared the NES witness upon arrival during the attorney-client conference, then conflicts arise. These conflicts are analytically different from the issue of borrowing the spoken language interpreter and leaving the NES party without access to counsel while interpreting at the witness stand which we have already discussed. This section explores the conflicts of interest that arise when the interpreter moves sequentially from interpreting privileged conversations to interpreting for the record – the witness interpreting function.

A number of cases have been appealed based upon the interpreter who works privately with either side and then interprets for the record. Courts have expressed concern about the appearance of impropriety in permitting court interpreters to work in privileged settings and subsequently to interpret witness testimony. Ethical codes prohibit the lateral move from interpreting privately for a party to interpreting for the record. The interpreter who huddles with first one side and then interprets that person's testimony appears aligned with that side. The interpreter should appear to be aligned with no one except the court.[80]

Ironically, courts are not overly concerned about the same interpreter interpreting privileged conversations and then interpreting the *proceedings* function because the NES consumer is the only recipient of the interpretation. However, when the court is the recipient of the interpretation of a NES witness with whom the interpreter has practiced the testimony, concerns arise about the accuracy of the record and the appearance of impropriety. When the interpreter moves back and forth between privileged conversations and witness testimony, the fear is that the interpreter will be unable to prevent privileged information from filtering into the testimony. The concern for the accuracy of the record is paramount.

As will be discussed shortly, some spoken language interpreters take offense at the suggestion that prior knowledge obtained from an interpreting assignment will interfere in any manner with a current interpretation.[81] ASL interpreters agree that consistency in interpreting is important for accuracy. In community interpreting, ASL interpreters try to keep the same interpreter on an assignment of any length and duration. This practice permits the interpreter to use all of the background information learned in the prior interpreting to create meaning within the current text. Courts fear that interpreters will not be able to simply interpret from the source language produced on the stand but will rely on their knowledge of the text from past interaction with the witness and will add information to the in-court testimony that the witness did not say on the stand. When ASL interpreters work with the same deaf person over time they do create "short hand" ways of referring to events that have previously been fully explained. This discourse strategy is an efficient method to avoid having to continually repeat understood information. Attorneys use the same strategies by referring to a case name or citation to stand for an entire principle of law. Sociolinguistics who study how people use language in practice agree that these elliptical strategies are efficient methods of communicating with people who share the same knowledge base.[82]

In the court, however, the interpreter who incorporates background knowledge from prior interpreting to construct meaning is considered to be adding information that was not present in the source language. Though the court's argument is faulty from a sociolinguistic perspective, as will be discussed in Chapter 6, it serves as one basis for challenging the accuracy of an interpretation from an interpreter who has previously interpreted privileged communications and witness preparation from the interpreting the witness' testimony. A sample cross-examination of a proceedings interpreter who had rehearsed the testimony of the deaf witnesses with one side or the other might look like the following:

Examination of Interpreter	
Counsel:	You have met Mr. X before, correct?
Interpreter:	Yes.
Counsel:	In fact you have interpreted for Mr. Witness before, isn't that a fact?
Interpreter:	You have interpreted all of this witness' conferences with the prosecutor in preparation for this case, haven't you?
Interpreter:	Yes.
Counsel:	You met with the prosecution and the witness at least 6 times over the past six months, correct?
Interpreter:	Yes I have.
Counsel:	And each of those sessions lasted about an hour or so?
Interpreter:	I think so.
Counsel:	And during those sessions, his testimony was reviewed, correct?
Interpreter:	Correct.
Counsel:	And during those sessions, the testimony of the other witnesses was reviewed, isn't that correct?
Interpreter:	I think so.
Counsel:	And during those sessions, Mr. Prosecutor practiced his examination with Mr. Witness, correct?
Interpreter:	Yes.
Counsel:	And during those sessions, Mr. Prosecutor told Mr. Witness the questions I would likely ask, didn't he?
Interpreter:	I believe so.
Counsel:	And Mr. Witness practiced answering those questions, didn't he?
Interpreter:	I think so.

Figure 7 -- Examining the Interpreter

Counsel might ask one more question regarding the interpreter's belief that he or she can interpret neutrally without influence from any of the prior preparatory sessions. Most attorneys would save that point for their legal argument, however, after the interpreter has left the stand and no longer in a position to respond. The point of the illustration is not to prove bias, but to plant the seed that the potential for bias exists. The interpreter is in a no-win situation: If the interpreter attempts to defend the practice, the attempt often appears defensive. If the interpreter answers truthfully, then the appearance is created that he or she might be unable to interpret without being influenced from the prior interpreting.

A. Ethical Prohibitions

Ethical constraints define a number of different conflicts of interest that challenge court interpreters to be vigilant in assessing the assignments they accept. The NCSC Code guides interpreters in this assessment.[83] Specifically, the commentary explaining the application of Canon 3 of the NCSC Code creates a number of bright-line rules by designating certain assignments which by definition constitute conflicts of interest for the court interpreter. In those instances, the interpreter should not serve as the proceedings interpreter. The relevant portion of the Code states:[84]

Per Se Conflicts of Interest

The following are circumstances that are presumed to create actual or apparent conflicts of interest for interpreters where interpreters *should not serve*:

> 2. The interpreter has served in an *investigative capacity* for any party involved in the case;

> 3. The interpreter *has previously been retained* by a law enforcement agency to assist in the preparation of the criminal case at issue. . . .

Figure 8 -- Per Se Conflicts

The Commentary to Canon 3 presents several factual situations that are understood as *per se* or automatic conflicts of interest. When a *per se* conflict exists, the interpreter should not accept the proceedings work. The primary rationale is that an appearance of impropriety surrounds the interpreter who works for both sides in an adverse legal proceeding.

The code specifically mentions law enforcement interpreting and prior interpreting for the investigation or preparation of a case as *per se* conflicts for which the interpreter should decline the later proceedings interpreting. Prior proceedings interpreting for the same parties in the same case is not prohibited because it is not private interpreting; it is interpreting for the court. The interpreter first contacted by the hiring party should keep these critical restrictions in the forefront of their mind while making recommendations for retaining the appropriate compliment of interpreters for the case.

Interpreters who work for the prosecution in the investigatory stages of a criminal case, whether they have worked with the police, the prosecutors, or the grand jury are precluded from accepting the proceedings work. In a geographical area in which there is a limited pool of interpreting talent, the limitations may require creative hiring recommendations. Law enforcement interpreting constitutes a *per se* conflict in Canon 3, not only for appearance reasons, but because the risk is high that those interpreters will also be called as witnesses at trial.[85] Interpreters who work in law enforcement (or any prosecutorial setting) are interpreting in non-privileged settings and their testimony may be necessary by the prosecution to authenticate the interpretation to avoid the evidentiary hurdles discussed in Chapter 3.

Likewise, criminal defense attorneys are advised to challenge the interpretation during the law enforcement investigation because of the traditional low quality of services rendered. Therefore, it is reasonable to assume that the law enforcement interpreter will be subpoenaed by the defense to testify about the prior interpretation. In such case, it is unethical to be appointed as the proceedings interpreter and then to be called to the stand as a witness. Because the likelihood is great that the prior interpreting will be an issue in the later case and the interpreter will be called to testify, it is a conflict of interest of the highest order for an interpreter to work for law enforcement and then to interpret the later proceedings. As a result of this concern, the drafters of the Code have defined prior law enforcement work as a *per se* conflict of interest.

Table interpreters for either side are included in those who are ethically disqualified by a *per se* conflict of interest from interpreting the proceedings. Table interpreters work with the parties to investigate and prepare their case.[86] Canon 3 of the NCSC Code specifies that it is a conflict of interest to engage in behavior that appears improper, even if the interpreter subjectively considers himself or herself to be neutral. The appearance is judged from how the conduct looks to a reasonable observer, not how it feels to the interpreter. Interpreting both the preparation work and the proceeding work in the same case appears improper to an objectively reasonable person. The deaf person's willingness to consult with counsel may also be impeded. It presents a potential internal dilemma for an interpreter heavily involved with preparation who then must neutrally interpret for the court.

A District of Columbia case illustrates the problems that can arise when roles are blurred because of a lack of interpreters in a particular language. [87] At trial, the NES defendants objected to using proceedings interpreters during court who had interpreted privately for the witnesses during the prosecution's preparation. The Chinese-speaking defendants each used a different dialect. The several interpreters were not equally fluent or certified in all dialects. The court "[did not] particularly like the notion of [using] house interpreters" but remarked that "skillful interpreting was not quite the same thing as sharpening a pencil."[88] Because not enough interpreters were available, the court required the prosecution's interpreters to interpret for witness testimony. To address the appearance of impropriety caused by mixing roles, the court instituted a "rule of celibacy" and prohibited the interpreters from talking with anyone connected to the case.[89]

The court's limitation on the proceedings interpreter was an overly restrictive way to try to reduce the appearance of impropriety. There may be times during a proceeding when the interpreters need to confer with each other or with counsel, to review documents or to meet new witnesses, among other things. The "rule of celibacy" precluded the interpreters from conducting their intra-trial preparation activities because they were seen as tainted from the initial pre-trial preparation with the prosecution. The interpreter's ability to perform his or her job effectively is hampered when the court is left to its own devices in fashioning a remedy for perceived conflicts. A better course of action is to hire an adequate number of interpreters early enough in the process to ensure that they are available for trial.

In another District of Columbia case, the shortage of interpreters caused the coordinator to hire a proceedings interpreter who had worked for the prosecution in the earlier grand jury proceedings. [90]

The court acknowledged that this sequencing presented a conflict of interest because the party's interpreter (the government in this case) had already interpreted portions of the investigation (the grand jury). In essence, when interpreters are in short supply, extra effort needs to be given to locating a sufficient number of interpreters with no prior involvement in the case. The interpreter first hired needs to keep these issues in mind when making recommendations to the court to avoid interpreter issues becoming the source of appellate issues.

As discussed earlier, *Bednarski* required the provision of separate interpreters to ensure that the deaf parties in a civil case had full access to counsel. The *Bednarski* court required separate table interpreters because of the appearance of bias surrounding one interpreter moving laterally between adverse parties in a contested proceeding: "For one interpreter to serve both principals in a court case is to place him in an unfair, awkward, and complicated situation."[91] Essentially, the court acknowledged the subjective component to the appearance of bias: Interpreting requires a relationship between the deaf person and the interpreter which is based upon trust. When an interpreter works for both sides of a case, it places the interpreter in conflicting roles with both sides who may view the interpreter's association with the opponent as an insurmountable obstacle to developing trust. Without trust, the party may not share critical information with counsel. *Bednarski* recognized the unfair, awkward and complicated situation this creates.

In California, the ethical prohibition regarding one interpreter preparing with a party and then interpreting the proceedings is now statutory: The California Evidence Code reads: "[u]nless the parties consent, an interpreter may not be appointed by the trial court to interpret in a proceeding after having previously interpreted on behalf of one of the parties, rather than on behalf of the court, in that same matter. An interpreter shall disclose that type of prior involvement to the trial court."[92] The California provision is not limited to preparing a witness, but includes any private interpreting for any of the parties. The provision recognizes, however, that it is *not* a conflict to interpret for different stages of the *same* proceeding. In that case, the final sentence requires the interpreter to disclose to the presiding official that he or she has interpreted in court previously for the same case.

New Hampshire is in accord: "No person who has assisted in the preparation of a case shall act as an interpreter at the trial thereof, if objection is made."[93] Like the California provision, the New Hampshire court rule does not differentiate between private interpreting that involves privileged communications only, or private interpreting that involves preparing witnesses to testify. The evil addressed is the same: The fear that the interpreter will be unable to separate out background information learned during those sessions and/or become biased, even unwittingly, through exposure to the theories, strategies and tactics of one side. The prohibition also protects the deaf or NES parties from having to use an interpreter who they may not trust because of the interpreter's involvement with preparing the opponent's case. The rule was discussed in a 2004 New Hampshire opinion which upheld the rule. In that case, the court agreed that interpreters who have interpreted for the preparation with either side of a case should be prohibited from interpreting the proceedings in the same case. [94]

Like *Bednarski,* these rules, statutes and cases recognize that an interpreter who interprets in succession the preparatory work for one side and then interprets the proceedings for both parties in an adversarial proceeding is faced with an untenable ethical conflict whether actual or apparent.[95] Other tenets of the NCSC Code caution interpreters from taking an active role in a case in which they are interpreting and will be discussed in greater detail in Chapter 6.[96]

B. *Van Pham*

State v. Van Pham involved three co-defendants who spoke Vietnamese and were convicted of first-degree murder.[97] Each defendant had his own interpreter at trial. In addition, the court had an interpreter for witness testimony. The court's native-Vietnamese-speaking interpreter had a heavy accent, was hard to understand and had difficulty speaking English fluently. One co-defendant wanted his native-English-speaking interpreter to interpret his testimony, rather than the court's interpreter. The state objected because the defendant's interpreter had interpreted all of the pretrial preparation with the defendant and counsel. *Van Pham* addressed both privilege-to-record conflicts and appearance-conflicts in refusing to permit the defendant's interpreter testify. The court stated:

> [W]hen you have been discussing the case with your client, he has made a *bona fide interpretation for an attorney of confidential nature.* And for him to now be appointed as the Court's interpreter would be twofold. First it would take him away from the defendant. I cannot appoint him as a court interpreter and then allow him to go back to the defendant. It would then throw discredit upon the present Court's interpreter because the jury would see immediately that she was not there and that all of a sudden the defendant's interpreter was there which would put greater reliance upon the defendant's interpreter. It's an irreconcilable conflict that the objection of the State must be sustained.[98]

The opinion stressed that the defendant's interpreter had been interpreting *bona fide* privileged communications prior to trial. The request to interpret then for the record presented a conflict of interest "approaching the greatest degree."[99]

In *Van Pham,* the appearance conflict was addressed because the court was concerned that the jury would view the court's interpreter as less able if she was replaced by the defendant's table interpreter who had a more fluent command of spoken English. The court commented on how the jury would perceive the court's interpreter if the defendant's interpreter made an appearance only for one witness (the defendant) and then resumed interpreting from the table. Appearance conflicts as well as privilege-to-record conflicts are critical factors for an interpreter to consider upon arriving at an assignment and being asked to interpret privileged communications.

C. *Extending the Privilege*

Based upon these cases, many ASL interpreters have informed attorneys that they cannot interpret privileged communications and then interpret for the court. ASL interpreters suggest that their status as officers of the court destroys the privileged nature of the communications. ASL interpreters have been willing to interpret select types of proceedings based upon the *Rioz* guidelines after the court extends the privilege to them. This reticence to interpret privileged conversations is not always well taken by attorneys given the universal exception that if a third person is necessary for communication, the privilege is not destroyed. Attorneys may insist because the need to confer with the client is immediate, and the attorney usually has no other interpreter available.

Conceptually, the issue is easer to appreciate and more likely to be successful if addressed in terms of the proceedings interpreter as an agent of the court, aligned with the court and who should not sequence from interpreting *ex parte* privileged communications to interpreting for the record. Attorneys understand that interpreters, like other court officers, should not be privy to *ex parte* contacts with either side.

The privilege-to-record cases suggest that the court interpreter, as an officer of the court, should not be interpreting privileged communications for several reasons. *Van Pham* suggested that the table interpreter and the proceedings interpreter are not interchangeable because of the partisan role placed on the interpreter who interprets pre-trial preparation. The California borrowing cases separate the interpreter performing the witness function from the interpreter performing the proceedings function because of the appearance of impropriety surrounding the interpreter who interprets privately for all hostile parties and for the court. The same California cases recognize the void at counsel table when the interpreter is occupied by interpreting for a witness on the stand. Authors have suggested that communication through a proceedings interpreter is not privileged because of the distinctly different role enjoyed by the court interpreter.[100]

Regardless of the conceptual paradigm, the proposition that a court interpreter should not be interpreting private conversations, and then interpreting testimony for the record is based in the court's fear that the record will be tainted by the interpreter's prior knowledge gained in a privileged setting and the interpreter's relationship to those parties. When there is no deaf witness testimony, this concern is lessened, though the California and New Hampshire provisions discussed in the previous section would still require separate interpreters, absent an express agreement (California) or upon objection to using the table interpreter to interpret the proceedings (New Hampshire). In instances in which there is no deaf witness testimony, in which the proceedings are not complicated or in which access to counsel is not critical, ASL interpreters often offer to have the court extend the privilege for them to interpret those conferences.[101]

Once the privilege is extended, or the parties agree they will not call the interpreter to disclose the interpreted communications, ASL interpreters are willing to interpret for privileged communications and then for the proceedings. There are times, however, when after an analysis of the requirements of the assignment, ASL interpreters should stand firm and require that a full compliment of interpreters are hired for specific proceedings. We will discuss matters for which the privilege should not be extended or a stipulation should be refused in section E.

D. Interpreter Privilege Statutes

Interpreter privilege statutes exist in some states which prohibit the interpreter from disclosing the content of an interpretation made *if it was made in a setting which would have been privileged without the interpreter.* The purpose of the statutes was to protect the holder of the privilege from losing the protection when the interpreter was subpoenaed to disclose what would otherwise have been a privileged conversation. This type of statute eliminates the need to extend the privilege in an attorney client conversation, but it does not solve the court's problem of privilege-to-record conflicts or of appearance-conflicts.

California has one such privilege statute, yet it coexists with the evidence code provision forbidding the use of an interpreter who has prepared privately with the parties from interpreting the proceedings, absent a stipulation. These conflicting statutes can be reconciled by looking at their purposes. The interpreter statutes were passed simply to protect the attorney-client privilege from challenge that the presence of a third person destroyed the privilege. The purpose of the evidence code provision is to ensure the sanctity of the record by prohibiting the interpreter who prepares the witness from providing the record testimony interpretation. In California, the interpreter who interprets privileged communications cannot be called to testify to the content of those communications. Likewise, the same interpreter cannot serve as the Court's proceeding interpreter. The two statutes exist side by side quite comfortably. If counsel needs to communicate with the client during a proceeding, a table interpreter is provided.

The privilege statutes involving interpreters for deaf people were written to provide sanctions against telephone relay operators and interpreters who reveal the content of interpreted conversations *in any setting*. These statutes protect deaf people in a wide array of settings from interpreters who may not respect their confidentiality mandate. These statutes place the deaf person in the same position as a person who can hear with respect to out-of-court communications. None of these statutes, however, were intended to limit the number of interpreters required for court proceedings or to prevent the attorneys from being able to subpoena the interpreter to authenticate their prior interpreting.

The interpreter privilege statutes are not even necessary to accomplish the desired purpose. The privilege statutes preserve the privilege when a third person is present in an *otherwise privileged* communicative setting and the third person is required for communication. At common law, a third person necessary for communication does not breach the privileged nature of the communication. Functioning as an extension of the attorney under agency principles, the interpreter was protected by this common law exception because the interpreter is assisting the attorney perform his or her function of giving legal advice. The common law exception and the interpreter privilege statutes are appropriately directed to the litigation team table interpreter who serves as an agent of the attorney rather than the proceedings interpreter who serves as an officer of the court. The table interpreter as an extension of the attorney is truly a third person necessary for communication; has duties in addition to interpreting; does not interpret any of the actual proceedings; and, is covered by both the statutes and the common law exception to the privilege.

The debate about whether the court interpreter falls under these statutes does not address the danger that the prior interpretation will skew the record interpretation which is the basis for the ethical prohibition. The interpreter who assumes that if an interpreting statute is in force, he or she can interpret privileged conversations, attorney preparation with deaf witnesses, and pretrial investigations creates potential issues for appeal and runs afoul of the court interpreter's ethical code.

E. Some Bright-Line Rules Regarding Extension

As discussed, ASL interpreters have sometimes sought an extension of the privilege belonging to the client in order to interpret privileged conversations just prior to interpreting the proceedings. The guidelines discussed in *Rioz* teach that there are cases in which this is acceptable and cases in which it is not. At times the interpreter should insist on ensuring that the courts provide for the appropriate complement of interpreters.

1. The Nature of the Proceeding

Seeking an extension of the privilege to interpret privileged communications and then interpreting for the court is a decision that should be made cautiously only after engaging in a thoughtful risk analysis. In cases in which the deaf person is not an active participant, when there is no deaf witness testimony, or where the proceedings are not complex, the risk of harm in extending the privilege and interpreting privileged conversations is attenuated. The reported opinions suggest that when the deaf person is not an active participant in a case, it is less critical to have full access to counsel. *Rioz* recommended that in rote proceedings such as arraignments, initial conferences, status hearings, non-evidentiary hearings or scheduling conferences, the deaf person is not normally an active participant. If the deaf person wanted to speak privately with counsel during such a proceeding, it would not be viewed as obstructionist to call the interpreter from the well to the table to interpret the communication. However, during trials, evidentiary hearings, whenever a jury is present or matters in which witness testimony is taken, the deaf person needs immediate access to counsel in order to assist him or her with the proceeding.

Rioz **Single Interpreter Proceedings**

- Arraignments
- Status conferences
- Non-evidentiary hearings
- Scheduling conferences
- Some change of plea hearings
- Initial conferences

Figure 9 -- Single Interpreter Proceedings

Some matters, regardless of length, cannot be adequately covered by one proceedings interpreter and a table interpreter should be hired. For example, in civil matters such as contested custody or divorce cases, with adverse deaf parties on both sides, it is manifestly inappropriate for the proceedings interpreter to interpret the private communications for one or both sides privately and then proceed to interpret the testimony for the record. Likewise in criminal cases in which there are adverse deaf co-defendants, each should be supplied with his or her own table interpreter and not be forced to share the same interpreter when access to counsel is critical. We have discussed the underlying reasons behind these rules in the previous sections; however, to summarize the rationale here is useful.

First, the deaf party is already in a room full of people who can hear and who may be perceived as having more power. The deaf person might feel hesitant to assert himself or herself into the process by calling the proceedings interpreter to counsel table and confer with his or her attorney.

Second, the borrowing cases suggest that considerations of how the defendant may be viewed by those with more perceived power should not be permitted to interfere with the exercise of a right. The risk that the jury might view the defendant as an irritant should be avoided. The court should hire a sufficient number of interpreters to avoid this perception.

Third, the chilling effect on adverse deaf parties sharing the interpreter is undeniable, even if the interpreter subjectively feels impartial. Interpretation is based, to a large degree, on trust. To convey critical private information through an interpreter who then goes to the opponent's table to interpret an attorney-client conference would tax even the most psychologically secure. The level of trust erodes, regardless of court and interpreter assurances that the interpreters are professional and impartial. The damage caused by the objective appearance of impropriety is too great to ignore for the sake of ego, efficiency or economics.

Matters Requiring Full Staffing

- Evidentiary hearings
- Complex matters
- Deaf parties & deaf witnesses
- Deaf co-defendants (or deaf adverse parties in a contested civil case)
- Active deaf involvement
- Need for immediate access to counsel

Figure 10 -- Table Interpreter Required

The interpreter must determine the nature of the proceeding and the deaf person's involvement prior to making any recommendations to the court about the wisdom of extending the privilege or fully staffing the case.

2. Some Thoughts on Interpreting Change of Plea Proceedings

When hired to interpret a change of plea proceeding (entry of guilty plea), ASL interpreters have long agreed to interpret privileged conversations preparing the defendant before interpreting the actual plea. ASL interpreters normally seek an extension of the privilege even though the deaf person *is an active participant.* The proceedings interpreter assists counsel in reviewing the plea offer and the waiver of rights form. In a change of plea proceeding, there is no trial. The defendant had initially entered a plea of not guilty, usually at an arraignment. After discussions with the prosecution, a plea bargain is reached and the defendant agrees to change his or her plea to guilty.

The court must ensure, on the record, that the defendant knowingly and voluntarily waives his or her Constitutional rights. The court will engage in active questioning of the defendant to ensure, among other things, 1) that the defendant knows what would happen if a trial were conducted, 2) that no one is forcing the defendant to change his or her plea, 3) that the defendant is, in fact, guilty of the crime alleged, 4) that the defendant understands the elements of the crime, and 5) that the defendant knows the associated minimum and maximum penalties. Counsel must thoroughly prepare the defendant to answer the court's questions properly.

The interpreter may actually spend more time preparing the defendant with counsel than interpreting the actual proceedings. Interpreting a change of plea involves some risk normally associated with the *Rioz* types of cases. The deaf person is an active participant who takes an oath to answer the court's questions truthfully. The proceedings interpreter is preparing the defendant for in-court testimony. The waiver of rights involves complicated Constitutional principles that may be foreign to the average deaf defendant. Having immediate access to counsel through an interpreter seems to be required. At the same time, no jury is present and judges are normally exceedingly patient in permitting conferences during the taking of the plea to ensure that the plea is entered knowingly and voluntarily.

The risk remains that if the defendant later tries to have the plea invalidated; the defendant will argue that he or she did not understand the interpreter or that the attorney did not fully explain the process and the attendant consequences. Regardless of whether the interpreter thought the work was protected by an attorney-client privilege statute, the likelihood is high that interpreter will be called to testify either about their skills or about the content of the attorney's explanation to the defendant.

By all accounts, the proceeding in which a guilty plea is taken meets the definition of a proceeding in which a full complement of interpreters should be provided. However, rarely are multiple interpreters provided when a plea is anticipated because the costs would be prohibitive. Plea bargains occur in about 9 out of 10 cases in criminal contexts. Courts simply could not function if forced to try each and every case prosecuted. Most of the time, an attorney will know whether the case will go to trial or enter into a plea prior to the proceeding. As a result, ASL interpreters typically find themselves working alone when the matter set for a trial is expected to result in a plea of guilty. Most of the time, the plea will go smoothly and the balance weighs in favor of hiring a single interpreter from the court's point of view. Though ASL interpreters typically agree to interpret a plea alone, they should do so mindful of the consequences that can result in a small percentage of pleas that are later challenged by the defendant.

Extending the privilege is a choice open to the proceedings interpreter when the courts are unwilling to hire a table interpreter. However, care should be taken that the guidelines are not over-generalized. Interpreters must use common sense, prudence and diplomacy to advocate for adequate working conditions. The interpreter who determines that his or her professional ethics would be compromised by inadequate staffing can and should decline even a change of plea.

To summarize: it is generally improper for the interpreter to interpret privileged communications and then interpret for the record. In some matters, is also improper to leave the deaf person without access to counsel even if there is no record interpreting when the need for the client to have immediate access to the attorney exists. If no record interpreting is foreseen, or if the proceeding is not conducive to accessing counsel, such as a status call or an arraignment, then it is less essential to provide a table interpreter and an extension may be considered. On the other hand, in matters in which the deaf person is an active participant or needs to be able to consult freely, quickly and unobtrusively with counsel, the interpreter should stand firm and insist that the case is properly staffed.

The proceedings interpreter must use professional discretion in advising the court about all of its interpreting needs. The proceedings interpreter must have adequate information to competently advise the court of its needs:

- Will the setting require table interpreters?

- Will there be record interpreting?

- Will counsel need to speak extensively with the deaf client pre-trial?

- Will the deaf person need a voice at counsel table to be effectively present?

- Will there be complicated testimony by expert witnesses?

- Will other deaf witnesses testify against the defendant?

- Will co-defendants also use interpreting services?

Of course, no interpreter can make an informed decision on these matters if he or she is not equipped prior to accepting the assignment with adequate data upon which to undertake the analysis. The implications for pre-acceptance preparation are weighty. As an officer of the court who has been qualified as the court's expert, the proceedings interpreter has a corresponding duty to undertake this preparation and analysis.

VIII. Ineffective Alternatives: A Chorus Line of Interpreters

At times, ASL interpreters have compromised their working conditions by separating the proceedings interpreting team and assigning each member the additional function of interpreting privileged communications for a designated party. In such cases, the parties watch the proceedings team while in court, and use the assigned team member during the breaks to interpret attorney-client conferences.

This compromise is inadequate for several reasons. First, if the interpreter is to interpret private conversations during a break, then the interpreter is not able to take a break. Interpreting is a mentally exhausting activity. The accuracy of the interpretation degrades in proportion to the amount of time the interpreter has been working without rest.

Second, while one proceedings interpreter is working during a matter, only the **off-mic** interpreter (typically called the **feed** interpreter by ASL interpreters) is available for privileged conversations. In other words, the deaf party is only able to speak with counsel when his or her designated interpreter is **off-mic**. While the deaf party's interpreter is working only the adverse party's interpreter is available for privileged communications with counsel. Sometimes interpreters agree that the off-mic interpreter is responsible to for *all* of the private conversations for both deaf consumers. This configuration forces the adverse parties to share the same interpreter for in-court privileged communications and the lack of trust remains a troubling issue.

Finally, when the off-mic interpreter is interpreting private conversations, the working interpreter has no teammate to monitor and assist with adjusting the accuracy of the interpretation. Hence, it is a compromise that creates more difficulty than it resolves.

Another arrangement that court interpreters have attempted to use, frequently at the behest of the court, is the spoken language interpreting model. As explained during the discussion of collapsed functions, the spoken language interpreting model does not fit ASL interpreting. The inappropriate use of the spoken language interpreting model was illustrated in *Bednarski*.

Recall that *Bednarski* was an important ASL interpreting case because it established the principle that when a state statute provided for all three interpreter functions, each function must be filled even in a civil case. Nevertheless, the configuration of the interpreters suggested in *Bednarski* was ineffective and illustrated what can happen when courts, and not interpreters, arrange and assign roles.

In *Bednarski* each deaf party had a single proceedings interpreter who also interpreted the assigned party's private conversations. In other words, two proceedings interpreters would stand side by side in the well and the defendant would watch "his" interpreter while the plaintiff watched "her" interpreter to understand the proceedings. When the deaf person wanted to speak with counsel "his" or "her" interpreter would approach the table from the well to interpret the conversation. In addition, a third interpreter, not affiliated with the parties, would be provided to interpret for the deaf witness testimony. All three interpreters would work alone. None of them would have the assistance of a team interpreter to ensure that fatigue did not jeopardize the integrity of the message. The court could have provided each interpreter with a team for a total of six interpreters – an unlikely scenario. The table function would still have been unfilled unless the off-mic interpreter also performed table interpreting services – a situation which is ineffective for the reasons mentioned at the beginning of this section. Providing "stereo interpreters" comported with the letter, but not the spirit, of the Michigan statute.

In principle, *Bednarski* sought to ensure that the deaf parties had access to counsel through interpreted privileged communications. The court was following the spoken language interpreting model when it required that the proceedings interpreters to provide both the privileged communications function and the proceedings function. It was clearly addressing the lack of adequate services during the initial custody proceeding when a single interpreter was provided for all three functions for both deaf parties and all of the deaf witnesses. However, the practical result was two interpreters standing side by side in the well interpreting the same content simultaneously and without any support. The *Bedarski* configuration is illustrated in the following figure.

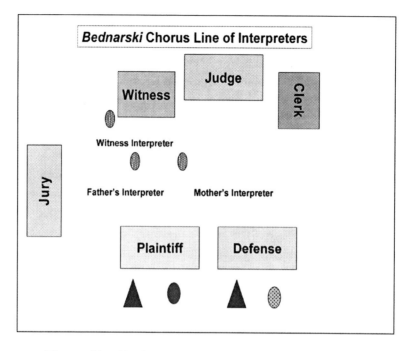

Figure 11 -- Ineffective Arrangement of Interpreters

This configuration is inefficient, overly burdensome and aligns the court's interpreters with the parties rather than with the Court. By adding one more interpreter, the case would be appropriately staffed and none of the interpreters would be working alone.

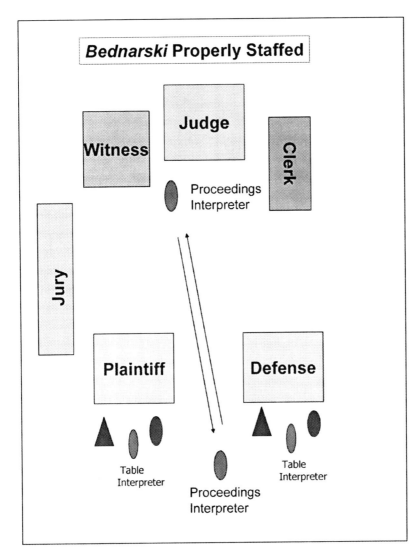

Figure 12 -- Effective Configuration

Two proceedings interpreters work together as a team for both deaf parties to watch and interpret all of the proceedings and all witness testimony for the record.[102] Each party has a table interpreter to provide access to counsel during the proceedings and monitor the work of the proceedings interpreters. This configuration assures the most impartial team is interpreting for the record. Each deaf person has full and unfettered access to counsel without the concern that the adverse party will be sharing the same interpreter for privileged communications. *Berdarski's* mission was admirable, and the intent of the statute can be effectuated while preserving favorable working conditions for the interpreters.

In this chapter, the definition of the court interpreter as a linguistic expert who takes an oath and functions as an officer of the court has been presented. The work of court interpreters has been illustrated by highlighting the differences between spoken language interpreter and sign language interpreter practices. The statutory and constitutional basis of the function-based definitions was explored. Finally, a number of cases, statutes and court rules have been discussed which provide justification for best practices in both criminal and civil matters. In the next section, the role and rationale for the ASL table interpreter will be explored in depth and the practice of monitoring the court interpreters to ensure fidelity to the record will be explained.

Chapter 5
Access to Counsel:
The ASL Interpreter at the Litigation Table

Chapter 5
Access to Counsel: The ASL
Interpreter at the Litigation Table

I. Introduction

Lawyers are taught that "[w]here there is an interpreter, there is a ground of appeal."[1] While it has been recognized that interpretation is an art and not a science, the legal system only grudgingly accepts this fact. If, for no other reason than the interpreter swears to interpreting to the best of their ability, the legal system expects that an interpreter hired by the court will in fact produce an accurate interpretation.[2] As lawyers become more familiar with the "best" of the interpreter's ability, the need for an independent method to review the proceedings interpreter's work becomes apparent. That mechanism, for ASL interpreters, is the interpreter who sits at counsel table, interprets privileged communications and monitors the proceedings interpreter's work for accuracy.[3]

II. A Review of the Function and Placement of Table Interpreters

Sign language interpreters, due to the visual nature of the language, are unable to sit next to the deaf litigant and render a whispered simultaneous interpretation which is the normal practice and placement for spoken language interpreters. Rather, ASL court interpreters must be situated in front of the deaf person in their direct **sightline** in the well of the courtroom. A separate interpreter, defined as a member of the litigation team, will sit at counsel table for privileged "whispered" communications between counsel and client and to watch the proceedings interpreters for accuracy.[4] Commonly referred to as the table interpreter, the sign language interpreter occupying this position performs two separate functions: (1) providing access to counsel by interpreting private conversations and (2) serving as a check on the accuracy of the court interpreter's rendition of the proceedings.

The differences in the work of the proceedings interpreter versus the work of the table interpreter have been explained as[5]

> the defense interpreter is party to privileged communications in non-structured conditions which may require something more than mere translation. At times the interpreter may have to accede to the desires of defense counsel whose work in the courtroom and in private conferences with the defendant may require the interpreter to vary the more routine services he would perform as a witness interpreter. His presence may assist defense counsel in assuring that testimony is being accurately translated. This *potentially partisan role* is to be recalled when we later consider the oath requirement.[6]

The role of interpreting private communications places the interpreter is a position inconsistent with that of **record interpreting.**

Nor should the table interpreter take an oath.[7] As has been explained: "[t]he work of the defense interpreter ordinarily does not become a part of the record, unlike the work of the witness interpreter."[8] The interpreting done by the ASL interpreter who sits at counsel table is privileged and does not become a part of the record either; therefore, the oath is not given. The table interpreter's role has been compared to that of a private investigator or a psychiatrist appointed to the defense team who would not also be called upon to serve the court.[9]

III. The Development of Table Interpreting

Historically, record interpreting (witness interpreting function) was the only type of interpreting formally recognized. Only when a *witness* did not speak the language of the court was an interpreter appointed to enable the judge and the jury to understand the foreign language spoken by the witness. In early times, a NES person would either bring an interpreter to sit at counsel table and relate the proceedings to him or her or, more likely, do without.[10]

In the landmark case of *United States ex rel Negron v. New York*,[11] the United States Court of Appeals abandoned the status quo of providing only witness interpreting services. *Negron* recognized that understanding the proceedings was a fundamental right for defendants faced with the adversary process. *Negron* established the principle that spoken language proceedings interpreters (who would sit at counsel table, interpret the proceedings and the privileged communications) were required to satisfy the Sixth Amendment's right to be present and assist counsel at trial. Recall that the spoken language interpreter who sits at counsel table collapses the functions of proceedings work and access to counsel work. *Negron* required both functions to be interpreted for a proceeding to comport with the Constitution. ASL interpreters by virtue of working with a language that requires them to be placed in front of the deaf person have staffed the function of access to counsel with a separate interpreter who sits at counsel table.

Table interpreting has been called by various names over the years, such as, defense interpreter, counter-interpreter, check interpreter, party interpreter, litigation team interpreter, monitor interpreter, and law office interpreter.[12] Regardless of the name, the functions of ensuring access to counsel before and during trial and of monitoring the proceedings interpreter for accuracy are not new functions. As early as 1918, a monitor interpreter was provided by one of the parties at their own expense, though the court admitted that it did not know what it would have done had the monitor actually challenged the court interpreter's work![13] As will be discussed, the processes and procedures for monitoring the proceedings interpreter's work have been refined in the ensuing years.

At the very birth of professional simultaneous court interpreting -- the Nuremberg trials -- monitor interpreters were present and working, albeit in a slightly different fashion than is currently used. Francesca Gaiba described the monitoring process used at Nuremberg:

Acknowledgement of the likelihood of errors led to a system of subsequent quality control in the form of a comparison between the various language transcripts (based on shorthand reporters' notes) and the original spoken material. This checking work was one of the duties of the "third" team of interpreters. On any one day, two full teams (three interpreters per language "desk") would work in court. . . . . When not actually interpreting, the other team listened to the proceedings in a separate room. This arrangement was introduced after the trial had begun in order to ensure continuity in terminology and familiarity with the material.[14]

The Nuremberg interpreters recognized a basic fact about all interpreting: There *will* be errors. Accepting this fact, the team established a creative quality control system to check for errors and to ensure that all interpreters used consistent terminology to avoid confusion. The driving force behind the system was the desire to ensure accurate interpreting and a fair trial for the participants.

IV. The Interpreting Function

Traditionally, courts presumed that they need hire only one ASL interpreter any time deaf people were involved in a case. Courts presuppose that the ASL interpreter functions much like a spoken language interpreter by interpreting both privileged conversations and the proceedings from the table. The unique positioning of sign language interpreters in the well of the courtroom, however, is not conducive to interpreting both functions. In order for ASL interpreters to interpret attorney-client conferences during witness testimony or other proceedings, the proceedings must be stopped and the ASL interpreter must commute to counsel table to interpret for the conference. To avoid disruptions caused by halting the proceedings, two ASL interpreters are required to perform the function that a single spoken language interpreter can perform, though the spoken language interpreter confronts similar challenges when faced with multiple NES participants.[15] As a result, a separate ASL table interpreter is retained to perform the function of ensuring that the deaf person has access to counsel and can meaningfully participate in his or her own trial.

A. The Legal Foundation

The challenge for the ASL interpreter is to articulate the differences between ASL and spoken language interpreting practices which are more familiar to the court.[16] In order for the ASL interpreter to present a cogent argument for best working conditions, there must be a firm understanding of the legal justification for the table interpreter – separate from the justifications underlying the proceedings interpreter.

The Constitutional basis for the table interpreter function derives from the Sixth Amendment guarantees of access to counsel which have come to mean: (1) the right to be present; (2) the right to assist in one's own defense; and (3) the right to have the assistance of experts. Courts have suggested that significant conflicts of interest arise when the interpreter is privy to private communications between counsel and client and then must also interpret objectively in the court proceedings role for the record. A table interpreter is a valuable protection for the court even when the proceedings interpreter is highly skilled. However, when the proceedings interpreter is shown to be biased or to possess deficient interpreting skills, a solution often resorted to is the appointment of an interpreter to monitor the interpretation for accuracy and neutrality. The cases that discuss the provision of a separate interpreter for this function remind us that this interpreter does not also interpret for the record.

The ASL court interpreter needs to understand these legal principles in depth.[17]

B. The Concept of Linguistic Presence

The argument for counsel table interpreter at public expense is strongest in the criminal arena. The Sixth Amendment states, in part, that "in all *criminal* cases, the *accused* shall enjoy. . . ."[18] The Sixth Amendment's protections do not apply in civil cases. As a result, interpreters are not constitutionally required in civil cases for the NES person to be linguistically present. The analogy to the right to be present and have assistance of counsel, however, is still useful.

In addition, for sign language interpreters, a statutory argument can be made that the ADA requires the provision of a table interpreter in order to assist counsel. Attorneys are considered public accommodations falling under Title III of the Act. Accordingly, attorneys are required to provide reasonable accommodations to deaf clients, as will be discussed later in this Chapter. The United States Department of Justice filed a complaint against a solo practitioner in Rochester, New York for failing to provide an interpreter for out-of-court consultations in a civil matter for a deaf client. A settlement was reached under which the attorney agreed to provide interpreters and to advertise to the deaf community that his practice was accessible.[19] In the civil arena, in addition to the protections offered by the ADA, court interpreting statutes may require that the function of the table interpreter be covered. Those cases will be discussed in further detail in this chapter.

In the criminal context, the Sixth Amendment provides that a defendant has a right to be present and to have the assistance of counsel during trial. The Supreme Court in *Dusky v. United States* held that the right to be present at trial requires that the defendant possess "sufficient present ability to consult with his lawyer with a reasonable degree of rational understanding."[20] One Florida criminal appeal involved a seventeen-year-old deaf male who was charged with second degree murder.[21] Invoking *Dusky,* the Court stated:

> Due process requires that a defendant not be made to stand trial unless he has sufficient present ability to consult with his attorney with a reasonable degree of rational understanding and a rational as well as factual understanding of the proceedings against him.[22]

Traditionally, this principle has been used to determine whether a person has the cognitive ability to stand trial. A person who is not mentally competent cannot be tried. More and more, as in Florida example, the competency argument has been extended to require that the defendant also demonstrate the linguistic competency required to communicate with counsel and assist in his defense.[23]

Linguistically incompetent has been defined as "a defendant who is unable to understand and participate in the legal proceedings because of his inability to communicate, is precluded from being subjected to trial by the state."[24] In the Florida case, no less than seven expert witnesses disagreed on whether the defendant had adequate communication skills to understand an interpreted trial and assist counsel with the defense. A small percentage of deaf people who interacted with the legal system lack a formalized language system. This segment of the community may have not been exposed to American Sign Language, may not have been educated, or may have other cognitive difficulties preventing them from being tried under *Dusky*. The majority of deaf people, however, use ASL and would only be considered linguistically incompetent to stand trial if they were denied access to interpreting services.[25]

Ironically, in a California case, an *English-speaking* defendant argued that he should be provided with an interpreter when the Spanish-speaking witnesses were testifying. [26] Though denying the request because the defendant could communicate with counsel in English, the court stated "the sound premises behind the constitutional provision are that a defendant *who cannot understand* the proceedings taking place is not truly present at his trial, and a defendant *who cannot communicate* with his counsel is ipso facto denied effective representation."[27] This case placed both the proceedings function and the access to counsel function squarely within the protection of the Sixth Amendment.

It may have been, however, that the defendant in the California case sought an interpreter at counsel table to point out any discrepancies between the witness' testimony in Spanish and the interpreted English version, though the argument was not clear from the reported opinion. In that instance, the defendant could have retained an expert consulting interpreter, at his own expense, to monitor the proceedings interpreters and serve as a check on their accuracy. If there are interpreter errors infecting the record, then the defendant is not able to fully confront the witnesses against him – a critical provision of the Sixth Amendment and should have expert assistance available to him. The argument is equally valid regardless of the native language of the defendant.

One 1985 federal criminal case placed the right to be present within the Fourteenth Amendment, suggesting that "a criminal defendant has a due process right to be meaningfully present at his or her trial."[28] A critical test was set forth to establish a procedural due process violation: "a defendant in a criminal proceeding is denied due process when: (1) what is told him [or her] is incomprehensible; (2) the accuracy and scope of a translation at a hearing or trial is subject to great doubt; (3) the nature of the proceeding is not explained to him [or her] in a manner designed to ensure his [or her] full comprehension; or (4) a credible claim of incapacity to understand due to language difficulty is made and the district court fails to review the evidence and make appropriate findings."[29]

Each prong of this test depends, at least in part, on the provision of an interpreter to perform the table function. The table interpreter monitors the proceedings interpreter for (1) comprehensibility and (2) ensures the accuracy of the translation is not in great doubt. The table interpreter inteprets privately for counsel to (3) ensure that counsel can adequately explain the proceedings. Finally, the table interpreter is (4) often the first person in a position to know about any capacity issue related to language.[30] When these functions are unfulfilled, according to *Negron,* "the adjudication loses its reasoned interaction … and becomes an invective against an insensible object."[31] The test presented above plays an important role in the table interpreter's actual monitoring duties, as will be discussed in more detail shortly. The table interpreter who must explain to the court a perceived error should keep in mind the standard by which the interpretation will be judged to violate the due process clause. In discussing the proceedings interpreter's work, the table interpreter should state how the errors in the interpretation affect the comprehensibility, place the accuracy in doubt, endanger full comprehension or create incapacity to understand due to the interpreter's language skills.

C. The Federal Court's Position

Recall that in the federal system, courts can borrow the defendant's interpreter to work with NES witnesses.[32] When the court borrows the spoken language proceedings interpreter from counsel table to interpret at the stand for the NES witness, the defendant is deprived of access to counsel. Federal courts have arrived at a compromise in an attempt to balance the right to counsel with the economics of administering justice in a time of shrinking federal budgets and burgeoning case loads. The Federal Court Interpreting Act, however, does not *prohibit* the court from providing separate interpreters when there are NES witnesses and defendants or when there are NES co-defendants. The Act simply does not require multiple interpreters and leaves the decision to the discretion of the trial court.[33] Several federal and state courts have rejected the federal compromise, refused to bow to economics, and held that meaningful access must be granted through the provision of a separate interpreter.[34]

A recent New York state judge denied the NES defendant the opportunity to have a bilingual investigator sit with him during those times when the court borrowed his proceedings interpreter to work with the non-English speaking witnesses.[35] After the defendant was convicted, he filed a writ of habeas corpus in federal court seeking review of the constitutionality of the state court proceedings. In federal court, the defendant presented the two strongest constitutional arguments for a table interpreter. He argued that while the court interpreter was occupied at the witness stand, he did not have access to counsel; therefore, was unable to assist with his defense – the Sixth Amendment argument. He also argued that he was denied access to the actual proceedings while the court interpreter was whisper interpreting for the witness at the stand – the due process/fundamental fairness argument. The defendant was left without a mechanism to communicate with counsel or to hear and understand the proceedings.

Though not granting the relief sought, the federal court admonished the state court for its handling of the proceedings:

> For a trial judge arbitrarily to deny permission for a translator
> to sit between defendant and counsel during the trial would be

an *unsettling departure from fair play.* While a trial judge has broad discretion to manage courtroom logistics, . . . both civil and criminal trials take place every day, in courtrooms across the country, with multiple lawyers, paralegals, legal assistants, police officers and other personnel assisting one side or the other at counsel table. Certainly a judge has and should freely exercise the power to limit the hordes in the interests of order, but it is not apparent how it threatens orderly courtroom procedure if a single lawyer in a one-defendant trial has the assistance of a single staff member, particularly for a significant reason such as facilitating communication between client and counsel. In this case, neither the prosecutor nor the judge suggested any reason why the assistant's presence should be denied and the State offers none to this Court.[36]

Essentially, the federal court, which does not have to provide a separate table interpreter, reprimanded the state court for not permitting a table interpreter. The court reasoned that there was no additional expense involved or obvious prejudice from permitting the investigator to sit at the table and keep the defendant apprised of the proceedings. Without discussing the double standard, the federal court essentially admonished the state court for not taking advantage of the resources available to ensure the defendant had full access to the proceedings.

Even if the state court had permitted the arrangement, however, the interpreting conditions would still have been inadequate. If *the investigator* was permitted to interpret the proceedings while the court's interpreter was otherwise occupied with the witness, the court should have first satisfied itself that the investigator was a qualified court interpreter. Ideally, the state court should have provided a separate *court* interpreter to interpret the *proceedings* while the court interpreter was with the witness. In the absence of providing a separate proceedings interpreter, the investigator should have undergone *voir dire* and been sworn to interpret the proceedings accurately during the time the court interpreter was at the stand with the NES witness.

In *Negron,* the court emphasized how witness interpreting can strip the defendant of his ability to both confer with counsel *and* understand the proceedings:

> Another factor adding to Negron's handicap during the trial relates to the crucial testimony of the Spanish-speaking witness Pagan. Negron testified upon cross-examination at his original trial and also at the hearing before this court that he was too far away to hear Pagan's testimony, which was translated to the jury in English through an interpreter. This claim is given credence by the realities of the situation where, as in the trial of this case, the interpreter approaches the witness on the stand and poses the English question in Spanish and receives an answer in Spanish which is then related in English to the jury. Because of the nearness of the interpreter to the witness, the Spanish portion of the translation is in a lower tone than the English portion since it is only the latter that interests the court, jury and attorneys. The defendant, however, sits at the counsel table some distance away. This is precisely what happened at the hearing before this court when the testimony of the Spanish-speaking Negron was translated in English to this court. In fact, at the original trial Negron's counsel, in summation, informed the jury that his client was unable to hear what Pagan was saying in Spanish because he was speaking too softly, and that his client 'did not know what most of the witnesses were saying because he doesn't understand English."[37]

Hence, best practices based upon the Sixth Amendment and the due process/fundamental fairness arguments suggest, though do not mandate, in the federal system, that a second *proceedings* interpreter should be provided to interpret the proceedings to the NES defendant at the table during NES witness testimony. In the context of ASL interpreting, a second interpreter should also be provided; however, that interpreter *only* provides access to counsel by interpreting table conversations. The ASL interpreter at the table does not take an oath to interpret accurately nor does the ASL table interpreter interpret any proceedings. Hence, the Deaf person, like the NES person, will have each of the three interpreting functions fully staffed through the work of two different interpreters.[38]

V. The Monitor Function

The Fourteenth Amendment's due process guarantees of fundamental fairness and the Sixth Amendment's right to be present justify the table interpreter's duty to inform counsel of any substantive errors made by the court's interpreter when NES witnesses are testifying. Obviously, if the defendant is receiving an inaccurate interpretation, he or she is not linguistically present and cannot confront the witnesses against him or her. The function of providing an independent check on the court interpreter's work falls to the ASL table interpreter who monitors the proceedings interpreter's work and informs the attorney of significant errors.

A 1984 California case described the problem of proceeding without ensuring the monitor function is staffed: "when no defense interpreter is available, it is impossible for the non-English speaking defendant to check the accuracy or competency of the witness interpreter's translation. This breakdown effectively precludes the defense from challenging or impeaching the interpretation rendered, because objection regarding accuracy of the interpretation must be made [in the court] below." [39] The same court later suggested in a different case that "when a showing is made at trial, that an interpreter may be biased or his skills deficient, one solution may be appointment of a 'check interpreter.' When no objection is raised to the competence of the interpreter during the trial, the issue cannot be raised on appeal." [40]

In a federal case most widely known for its discussion regarding deaf jurors, the Court of Appeals in *United States v. Dempsey*, explained the value of the monitoring function while justifying the reasons a deaf person should be permitted to serve on a jury.[41] According to *Dempsey*, "[a]ny problems with inadequate interpretation, because the interpreter either interjects opinions or incompetently interprets can be monitored by the parties to the suit because the proceeding is in open court."[42] The court further explained that "[i]f the interpreter's adequacy comes into question, the parties can have another interpreter present to review the quality of the translation. And a court might possibly create a record by videotaping the proceedings."[43] The use of a monitor to check the proceedings interpreters' work was recommended even though the only deaf participant was a juror – an intriguing idea that is not standard practice currently with respect to jury duty interpreting.

An early federal case involved interpretation for a Native American defendant charged with assault with a dangerous weapon.[44] Due to the isolated nature of the setting, the community of bilingual speakers was quite small and the court-appointed interpreter happened to be related to several of the witnesses. The defendant objected to using this interpreter because of the family connection. The trial court conceded that it was inappropriate to use a family member as the court's interpreter and sought to find a replacement. However, no suitable neutral interpreter could be found.[45]

Out of necessity, the trial proceeded with the court-appointed interpreter. As a precaution, however, the court formally appointed another interpreter "representing the defendant as a "counter-interpreter" to check the court's interpreter for accuracy and ethical behavior."[46] During the state's witnesses, this counter-interpreter sat at counsel table and "from time to time made suggestions and corrections concerning the interpretation of the testimony by the official interpreter."[47] In instances when the skills or ethics of the court interpreter are in question, a separate interpreter should be hired to monitor the proceedings interpreter's work. Other federal courts have agreed even though providing a "counter-interpreter" is not recognized as a matter of right in the federal system under the Court Interpreter's Act.

VI. Monitoring by Committee

The monitor function has not always been so formally recognized, though it often takes place on an *ad hoc* basis. It is a common experience for interpreters that there will be someone in the room, not paid as an interpreter, but with an opinion regarding the interpretation. Challenges to the interpretation are more frequently made by these non-interpreter participants than by retained professional monitor interpreters. As a result of knowing the interpreter's working languages, it appears impossible for bilinguals to not monitor and not to become involved when there are interpreted errors. Court interpreter ethical codes advise court interpreters to treat these challenges professionally, without becoming defensive, and to objectively analyze any challenge to their interpretation.[48]

The inability of observers to refrain from monitoring interpreters is best demonstrated by the experiences of bilingual jurors. Frequently there are challenges to seating bilingual jurors out of a fear they will rely upon their own understanding of the foreign language testimony rather than the official interpretation. The Supreme Court of the United States considered a peremptory challenge to a bilingual juror on the grounds that the juror would not attend to the official interpretation and in essence would be deciding the case on evidence different than that received by the remainder of the jury in *Hernandez v. New York*.[49]

Bilingual legal commentators have been critical of the analysis in *Hernandez* and have accused the Supreme Court of being insensitive to the character of bilingualism. University of Wisconsin Associate Professor, Debrorah A. Rameriz, published psycholinguistic research that convincingly demonstrates the impossibility of the task asked of bilingual jurors by the Court. As a starting point, Rameriz described the instruction to bilingual jurors as:

> [T]he prosecutor was asking the bilinguals to hear and process the foreign language testimony in the following way: (1) listen to the words spoken in Spanish by the witness; (2) do not process or derive any meaning from the Spanish words or, alternatively, process what you hear in Spanish, but disregard any information derived from the Spanish testimony; (3) listen to the words spoken in English by the interpreter; (4) process those words; (5) then, rely solely upon the information derived from the English words spoken by the interpreter.[50]

According to Rameriz, this task is cognitively impossible. The following test with dramatically illustrates Rameriz' point:

> [L]ook at a billboard which had on it the English sentence: "A mind is a terrible thing to waste." Now assume that she is instructed to look at the billboard, but refrain from reading the sentence. She is instead to focus solely on describing

how many of the letters are round in shape and how many are linear or curved. The monolingual would not be able to comply with that instruction. She would discover that she could not deactivate her ability to understand the written words on the billboard. Unconsciously, she would process the words and understand their meaning, even when instructed not to do so.[51]

Rameriz presents intriguing psycholinguistic justification for the underlying reasons why bilingual individuals find themselves actively involved in monitoring the interpretation. Many cases in which bilingual jurors have thrust themselves into the role of monitoring the working interpreters have been appealed on these issues. Nevertheless, courts rely on the fiction that a jury can be ordered to turn off their comprehension of the other language and attend only to the official interpretation. Despite the admonition, many more appeals are likely because monitoring by non-practitioners is a practice not likely to stop as long as there are bilinguals in the courtroom.

A. Bilingual Judges

In an early Nebraska case, the judge understood Bohemian and monitored the interpretation interrupting several times to correct serious errors. [52] The trial judge "warned the interpreter a number of times as to his duties, such as, that he must not ask any questions except those which were asked by the attorney, and must directly interpret her answers as given; again, that he must stop [the witness] and have her restate any part of the answer which he did not recall."[53] Though it is hard to imagine how a judge has the time during a proceeding to monitor the interpreter, bilingual non-interpreters feel compelled to "second chair" the interpretation. This case also demonstrates an important point: The monitoring function is not limited to issues of accuracy. Rather, in most of the cases, courts want the person monitoring to note ethical or protocol errors such as when the interpreter goes beyond the role of interpreting and holds private conversations with the witness.

B. Bilingual Parties

A deposition of a key witness was taken in Liechtenstein where the national language is German in a 1990 Florida case.[54] The deposition interpreting formed one basis for appeal. The judge who oversaw the foreign deposition noted that one of the *defendants* spoke both German and English and was not in the least bit "bashful about disagreeing with the translation on the rare occasion that it occurred."[55] On appeal, the court held that the defendant's rights were adequately protected because he *personally* could monitor and correct the interpretation to the witness. In spoken language cases, a party or even the witness using the interpreter could be bilingual to some extent and able to function as an additional check on the interpretation. For the vast majority of deaf people, however, the lack of meaningful hearing ability precludes them from accessing the spoken English. Some deaf people are bilingual in ASL and written English; however, the oral channel of transmission in court constitutes a bar to successfully monitoring the interpretation. In addition, defendants, witnesses and other parties should not be required to spend their energy monitoring the interpretation when their focus is needed upon the content of the case.

C. Bilingual Jurors

As mentioned previously, bilingual citizens can be stricken from a jury because of their language ability. One personal injury case demonstrates how bilinguals assert themselves into the process. The civil case was appealed on grounds that a bilingual juror challenged the court interpreter's rendition of a word spoken in "Spanglish." [56] On appeal, the court undertook a lively analysis of **contact language varieties** in spoken English and Spanish in New York City. The plaintiff spoke Spanish and sued the transit authority for injuries she received after falling when a subway train stopped suddenly. In her testimony, the plaintiff used the word "chocar" to describe how the train stopped. The interpreter rendered the term as "bumped." A juror challenged the accuracy of the interpretation because, in the juror's estimation, the word meant "crashed." Obviously a crash is more likely to produce serious injuries than a bump. From a damages perspective then, the discrepancy was important.

In chambers, "the juror, with interpreter, court reporter, and counsel present . . . explained that the verb "chocar" translates into English as 'to bump' but was used by the plaintiff to mean to "crash."[57] The juror contended that if the plaintiff truly meant "bump," she would have used the Spanglish word 'bompiar' which is commonly used by New York Puerto Ricans similar to the plaintiff. After consultation in chambers, the plaintiff agreed with the juror's version of the interpretation.

Not surprisingly, the court was concerned about whether the juror would be able to attend only to the official court interpretation for the remainder of the trial. When the juror was asked if he could ignore interpreted errors, he responded affirmatively; however, he noted that "if there was a large discrepancy, he would bring it to [the Court's] attention."[58] In essence, the juror would continue monitoring the court's interpreter. The juror's experience confirmed Professor Ramirez's theory that one simply cannot turn off language comprehension skills at the direction of the Court.

In one rather embarrassing reported case, a juror was dismissed for questioning the proceedings interpreter's work.[59] When the juror disagreed in open court with the interpreter's rendition, the court interpreter retorted: "[I]n the first place, the jurors are not to listen to the Spanish but to the English. I am a certified court interpreter" to which the juror responded, "you're an idiot."[60] The juror later denied saying *idiot*, claiming that she actually said "it's an *idiom*." The court determined that the juror could not remain impartial because her attitude would likely infect the other jurors.

It is interesting to note the defensiveness on the part of the certified court interpreter. The interpreter's immediate concern was not for accuracy of the record, but for appearances. The immediate defensive reaction was to blame the juror for acting outside of the juror's role by questioning the interpretation. The interpreter did not consider whether the juror's position was correct or objectively analyze the challenge as her ethics require. Rather disturbingly, instead of delving more into the validity of the "monitor-juror's" challenge, the Court summarily removed her from the case.

As mentioned earlier, bilingual jurors pose special problems for court not only because of the tendency to monitor the interpretation but also because the fear that in attending to the testimony in a language different from English, the bilingual juror may hear different testimony than received by English speaking jurors who must rely upon interpreters. As a compromise, bilingual jurors are instructed to ignore the source language testimony and attend only to the interpreted version. Bilingual jurors must be questioned on *voir dire* about their ability to consider only the interpretation and ignore the source language. In a 1999 Delaware case, it was stated that "[b]ilingual jurors must be questioned individually regarding their ability: to treat their own foreign language translation as inadmissible evidence; to base their judgment solely upon the official interpreter's translation that is admitted into evidence; and to refrain from discussing inadmissible evidence (their own translation) with other jurors."[61] A typical instruction reads:

> Languages other than English may be used during this trial. The evidence you are to consider is only that provided through the official court (interpreters) (translators). Although some of you may know the non-English language used, it is important that all jurors consider the same evidence. Therefore, you must base your decision on the evidence presented in the English (interpretation) (translation). You must disregard any different meaning of the non-English words.[62]

What is disturbing about the instruction is that the court is not concerned about ensuring an accurate interpretation. Ostensibly, courts would prefer that the entire jury hear inaccurate interpreted testimony, rather than to concede that errors in language interpretation will happen. A better alternative would be to create a system which would reduce the impact of the errors such as by videotaping the proceedings or by retaining monitors in interpreted cases. In fact, courts know that jurors will continue to monitor the proceedings regardless of the warning to disregard the source language testimony. The Delaware opinion repeated a point made by Justice Kennedy in the Supreme Court's *Hernandez* decision: If a discrepancy was noted by a bilingual juror, the juror could discreetly advise the trial judge through a note to the bailiff. [63] This implicitly admits that courts know that bilingual jurors will actually monitor the proceedings even sanctioning the process of discreetly bringing an error to the attention of the trial court.

D. Bilingual Attorneys

Many cases have discussed whether bilingual attorneys are also in a position to monitor the work of the proceedings interpreters. In a federal case, the defendant objected to the use of a non-court certified interpreter for the Spanish-speaking witnesses against him. [64] The Court made two recommendations: (1) tape record the interpretation and the witness testimony; or, (2) have defense counsel monitor the interpretation for accuracy. Both suggestions were objected to, and the court recessed to give the government attorney an opportunity to locate a court certified interpreter. The prosecution was unable to locate a replacement interpreter in the *twenty-four minute* recess allotted and the Court ultimately declared a mistrial. Even in relatively recent times, courts still suggest that bilingual counsel should monitor the skills of the court interpreter.

Practically, bilingual attorneys – as bilinguals -- probably do monitor the interpretation at some level. Though the quality of legal work likely suffers in direct proportion to the amount of energy they spend on attending to the interpreting services. If there is a disagreement involving the interpretation; however, that places the attorney in the untenable position of being a witness supporting one version of the interpretation against the proceedings interpreter who may disagree with the attorney's interpretation. Ethically, an attorney is not permitted to become a witness in their own case.

VII. The Process of Making a Challenge

Often, sign language interpreters interested in court interpreting think that the table interpreting position is the safest place to begin their legal interpreting careers. Because the ASL table interpreter does not interpret the proceedings, the reasoning is that he or she does not have to worry quite so much about understanding the legal terminology or the proper procedures for interpreting in court. On the face of it, the risk of harm from an inexperienced interpreter is reduced if that interpreter is limited to counsel table interpreting. While this logic has some appeal, novice legal interpreters should take on this role with some circumspect.

Because the table interpreter functions as an expert for the team when not interpreting privileged conversations, the interpreter must have defensible credentials. In other words, the table interpreter should be fully qualified as a court interpreter. Once a challenge is made, opposing counsel has the right to question the qualifications of the challenger.[65] Hence, when challenging the proceedings interpreter's work, the monitor must also be prepared to testify professionally and convincingly to challenges to their own qualifications to monitor.

A. To Interrupt or Not to Interrupt

As the table interpreter, the privilege to interrupt the Court and report an error must not be abused -- because it is truly a limited privilege. Court interpreter ethics caution that any interruptions to the court process should come only as a last resort.[66] Court interpreters strive to be unobtrusive, and even though the table interpreter's role is not that of a court interpreter, a table interpreter should be aware that interrupting the proceedings distracts from the important work of the Court and can have a detrimental effect on the process. There are a number of other less intrusive options for the monitor to employ to correct errors. Interrupting the Court is reserved for serious, immediate non-recoverable errors typically of interpreted testimony. Courts loathe interrupting testimony for trivial disagreements, particularly about stylistics. Such pettiness as "I would have signed it differently" will not be countenanced frequently and only serves to waste valuable time and damage the table interpreter's credibility.

B. Bump v. Crash: The Standard for Accuracy

Courts recognize that different interpreters will produce varying interpretations and they expect that only egregious errors affecting the substance of the testimony will cause the interpreter to interrupt the court.

In 1987, a Minnesota court said:

Translation is an art more than a science, and there is no such thing as a perfect translation of a defendant's testimony. Indeed, in every case there will be room for disagreement among expert translators over some aspects of the translation. Defense counsel, with the assistance of the defendant's own interpreter, is always free to object contemporaneously if counsel believes that the court-appointed interpreter has significantly misinterpreted or omitted parts of the defendant's testimony. [67]

Hence, courts know that there will be room for disagreement about interpretations and want to be interrupted only for those errors that go to the substance of the message, and that cannot be remedied in a less obtrusive non-prejudicial manner. For good or for bad, courts are reluctant to reverse a case and free a convicted defendant upon a perceived technicality such as interpreting errors. When the substance of the testimony is conveyed, despite the errors, the conviction generally will not be reversed.[68] At times, courts have commented that though minor errors can affect the perception of the witness by the jury, only an error in translation that has a prejudicial effect will form the basis of a reversal on appeal. [69]

The Court explained,

Although this subtle impact of the translation may be relevant, our focus must be on the tangible effect of the translation errors shown. The Supreme Court has noted that trial interpretation is necessarily imperfect. Any translation is inevitably a screen placed between the witness and the jury, affecting the jury's ability to assess credibility from demeanor, inflection of voice, nuances of language, and details of testimony. ... Translation is more than simple two-way street between two languages. While the translation here may have inadvertently benefited the state, [Mr.] Her has not shown tangible prejudice from the specific errors identified.[70]

The legal definition of prejudice is quite specific and varies significantly from the word's usage in the common manner of speaking. Legally, a defendant suffers prejudice if he can demonstrate that without the prejudicial event, the outcome of the case would have been different. In other words, in the proceeding example, Mr. Her must have been able to demonstrate that if the interpretation had been accurate, the jury would have acquitted him – a very tall order for any defendant.

This discussion does not suggest that the interpreter should only note prejudicial errors, even if the interpreter could determine which errors would lead the jury to arrive at a different outcome. Only an appeals court can make the decision regarding prejudicial effect of an error in interpretation. The table interpreter must note all important errors and deal with each in the least intrusive manner.

C. Is It Substantive?

The table interpreter's choices depend on the nature of the error and the place in the process in which the error occurs. The table interpreter must know the options available and the legal standard by which the courts understand errors to be substantive. The standard for establishing when an interpretation falls below the constitutionally permitted due process level has been described as, "the faulty translation [must have] prejudiced [the] hearing . . . in a manner so as to potentially to affect the outcome of the proceedings." In evaluating an error, interpreters can use the suggested three-prong approach: "(1) direct evidence of incorrectly translated words; (2) circumstantial evidence related to unresponsive answers; and (3) the petitioner's expression of difficulty in understanding the translation."[71]

If there was evidence of a gun admitted in a particular case, yet the interpreted testimony indicates that the weapon was a knife; direct evidence of an incorrectly translated word may exist. The second example is frequently described in ASL as OFF-POINT[72] when the witness gives irrelevant answers which can be circumstantial evidence of an interpreted error, or an indicator of cognitive difficulties processing the language input. Finally, if the deaf speaker himself or herself speaks up and indicates that he or she is having difficulty understanding the interpretation, there is a fairly strong indication that the translation may have fallen below a constitutionally permitted due process level. Hence, in addressing the errors, the monitor interpreter should keep these tests in mind to assist in the analysis of the substantive nature of the error.

1. Some Guidelines on Options

With experience comes the intuition necessary for determining the most appropriate course of action considering all of the circumstances. The following general principles and skills serve as a useful guide. Generally, the table interpreter must

- Have a thorough understanding of the case;

- Analyze whether the error is recoverable;

- Choose the least disruptive method of correction;

- Interrupt through the attorney;

- Interruptions should be taken out of the hearing of the jury;

- Allow for adequate time for the proceedings interpreters time to self-correct;

- Know the various options such as:

    o   Passing a note to the attorney;

    o   Having the attorney re-ask the question;

    o   Notifying the deaf person though a short note;

    o   Notifying the deaf person though a short clarifying statement in sign, unless the deaf person is also on the stand testifying;

    o   Discussing interpreting issues on a break with the proceedings interpreters.

At times, the error will be patently obvious to all of the participants, including the deaf person. In that case, the attorneys might initiate the discussion of the error or set about to correct it themselves. The attorneys might also seek advice from the monitor interpreter or occasionally swear the table interpreter as a witness to address the linguistic issue. In any event, there are a range of options available to the table interpreter other than interrupting the proceedings through the attorney, which should be resorted to only if no other viable option exists.

2. Non-record Interpreting

In some parts of a trial, the interpreter should simply *not interrupt* unless the interpretation is utterly incomprehensible, and the content is irretrievable by any other method. The interpreter should choose one of the alternative methods for correcting the misinterpretation. In other parts of the trial or proceeding, the interpreter may be compelled to interrupt the proceedings through counsel. The interpreter should have a sufficient grasp of the structure of trial work to apply the appropriate method of error correction at the appropriate juncture.

For example, opening statements are generally not disrupted to correct interpreted errors. Opening statements are interpreted in the simultaneous mode and as a result, errors are statistically more likely to occur.[73] The proceedings interpreters are less familiar with the content of the case at this stage. In warming up, the proceedings interpreters will be learning some of the details of the case. As a result, the interpretation may be less effective than at a later part of the proceeding.

The goal of opening statements is for the attorney to explain what the evidence will show and to create a relationship with the jury. No evidence is presented. If an interpreter initiated disruption occurs, the attorney's opportunity to connect with the jury can be derailed. Repeated interruptions at any stage annoy the court and focus attention on the interpreting process, rather than on the content of the trial. Because opening statements are a preview, the deaf person will be presented with the same information in the form of witness testimony during the trial. As a result, typical errors during opening statements can be remedied by less intrusive measures than interrupting.

During opening statements, it is relatively easy to either pass a note to the deaf person or sign the correction because of the ASL table interpreter's proximity at the table. Additionally, errors in opening statements are often recoverable because the deaf person has lived with the case from the beginning and will have a great deal of information with which to remedy defects in the interpretation. Finally, the deaf party will be present for the entire trial and have plenty of opportunity to speak with counsel about the opening statements during breaks in the trial. Though the deaf person may not agree with the presentation of the opponent's version during opening, the underlying facts will not be new. An error in the interpretation can easily be fixed by a swift note or brief utterance in sign language to the deaf person.

Closing statements present similar issues and should be handled in a like manner. The trial is concluding and the attorneys are assisting the jury to frame the evidence in a manner most favorable to their side. Because summations review information already known by the deaf person, interpreted errors are more easily recovered by the deaf person. The interpreter can correct these errors by choosing less intrusive measures than interrupting the process. As with all professional conduct, the interpreter naturally has a measure of discretion to adapt these suggested guidelines to the particular facts of each case. The matter of correcting errors during deaf witness testimony, however, presents more complex issues for the interpreter to consider. To managing errors in record interpreting, then, we turn next.

3. Record Interpreting

During record interpreting, on the other hand, the witness' presentation is critical, and the monitor must be hyper-sensitive to errors that might give the jury an erroneous impression of the deaf witness. Errors in **voice interpreting** are not easily retrievable by the deaf person. Record interpreting errors cause the greatest damage to the witness' credibility. Credibility derives from far more than the witness' words. Credibility determinations, like first impressions, are based upon the witness' communication style, the demeanor, and the manner of responding to the examination questions.[74] Corrections to the interpretation are critical to ensure that the jury's impression of the witness is not distorted by interpreter errors.

As an aside, it should go without saying that the interpreter never speaks directly with the jury. Rather errors regarding the interpretation are discussed privately, at the bench, out of the hearing of the jury. The court makes the final determination about the most appropriate method for informing the jury of the correct interpretation.

Physical factors can limit the table interpreter's options while monitoring. During record interpreting, the deaf party may be on the stand and no longer at the table interpreter's side. The attorney may also be standing at a podium or near the witness. The table interpreter does not have easy access to the attorney. The table interpreter should discuss this issue with counsel as a part of normal preparation for the case.

Aside from the physical difficulties when the deaf person or attorney is not in close proximity to the table interpreter, record interpreting is the stage of a proceeding where the table interpreter most likely will be forced to interrupt the proceedings, through the attorney, for egregious errors. The table interpreter must have an effective system in place to inform the attorney of substantive errors. Correction methods should be discussed ahead of time. The table interpreter should remind the proceedings interpreter of the monitoring function and the options for remedying substantive errors.[75] All interpreters should keep in mind the import of accurate interpreting and work diligently to ensure that errors are corrected in the manner most conducive to the proceedings. Interpreter-related interruptions must be restricted or the system will lose faith in interpreters and ultimately, deaf people will not receive adequate services. Handled correctly, the table interpreter should be viewed as an additional layer of protection for the record. Once the table interpreter has brought a substantive error that must be rectified immediately to the attention of the attorney, the attorney will stop the process and ask to approach the bench. The next section outlines the procedure the court uses in ruling on a challenge to the interpretation.

D. The Rebuttable Presumption of Accuracy

When there is a challenge to the interpretation, a Court must determine whether the translation was deficient. The inquiry examines whether the interpreting deficiency made the trial fundamentally unfair.[76] In a criminal case, the standard will be whether "the testimony as presented through the interpreter [was] understandable, comprehensible, and intelligible, and if not, whether such deficiency resulted in the denial of the defendant's constitutional rights?"[77] Recall the due process test set forth earlier, which suggested that "a defendant in a criminal proceeding is denied due process when: (1) what is told him [or her] is incomprehensible; (2) the accuracy and scope of a translation at a hearing or trial is subject to great doubt; (3) the nature of the proceeding is not explained to him [or her] in a manner designed to ensure his [or her] full comprehension; or (4) a credible claim of incapacity to understand due to language difficulty is made and the district court fails to review the evidence and make appropriate findings."[78] The table interpreter should know that these legal standards will guide the attorney in arguing and the court in making its determination.

The table interpreter should also keep in mind that the court-appointed proceedings interpreter enjoys a rebuttable presumption of accuracy in their interpretation. The Missouri Court of Appeals explained that "[a]n interpreter who functions with the sanction of the court necessarily enjoys a preferred position. . . ."[79] The table interpreter must overcome this presumption and demonstrate convincingly that the court-appointed interpreter is making serious interpreting errors. In essence, a challenge to the proceedings interpreters' work constitutes a challenge to the court because the court interpreter had been sworn and appointed by the court.

Though the presumption can be criticized, it provides the court with a guideline to resolve challenges to the interpretation.[80] Writer Debra Hoveland has suggested that this preferred position enjoyed by the court interpreter is simply a fiction which obscures the substandard quality of interpretation traditionally provided to NES persons.[81] Hoveland suggested that the presumption of accuracy should be reversed and that court interpreters should be presumed to be interpreting *inaccurately* until the prosecution could prove otherwise.[82] Though this reversal of the presumption might result in more effective interpreting services provide, courts are unlikely to adopt the recommendation.

Under the current state of the law, the challenger must prove that the proceedings interpreter made an error to the satisfaction of the Court.[83] The table interpreter must be able to skillfully articulate the error in a manner which will convince the Court of the proper interpretation and overcome the presumption of regularity that adheres to the work of the proceedings interpreter. This is a daunting task for those unfamiliar with speaking in court. It is the primary reason new interpreters should think carefully about beginning their careers in this position.

E. The Mechanics of a Challenge

As mentioned, in addition to knowing how to present an explanation of the error, the table interpreter must have a system devised for informing the attorney of the need to interrupt, when necessary. The system should be carefully thought through and explained to the Court, the parties and the attorneys prior to the beginning of the proceeding. The monitor should confer with and obtain agreement from the proceedings interpreters regarding the mechanics of interrupting the proceedings in advance of the trial. This procedure assures that the monitoring function is carried out in the least disruptive manner.

It is dangerous to confer this responsibility, by inaction or otherwise, to anyone other than a trained interpreter. When courts take on the duty to set interpreter working conditions, a circus-like atmosphere can result. Attorney Helen Reagan provides the following example of the confusion that can result when the court attempts to determine the best approach for handling objections through an interpreter:

Question:	Did you accept the offer of employment?
Opposing Attorney:	Objection.
Witness:	(Through Interpreter before the court ruled) No it was in Florida.
Court:	Wait. If there is an objection – go ahead

and translate the question or maybe we should have the objection before the question is translated, but before there is an answer, we'll have the objection. What's the objection?[84]

In the above example, the judge is unsure whether the interpreter should go ahead and interpret the question up to the point of the objection, or whether the interpreter should stop and have the objection ruled upon before completing the interpretation of the question. With advice and suggestions from the court interpreters in conjunction with the table interpreter, courts can manage the flow of the interpreted testimony better.

Any interpretation-related interruption should also be taken out of the presence of the jury. The table interpreter should inform the attorney of the error and the attorney should ask to approach the bench. In *State v. Van Pham,* the Kansas court gave the following instruction to the table interpreters:

I am going to issue an order that in the event any of your interpreters disagree either among yourselves or disagree with what the Court's interpreter interprets [as] the testimony of any Vietnamese witness, then no counsel is to stand up and relate that fact to the jury. What I want to happen is the attorney can make objection – we'll stop the proceeding – to approach the bar and advise me in a voice that cannot be overheard by the jury that we have a dispute over what is said by one of the witnesses. At that time I will excuse the jury to go back to the jury room and we will get to the bottom of it. [85]

On appeal, the court agreed that the jury should be insulated from any interpreter-related disputes: "To have the jury hear various interpretations involving fine shadings of meanings of the same word or phrase and then have the court, as it did here, accept the official interpretation could certainly confuse the jury."[86] Taking all interpreter-related issues outside of the hearing of the jury is consistent with the Federal Rules of Evidence requirement that evidentiary matters should be handled privately.[87] The intrusion caused by a bench conference has far less effect on the process than a badly timed exclamation about the accuracy of the interpretation from the mouth of a table interpreter in open court.[88]

Once at the bench, the table interpreter has the burden to present the error to the court. The table interpreter can rely upon notes taken of the interpretation if necessary while discussing the error. The table interpreter should state the nature of the error, succinctly and without unnecessary elaboration. The table interpreter should indicate what the witness signed and how the interpretation was rendered. If the error is not obvious, a short description of the miscue can be made. The court will defer to the appointed proceedings interpreters to determine whether there is agreement or not. If the court interpreters agree, the record is corrected by the court through an instruction to the jury. If the court interpreters disagree, the court decides the correct interpretation.

F. The Contemporaneous Objection Rule

Only errors in the interpretation that are prejudicial will warrant reversal on appeal.[89] If an objection is not lodged immediately, an appellate court will not consider the objection.[90] Errors must be brought to the attention of the trial court through an objection unless they rise to the level of **plain error** and affect a substantial right of the party. In order to comply with this rule, monolingual counsel must have a method to determine the accuracy of the interpretation as it is occurring.

In a Texas case, the court warned that "[t]he attorney representing each party in a case [should] have an interpreter available to call the court's attention to any errors or mistranslations asserted by the interpreter who is translating the witness' testimony for the jury. By following this procedure, asserted discrepancies can be timely presented to the court for a decision."[91] The contemporaneous objection rule requires all objections to be presented immediately to the court or the opportunity to appeal will be lost. The principle of evidence law is based upon fairness notions. In life, it is generally viewed as unfair to "go over someone's head" when there is a grievance. Rather, it is fairer to first address the issue with the person involved before appealing to a higher authority. Consequently, all objections, to the interpretation or otherwise, must be presented immediately to the court for consideration. As will be shown, in the absence of a table interpreter, the attorney will not be able to make a timely objection.

The rule that an objection based upon the interpretation should be presented immediately is logical. Otherwise, "[i]t would be an open invitation to abuse to allow an accused to remain silent throughout the trial and then, upon being found guilty, assert a claim of inadequate translation." [92] A defendant could create an issue for appeal by remaining silent, later claiming that the judge erred in admitting an inaccurate interpretation. In evidentiary terms, then, the contemporaneous objection rule permits the judge to address the issue of an alleged error in interpretation prior to appealing to a higher court for a decision that the judge was wrong in admitting the supposedly erroneous interpretation.

A Minnesota case illustrated the consequences of failing to object immediately to misinterpretations. [93] A young girl who was a recent immigrant alleged that her job counselor, Mr. Her, had lured her to a motel where he raped her. The trial was interpreted by two Hmong interpreters. The original transcript of girl's testimony had been preserved, though no table interpreter was present at the trial to monitor. After the trial, each side hired experts to review the girl's interpreted testimony and the experts disagreed with each other. The Hmong word "mos" had been interpreted as "rape" and Mr. Her alleged on appeal that the proper interpretation should have been "wrestle."

The court agreed that the interpretation was poor, and helped the prosecution's case because it made the girl appear inexperienced, vulnerable and inarticulate. However, the court faulted the defense for not immediately objecting to the errors in the interpretation. Even though on appeal, consulting interpreters and others in the community had pointed out the serious errors made by the court interpreters, the court held that the issue had been waived.[94] In the absence of a table interpreter at trial, the recording of the original testimony was ineffective in securing a new trial with competent interpreting.

A similar waiver scenario was presented by a defendant in a federal criminal matter who "somewhat belatedly challenge[d] the competence of the interpreter who translated his testimony at trial."[95] Because the defendant's "contentions in this regard [were] raised for the first time on appeal, and, indeed, at the outset of the trial, [his] counsel fully conceded the interpreter's qualifications," the appellate court was not eager to find error.[96] Misinterpretations must be presented promptly or lost. Misinterpretations cannot be presented unless first discovered. At trial, if counsel is without expert assistance, he or she will not have the skills to uncover misinterpretations. As happened in the federal case, counsel commonly makes no objections to the interpreter's qualifications in the beginning of the case. The attorney is likely laboring under the same fiction as the court: If the interpreter is appointed by the court, he or she is qualified. Counsel has not had the benefit of expert assistance of a table interpreter in preparing *voir dire* questions for the proceedings interpreter to inquire into the interpreter's abilities. Essentially, in order to preserve an interpreting-related error for appeal, counsel must have retained an expert interpreter to monitor the proceedings work. In the absence of a counsel table interpreter, counsel runs the risk that objections relating to the interpretation will be waived.

Many interpreters might take umbrage at the suggestion that errors of any kind might be permitted once discovered. However, from a criminal justice perspective, appellate courts are not quick to reverse convictions on appeal unless an injustice at trial was, in the Court's view, prejudicial. As a result, appellate courts look to whether the error complained of on appeal was brought to the attention of the Court and remedied, whether it was a significant error, and whether there was an opportunity for cross examination of the witness with respect to the disputed testimony.

In at least one state, interpreted errors, even if brought to the court's attention below, are simply non-reviewable on appeal. The Texas Court of Appeals explained that accuracy of an interpretation is a factual question not presenting a legal issue for review on appeal.[97] The court compared evaluating a discrepancy in two competing versions of an interpretation to evaluating a discrepancy in two competing versions of witness testimony and concluded that only the jury can make a determination as to the accuracy of each. The parties' recourse is to impeach the interpretation through cross-examination just as one would impeach a lying witness. In order to impeach an interpretation, it is required that a bilingual expert be available, immediately, to the litigation team in order to present an objection and to effectively cross-examine the interpreters.

G. *Videotaping: Table Interpreter Still Required*

A recording is the only way to preserve the **source language** testimony and the interpretation for review by an independent expert for accuracy. Court interpreters frequently request that their interpretation be videotaped, including interpretation of deaf witness testimony. However, standing alone, a video or an audio tape will not preserve an objection for appeal in the immediate context of a trial. One court explained that attorneys can always choose to "have the original testimony recorded and make the recording part of the official court record for review. With this alternative, however, the error would only be seen upon review and not in court when the testimony is given."[98] Likewise, in *Van Pham,* the court devised its own recording technique to assist with resolving immediate challenges, but not to become part of the official record since the source language was preserved only for the duration of one side of the tape. The court explained:

> If there is an error in any translation, I'm also going to tape record the testimony given by the Vietnamese. That testimony will not be preserved, please understand, on the tape recording. It will merely be preserved for short durations at a time being the time limit on each side of the tape cassettes. The reason for that being that if there is a disagreement on what a Vietnamese witness testified to, including the defendants, then I would have the actual recording of what was said so that it could be played back. . . . And in his way it would preserve that testimony so that should a conflict arise as to the proper translation it could be played back until we could arrive at what the proper translation was.[99]

Attorneys are simply not in a position to determine whether the interpretation is correct even if recorded without the assistance of a table interpreter to immediately point out the errors.[100] Because of the contemporaneous objection rule, the parties do not have the luxury of time to permit extensive and independent review of a videotape by an expert after trial. Additionally, an uncorrected error can affect other parts of the proceedings and cause confusion when attorneys expect to hear specific facts that are misinterpreted. Hence, the recording does not obviate the need for a live table interpreter to be present to monitor the proceedings interpreters.

The Federal Court Interpreting Act authorizes counsel to request a videotape of the original testimony and the interpretation to be reviewed for accuracy by a linguistic expert.[101] The statute provides:

> Upon the motion of a party, the presiding judicial officer shall determine whether to require the electronic sound recording of a judicial proceeding in which an interpreter is used under this section. In making this determination, the presiding judicial officer shall consider, among other things, the qualifications of the interpreter and prior experience in interpretation of court proceedings; whether the language to be interpreted is not one of the languages for which the Director has certified interpreters, and the complexity or length of the proceeding.[102]

The section supplies an additional tool for languages which the Director has not approved of a certification examination. When there is no other guarantee of minimal effectiveness, the court is authorized to record the original testimony and *voir dire* the interpreter prior to appointment. Any party may request a videotape under this section. A videotape can be an extremely useful method of providing review of the interpretation for accuracy as long as it is immediately available for review by the table interpreter while the trial is in session.

Proceedings interpreters should continue to suggest videotaping of their interpretation with the caveat that the video should be used in conjunction with a table interpreter. Without a record of the original testimony or without the provision of an expert there to check the accuracy of the interpretation, there is no guarantee that the interpretation is accurate. Mistranslations would go unnoticed and uncorrected, thereby infecting the record. Even if the mistranslations were subsequently discovered, most courts would find that unless the errors were plain and prejudicial, the objection to the interpretation was waived.

H. The Downside to Monitoring

In 1950, Luis Lopez Mendes was convicted of murder in the first degree in the Superior Court of Colusa County, California.[103] One issue on appeal was that the court interpreter had admittedly made numerous errors and should have been replaced. Throughout the trial, Mr. Mendes had the assistance of interpreters from the Mexican Consulate who monitored the court-appointed interpreter. Later, the consulate interpreters provided affidavits to the appellate court regarding the court-appointed interpreter's inadequacies.

At trial, if the consulate interpreters disagreed with the court-appointed interpreter, the witness would be re-asked the questions for the purpose of clarification of the interpretation. On appeal, the court held that "since the court interpreter and the defendant's interpreter were generally in agreement and the affidavits set forth no errors that were not corrected in the course of the trial, the trial court was justified in concluding that the court-appointed interpreter was competent."[104] Sadly, the conclusion that the court-appointed interpreter was competent simply does not follow from the evidence that both the court interpreter and the monitoring interpreters found many errors. The only conclusion that logically follows is that the interpretation was not effective and was salvaged by virtue of the consulate monitors. Because some of the errors were fixed does not mean that the interpretation overall was effective. The court was not justified in concluding that the presence of monitors created a competent and comfortable interpretation for the defendant. It can be more accurately said that a substandard court interpretation will not justify a reversal as long as monitor interpreters are present and functioning as a linguistic safety net to fix the most egregious of the errors.

I. The Final Arbiter: Court as Linguistic Expert

Curiously, in matters related to the accuracy of the interpretation, the judge has the final word. The judge is normally not linguistically qualified to make language interpreting decisions. A federal court demonstrated how the judge typically determines the merit of an interpreted errors suggesting that "the 'errors' in the translation cited by the appellant uniformly appear of minimal significance."[105] The court was not "willing to say, for example, that the interpreter's occasional transpositions of [the NES witness'] remarks from the first to the third person precluded the possibility of a fair trial."[106] Minimizing the errors made by the interpreter and their effect on the jury is a dangerous strategy. The judge does not know the cumulative effect of these errors on the jury or on the credibility of the witnesses.

For professional interpreters, when another interpreter uses third person while interpreting for the witness, a good deal of information is imparted about the level of training and sophistication of the interpreter. To the judge, these errors may seem minor; however, these may be the only types of errors that were recoverable from the English transcript. The court cannot know the extent of the adequacy of the interpretation without bilingual skill from some corner. Given what is known about the quality of ASL interpretation from the literature in the field, a cursory analysis only of the English transcript does a disservice to a deaf litigant.[107]

The court jealously guards the power structure in the legal system. The judge normally has the final word on all things, including matters of interpretation. In one case the prosecutor, on his own and without consultation, replaced an interpreter who admittedly was interpreting terribly on the first day of a trial.[108] The prosecutor's Spanish-speaking officer had informed him of errors made by the interpreter. On the prosecutor's request, the clerk replaced the interpreter.

On the second day of trial with a new interpreter, both the prosecution and the defense objected to the accuracy of the interpretation. The interpreter also made some disparaging remarks about the witness.[109] At the recess, the judge then replaced this interpreter. On appeal, the prosecutor was reprimanded for his unilateral rejection of the first interpreter. However, in affirming the conviction, the court found no prejudice to the defendant in replacing the admittedly ineffective interpreter. The court explained that "during a trial, both the opposing counsel and the judge should be informed of any difficulties which develop with the court-appointed interpreter. It is the duty of the trial judge, not the prosecutor, to appoint and replace interpreters."[110] The Court determined that the prosecutor was not acting to gain a tactical advantage but purely from the desire to obtain a more accurate interpretation. Nevertheless, the interpreter's competence is determined by the trial judge.[111]

In the reported opinion, the court admitted what interpreters have long known — errors cannot be detected in a record that consists solely of the English transcript. Congress discussed the issue in hearings before passing the Court Interpreters Act and stated that "nobody knows how accurate the interpretation may have been except the interpreter. And he is the wrong person to look to for an impartial assessment of his performance."[112]

The position that if errors were fixed, then the interpretation was adequate ignores the effect that repeatedly interrupting the proceedings to hash out interpretation errors can have on the jury. The analysis also presumes that a jury can hear an interpretation and then effectively erase it from their minds. How likely is it if the jury first hears "rape" it will be able to later ignore the effect of that word and replace it entirely with "wrestle?" In the case just discussed in which the prosecutor replaced the interpreter, the defense attorney was bilingual. The court assumed the attorney would monitor the process. The attorney should not have to perform this additional burden while simultaneously defending the client. If the attorney had not been bilingual, then the challenges would depend entirely upon the credentials of the Spanish-speaking agent, who while possibly a good agent, may not have the skills or credentials to perform the monitor function. While the court may reserve to itself the right to make a final determination on the accuracy of the interpretation, it should, at the very least, ensure that it is acting on competent advice from an expert in language and interpreting issues.

VIII. The Expert Function

While the table interpreter's primary function is to interpret between the attorney, the client and various members of the defense team, there is a great deal more expertise the interpreter can provide to the litigation team. At times, this service has been provided incidental to the role of table interpreting. In other instances, consulting with the legal team is the primary role, with interpreting incidentally if at all. The configuration depends upon the seriousness of the case and the sophistication of the legal team. The Constitution has been interpreted to mean that in order to present an effective defense; the defendant has the right to associate experts to form a defense team.

In *Ake v. Oklahoma,* Justice Marshall explained "that when a State brings its judicial power to bear on an indigent defendant in a criminal proceeding, it must take steps to assure that the defendant has a fair opportunity to present his defense." [113]

Marshall continued:

> We recognized long ago that mere access to the courthouse doors does not by itself assure a proper functioning of the adversary process, and that a criminal trial is fundamentally unfair if the State proceeds against an indigent defendant without making certain that he has access to the raw materials integral to the building of an effective defense. [114]

Ake created an indigent defendant's right to have the state pay for an expert psychiatrist to assist counsel in preparing the trial defense. The Supreme Court held that a psychiatrist was an integral part of the defense team in the case in which the defendant has placed his mental capacity into issue. Access to the courthouse door has been extended to other types of experts who supply the raw materials needed by counsel to present a constitutionally adequate defense. The attorney has the duty to hire various experts required in the case including investigators, doctors, forensic specialists and linguistic experts such as interpreters. [115]

As a part of the litigation team, the table interpreter should serve as a resource on linguistic matters uniquely within the interpreter's training, experience and education. Of course, this function is not carried out during the actual interpreting process. The interpreter performs this duty by advising counsel regarding matters such as proper interpretation techniques, theories, best practices, language issues, cultural information and other issues specific to the case at hand. For example, it is appropriate for the table interpreter to provide counsel with relevant law review articles, texts regarding interpretation and deaf culture, RID standard practice papers, brochures, interpretation literature, interpreter *voir dire* questions, jury instructions and oaths, among other items.

Legal writer Helen Reagan explained that "the interpreter fulfilling this role functions as part of the attorney's law office, and will have a relationship with the client that is very different from the interpreter used for depositions or trial."[116] The interpreter has a duty to correct misapprehensions and misunderstandings created because of the cultural differences between counsel and client. Reagan contends that the initial meeting in which counsel must appraise the client and develop a bond of trust is impeded if the interpreter is not able or willing to assist in this process.[117]

Because deaf people have not been informed of this role, the interpreter must carefully explain to the consumer during the preparation process the exact parameters of this different role and the functions of the table interpreter *vis a vis* the proceedings interpreter. Reagan agrees that it is critical that the client "understand the different relationships that exist with the court interpreter, who will be conveying information to and from counsel, the opposing attorney, and the judge, and the client interpreter employed by counsel at the outset of the case for information gathering."[118] The obligation to provide this explanation falls to the table interpreter hired as part of the litigation team.

IX.   Proceedings Interpreting: Just Say No

The table interpreter is a member of the litigation team, aligned with the deaf person on the team -- whether a party or a witness. The proceedings interpreter is an officer of the court responsible for the linguistic integrity of the interpreted proceedings, and most critically, of the record. Only the proceedings interpreter takes an oath to fulfill this function. The court interpreter's oath is to interpret all of the proceedings accurately. The table interpreter should not take an oath.

The ASL table interpreter does not interpret *any* of the proceedings and most importantly, the ASL table interpreter *does not interpret* for the deaf witnesses. This is true, even though according to traditional best interpreting practices, the table interpreter might render the most accurate rendition given the familiarity with the deaf person and the case. Nevertheless, accuracy must yield to the appearance of impropriety that shrouds the table interpreter due to their work on the defense team.

Many of the cases discussed in Chapter 3 and earlier in this chapter have discussed the impropriety of a party's personal interpreter also interpreting the party's testimony. Appeals courts generally have "sustained a judge's refusal to allow testimony by the accused through [a] personal interpreter rather than the court's interpreter (witness function), where a statute required the use of court-appointed interpreters for testifying criminal defendants, or using the personal interpreter might place him in a conflict of interest."[119]

In *Van Pham,* one co-defendant wanted his table interpreter to interpret his testimony.[120] The table interpreter was a native English-speaker who "was more conversant in English than the court interpreter."[121] The judge ruled that "to serve in dual capacities at the same time would be approaching a conflict of interest in the greatest degree."[122] The Court was concerned with the appearance of replacing mid-stream the court interpreter with an interpreter who was aligned with one of the parties and the impression that would make on the jury.

Further, the Court reasoned that it was inappropriate to permit a table interpreter who had been privy to private conversations to then interpret for the court. This sentiment was echoed by a federal court which would not permit the defendant to waive the use of the court-appointed interpreter and testify using his personal interpreter.[123] The court "recognized that this interpreter is affiliated with the party and does or may not possess the neutrality necessary to interpret the witness' testimony. It is not because of the fact of payment coming from one private party only, but also the affiliation with that party."[124]

The California Supreme Court agreed that the interpreter who works with the defense team cannot also interpret the proceedings.[125]

The Court stated: "Requiring two interpreters in cases such as the one before us has additional benefits to the criminal justice system because 'it is difficult for an interpreter who has worked closely with the defendant and his counsel in the preparation of the defense from the pretrial stage to translate the court proceedings impartially. Finally, a separate defense interpreter would serve to ensure the accuracy of the proceedings and witness interpreters.'"[126]

Resendes was in accord with these other cases and suggested that

> requiring a defendant to relay confidential communications to counsel through the interpreter for his codefendant with conflicting interests introduces another possible chill to the communication process. Respondent makes light of the Supreme Court's suggestion in *Aguilar* that the defense interpreter may be torn by feelings of partiality. . . . Respondent likens the interpreter to a court reporter, 'impartial servants of the justice system, doing an objectively measurable task.' *The court reporter analogy may be valid for a [proceedings] interpreter. It is singularly unpersuasive when extended to a [table] interpreter. Unlike a court reporter, a [table] interpreter is privy to confidential attorney client communications. In a very real sense, if only because of linguistic necessity for the duration of the trial he is part of the defense team.*[127]

Courts should not place an interpreter in a position in which temptation exists. Courts should not "be blind to the appearance created by forcing [the interpreter] to be privy to confidential information from multiple defendants whose interests conflict. ... even accept[ing] the moral imposition on the interpreter himself, we cannot ignore the risk that the defendant's subjective fears may deter him from relaying confidential information to his counsel through his codefendant's interpreter."[128]

Though many interpreters take issue with the suggestion that they may not be able to neutrally serve all parties, this all-things-to-all-people philosophy ignores the outward appearances that are simply out of the interpreter's control. These cases take into consideration the perception the jury may have or the NES participants may have of the interpreter's conduct. Prohibiting the interpreter who has been privy to privileged conversations from serving as proceedings/record interpreter is grounded in sound policy and not meant as an affront to the professionalism of the interpreter.

There are also cognitive psychological reasons for insisting upon a separation of interpreters performing the record interpreting function (witness) and the privileged communications interpreting function (table). According to Professor Ramirez in her critique of the Supreme Court's opinion in *Hernandez,* people learn information in a variety of modalities and "whether the information is acquired linguistically, linguistically and visually, or visually and through other senses, . . . most of the information is integrated into one semantic framework."[129] Professor Ramirez's work suggests that it is impossible for interpreters to remember whether they learned facts from preparation sessions or from the witness' testimony on the stand because "while the gist of the information becomes integrated into a global semantic framework, the form in which it was acquired does not"[130] Finally, she suggests that this global framework is relatively alinguistic and conceptual in nature allowing the meaning to be retained but the form lost.

The implications of this cognitive processing theory on interpretation are enormous. If it is true that the brain loses the ability to recall whether information was learned in ASL, spoken English or written English, then when an interpreter prepares with each side of the case, the information learned will be integrated into the global semantic framework alinguistically. The language and mode through which the information was initially received will fade. Hence, though many interpreters claim that they can interpret for all sides for any aspect of the case neutrally and impartially, it may be that they cannot cognitively separate confidential information learned from preparing the witnesses on one side of the case from the other. The brain is always looking for meaning, and faced with gaps in testimony, the brain may unconsciously fill those gaps to construct a logical product. The danger is that interpreters will fill in those gaps with information that was not present in the testimony but was learned during rehearsal. When proceedings interpreters do not interpret preparation sessions with witnesses, and when table interpreters do not interpret testimony after preparing a witness, the risk is reduced that the in-court interpretation will be affected.

X. Payment for Services Rendered

When interpreters suggest the use of a table interpreter, attorneys may be interested until the issue arises of payment for the services. Often payment for table interpreters for pretrial out-of-court services becomes problematic. Under the ADA, overlapping obligations exist between the court which is required under Title II (state and local government) and attorneys who are required under Title III (public accommodations). Under the ADA, attorneys are not permitted to pass the costs of an ASL interpreter on to the client.[131] In general, attorneys are not used to paying for any costs associated with representing a client; the client is typically billed for all costs in addition to the attorney's hourly fees. Attorneys are not legally obligated to provide interpreting services for other languages, except sign language. Because attorneys are used to passing all costs along to the client, it comes as somewhat of a shock to learn that, under the ADA, representing a deaf client will cost the attorney money.

Like attorneys, courts are not permitted to pass along the costs of the interpreter, though traditionally, costs are apportioned to the losing party. Any state law permitting ASL interpreting costs to be passed along to the losing party conflicts with and violates the ADA, when the losing party is also deaf.[132] Courts have tried creative strategies to obtain free or low cost interpreting services. Most often, courts have tried to force interpreters to interpret in court for free through the threat of contempt. A Massachusetts judge was reversed for subpoenaing an interpreter to court for the purposes of interpreting. [133] The judge had issued an arrest warrant to compel an interpreter to appear. On appeal, the court explained "an interpreter, like an expert witness, cannot be compelled to attend proceedings and testify for an ordinary witness fee."[134]

In some places, courts agree to pay for in-court criminal proceedings and the table interpreting services. Privately-retained counsel pay for out-of-court table interpreting services. Other courts require privately retained counsel to pay for their own table interpreting services both in and out-of-court. The analysis is different if the deaf person is *indigent.*

Courts pay for the legal services provided to indigent defendants in criminal matters, including interpreting services whether in or out-of-court. Constitutionally, indigent defendants are entitled to counsel and interpreting services are seen as a necessary part of this protection. This applies to both deaf and NES criminal defendants because of the Sixth Amendment's right to counsel provisions. In some states, the public defender service may provide representation or contract with individual attorneys to provide representation for indigent clients. In that case, the public defender normally pays for the table interpreter.

One civil lawsuit pitted the Wisconsin public defenders service against the court administrator.[135] The public defender's office filed suit to force the Director of State Courts to pay for the table interpreter's work outside of court. The Director had been ordered to pay for the public defender's in-court interpreting services. The public defender sued to force the Director to also pay for the table interpreter's out-of-court services.

The Wisconsin statute spoke of the Director's in-court obligation to pay for interpreters. The statute was silent about out-of-court expenses. The Director contended that the public defender should pay for its own interpreting costs in preparing cases. On review, several factors were considered in concluding that the public defender should pay its own interpreting costs. First, the public defender was most directly involved with providing the services at issue. Second, the public defender was in the best position to monitor and economize in the use of the services. If someone else was paying the bill, the public defender might be less conservative and might use unnecessary interpreting services. In light of the overlapping obligations to provide access to interpreting services, the parties tend to come to equitable resolutions without the aid of litigation. Through litigation, here, the parties were forced to divide the costs based upon a fairness rationale of who benefited most from the services and who was in a better position to regulate the costs.

There is a paucity of case law on the division of payment responsibilities for the table interpreter function. However, there are a number of sources who have overlapping responsibilities to ensure full constitutional presence of the deaf person. Because the practice is not standardized, there can be great variations in local practice. Particular jurisdictions might have enacted statutory obligations that dictate payment by one entity or another. Although payment is not necessarily the interpreter's responsibility, it is helpful to know the variety of potential arrangements for payment and to ensure that the interpreter hired knows how and to whom to look for payment. The only uniform prohibition is that the ADA and Section 504 of the Rehabilitation Act forbid the entity from charging the deaf consumer for the services.

The table interpreting function plays a vital constitutional role in the protections given to criminal defendants to ensure adequate access to counsel. The table interpreter ensures the defendant is able to effectively confront the witnesses against him or her. Serving in the role of table interpreter requires skill and diplomacy. The interpreter must know how to identify, classify and address non-equivalent messages. The interpreter functions as an expert to the team and provides a critical service as a resource to the litigation team. The interplay between the functions of the table interpreter and the proceedings interpreter are rife with ethical considerations such as preparing witnesses and then interpreting their testimony which have been partially addressed in Chapters 4 and 5. In the final Chapter, however, we turn to a fuller discussion of certain ethical rules, practices and conventions that dictate working conditions and best practices for ASL interpreters.

Chapter 6
Ethics Based Interpreting Issues

Chapter 6
Ethics-Based Interpreting Issues

I. Divergent Views on Accuracy

Because judges cannot monitor the accuracy of the interpretation, they are in the unusual position of having to rely upon individuals whose effectiveness they cannot directly verify. Courts fear the unsupervised interpreter will usurp the court's power. If truth be told, courts would prefer not to have to use interpreters at all. In New Jersey, one court declared:

> An interpreter should never be appointed unless necessary to the conduct of a case. That is, interpretation should be resorted to only when a witness' natural mode of expression is not intelligible to the tribunal.... This is so because no matter how disinterested an interpreter might be, there always exists a possibility that he will inadvertently distort the message communicated by the primary witness."[1]

Other courts agree. A Florida court confirmed that "it is far better to testify in English" rather than through an interpreter.[2] Another court explained its fear that "[p]roblems of distortion and confusion obviously may arise when an interpreter is placed between the witness and counsel, the judge and the jury, even in the best of circumstances."[3] The common theme is a concern that the presence of an interpreter will distort the testimony. This section explores the source of the legal system's paranoia about interpreters and their work. In doing so, the chapter attempts to provide guidance for how the legal system can come to terms with the interpreter – a necessary part of justice.

A. A Fiction Is Born

Courts have not dealt with interpreting issues entirely honestly. Recognizing the potential danger that unskilled interpreters pose, courts announce that interpreters are nothing more than language machines calibrated for accuracy. Automated, interpreters are switched "on," and the deaf person is transformed into one who can hear. All supposed cultural and linguistic differences disappear and the court proceeds with business as usual.[4]

Rather than acknowledge that interpreters function in an unsupervised parallel universe, the legal system has created a **fiction** by which it can ignore the latent disaster. The fiction proceeds as follows: If hired by the court, the interpreter is competent, and the interpretation will be accurate. One New York court confirmed that the fiction is alive and well when it denied a defendant's request for a monitor interpreter.[5] The court described the request as "suffer[ing] from a logical flaw inasmuch as it implicitly attacks the premise – *accepted universally in the court system and in the case law* – that a court-appointed interpreter is capable of providing an accurate translation."[6] Considering all that is known about the quality of court interpreting, courts that labor under this illusion endanger the rights of those who rely upon interpreters to receive accurate information in court.[7]

Courts, by virtue of the power to define, subscribe to the outmoded **conduit model of interpreting** which defines the interpreter as a telephone or machine.[8] According to this view, the interpreter is a transparent non-entity. The interpreter's presence has no effect on the parties or on the communication process. The model fails to recognize that an interpreter aims to convey equivalent meaning between people from at least two vibrant and living communities which naturally have differing values, mores and language practices. The conduit model interpreter has been described as the functional equivalent of a dial tone[9] – a view which has been long discredited in the ASL interpreting field. Courts seek to achieve this colorless transmission by instructing the interpreter to interpret accurately. In other words, the very act of telling the interpreter to interpret correctly (often heard as "translate, don't interpret" or "interpret word-for-word" or "interpret verbatim"), ensures that there will be no "static" on the line.

Court opinions perpetuate the fiction by describing the computer-like functions which interpreters serve in enabling the defendant to understand and to be understood.[10] The interpreter has been described as "a conduit from the primary witness to the trier of fact .. . [who] should not aid or prompt the primary witness in any way . . . instead, as far as is possible, he should translate word-for-word exactly what the primary witness has said."[11] Another court instructed a jury that "an interpreter really only acts as a transmission belt or telephone. In one ear should come in English and out comes Spanish. . . ."[12] Plainly, the real concern is that interpreters will not interpret accurately. For this reason, interpreters are told not to change, add or omit any information while carrying out their duties. Although accuracy is critical in court interpreting, it is foolishness to think that a judge can make an interpreter effective simply by telling the interpreter to render the message accurately.

B. Ethics Codes Contribute to the Fiction

Ethical rules governing interpreters reflect the legal system's concern for accurate interpreting. Without exception, accuracy is a fundamental theme of interpreter codes of professional responsibility.[13] The NCSC Code's first principle describes the interpreter's duty to produce an accurate interpretation. Interpreters are admonished to "never interject their own words, phrases, or expressions."[14] Interpreters are informed that they have an "obligation to conserve every element of information in a source language communication when it is rendered in the target language."[15] Canon 1 of the National Association of Judiciary Interpreter and Translator's ("NAJIT"), Code of Ethics and Professional Responsibilities states:

> Source-language speech should be faithfully rendered into the target language by conserving all the elements of the original message while accommodating the syntactic and

semantic patterns of the target language. The rendition should sound natural in the target language, and there should be no distortion of the original message through addition or omission, explanation or paraphrasing.[16]

This provision recognizes that linguistic patterns in the target language differ from those of the source language. For the interpretation to sound natural in the target language, the interpreter may be required to reorganize some elements into an order different than a verbatim rendition would suggest. For the most part, however, the accuracy principles reinforce the instructions given to interpreters during the proceedings by the court.

The NCSC Code suggests that "verbatim, word-for-word or literal oral interpretations are not appropriate *when they distort the meaning of the source language*, but every spoken statement, even if it appears non-responsive, obscene, rambling, or incoherent should be interpreted."[17] Ostensibly, the drafters of the code recognized that word-for-word interpreting has the potential to skew the meaning of the target language. The unspoken message remains, however, that verbatim, word-for-word or literal oral interpretations are expected when they do *not* distort the meaning of the source language. To some extent, the NCSC code embodies the same institutional paranoia about interpreting that the legal system embraces. Many reported cases give lip service to the ideal that verbatim interpreting is ineffective, yet in the next breath, admonish interpreters to interpret in as literal as a manner as possible.

One Virginia criminal appeal was based upon the protracted private conversations the interpreter had with the witness while interpreting a question. After the long colloquy with the witness, the interpreter produced a short one word interpreted answer. [18] Each time this happened, the defense would move for a mistrial. In a twisted kind of logic, the court stated that "an interpreter's version of a witness' answer need not be literal, *as long as the answers of the witness and the interpreter amounted to the same thing!*"[19] Another court suggested that while "the general standard for interpretation requires word-for-word translations, occasional lapses in the standard will not necessarily contravene a defendant's constitutional rights."[20] In reality, courts are more apt to forgive minor errors in interpretation than reverse a conviction, regardless of the general requirement of accurate interpretation.

The other suggestion in the NCSC Code's accuracy section is equally telling of the judicial system's fear of the interpreter's potential reach. The Code counsels the interpreter to interpret *all* statements even if they appear non-responsive and the like. Without this admonition, interpreters could make judicial decisions by choosing not to interpret testimony the interpreter felt was not important.[21] The National Association of Judiciary Interpreters and Translators' position paper on summary interpreting explains: "When an interpreter is allowed to summarize, she is being permitted to decide or evaluate what portion of testimony or statements given by the parties is relevant. An interpreter is not qualified to make such determinations."[22] It is solely within the court's province to determine whether testimony is admissible. The duty cannot be delegated to the interpreter.

Courts have been reversed for violating this principle. One case involved a defendant who was proceeding without a lawyer, and who spoke no English.[23] Because the defendant was unfamiliar with the rules of evidence, while he was cross examining the prosecution's witnesses, he would make improper statements. When this occurred, the Court would direct the interpreter not to interpret the statements."[24] The following exchange took place:

COURT: Miss Interpreter, he is there to ask questions, not to make statements, so don't translate any affirmative representations he makes as to the facts. He will have a chance to testify if he wants to exercise that right. Miss Easman, please do not translate these can [sic] statements. He is only entitled at this stage of the game to make comments, not make statements."

INTERPRETER: When the defendant starts to speak, I don't know if it is a question or a statement. I don't have any way of knowing.

COURT: Wait until you hear the end of it. Don't start translating until you know it's a question or a statement. When the government's putting in its case, he's entitled to ask him questions on it, but not make statements. If he wants to take the stand and make a statement when the government is finished, he can do it.

INTERPRETER: Your Honor, may I wait until he finishes, then you will instruct me if I should state it?

COURT: If you can't tell whether it's a question or a statement, then come up here and I will instruct you.[25]

The court inappropriately altered the interpreter's role by relegating important judicial duties to her.[26] The interpreter was placed in the impossible position of deciding whether a question was in the proper evidentiary form before interpreting. In a similar case from Massachusetts, the court explained the approach to be used in managing NES witnesses who provide narrative answers on cross-examination:

It may be appropriate for the judge to instruct the interpreter that if the witness is not responding to the question he should indicate this to the judge. The judge would then stop the witness, have the interpreter translate all of what the witness has said, pass on the admissibility of the answer as given, and further instruct or inquire of the witness as appropriate. However, the judge should not delegate to the interpreter the ultimate decision on admissibility. For example, an instruction to the interpreter to translate only that part of the answer that is responsive to the question would be error.[27]

The interpreter should not be asked to determine what is relevant to the case. The ultimate decision on admissibility always lies with the court. Even the approach suggested by the appeals court required the interpreter, after hearing the witness' full answer, to determine whether it was non-responsive and inform the court who would make a determination. In the first example, Ms. Easman was placed in an untenable position *vis a vis* the *pro se* defendant. When the defendant made a statement instead of a question, only the interpreter and the speaker knew the content of the statement. If the interpreter had acceded to the judge's instruction, she would be the only person who knew for certain which part she had interpreted and which part she had determined not to interpret because it was not a properly formed question.

These cases place the interpreter in the position of being the sole holder of information. Interpreters should avoid being placed in these situations. Though in the first case, the interpreter protested, she objected on the grounds that she did not know if the utterance was a statement or a question. The interpreter should have informed the court that it was asking her to violate her oath by editing testimony before interpreting. Had the interpreter informed the court that she was ethically obligated to interpret everything without editing or evaluating; the court might have reconsidered its position. In the event the court did not reconsider, at least the interpreter's statements on the record would be accurate for the inevitable appeal.

C. *Verbatim Issues: Words Are Not Widgets*

The difficulty of the interpreter's task is compounded by the court's definition of accuracy as a word-for-word or verbatim rendition in the other language. It is useful to contrast the court's view with a translator's definition of a verbatim translation. Larson suggests:

> A word-for-word translation which follows closely the [surface structure] of the source language is called a literal translation. A literal translation is useful if one is studying the structure of the source text as in an interlinear translation, but a literal translation does not communicate the meaning of the source text. It is generally no more than a string of words intended to help someone read a text in its original language. It is unnatural and hard to understand, and may even be quite meaningless, or give the wrong meaning in the receptor language. It can hardly be called a translation.[28]

a. Not Widgets: Form v. Meaning

Spoken English can be effectively represented in ASL, but not on a one-word-for-one-sign basis. The drafters of the NCSC Code implicitly recognized that words in languages are not interchangeable like parts for a car. When interpreters are faced with a "term or phrase with no direct equivalent in the target language. . . .," the NCSC Code permits them to interrupt to explain the term or phrase.[29] Still, the NCSC Code misunderstands the task of interpreters who work with languages far different in structure than English. The quoted language presumes that, in most cases, there *will* be a direct equivalent in the target language, and that the need to interrupt the proceedings will be relatively rare. In many languages, such as ASL, there simply are no direct equivalents to everyday English words, much less words and phrases used in technical legal settings.

ASL is not the only language community which faces this issue. For example, in Aguaruna, used in Peru, the English word "sad" is expressed by saying "stomach-being-broken-feeling."[30] Likewise, the Aguaruna equivalent for the term "wilderness" is "people where-they-are-not-place."[31] In Mbembe, a Nigerian language, the word "embezzle" is represented by the idiom "chi akpuka" literally meaning "eat money."[32] By directing the interpreter to perform a verbatim interpretation, does the court intend for the interpreter say "eat money," "embezzle" or is this an instance in which the interpreter's discretion should be triggered to stop the proceedings and inform the court than no direct equivalent exists?

English has many examples which, upon reflection, would make no sense if interpreted literally. For example, the statements, "I'm done for," "look up a friend," "I made it up," "he's all over it" or "under the weather" would make no sense if translated word-for-word. The meaning can easily be conveyed though not in a such a manner. If the interpreter read the NCSC Code provision literally, he or she would be interrupting the court constantly to inform it that no direct equivalent existed. Needless to say, little court business could actually be concluded. Most judges would likely agree that the proceedings would be conducted more efficiently if a meaning-based interpretation was rendered in these instances.

Courts are more concerned about egregious deviations from the source language which change the content of the message. For example, a Texas appeal of a murder conviction concerned the interpretation of a phrase which literally translated as "I've marched him," yet a meaning-based interpretation was "that's it, he's gone," in referring to the victim.[33] The court agreed with the prosecution that a literal translation would cause the phrase to lose all meaning. The defense, on the other had, wanted the interpreter to interpret the phrase literally which removed the incriminating connotation.

b. Not Widgets: Leading Questions

Attorneys have good reason to worry about form when it comes to certain question types that are extremely controlling. Leading questions used on cross-examination are characterized by tag questions affixed to short declarative statements seeking the witness' agreement or disagreement. The witness is constrained to respond in a yes-no format. The opportunity to explain comes later on re-direct examination. Qualitative research conducted by Susan Berk-Seligson examining the **pragmatic equivalence** of leading questions interpreted by Spanish interpreters demonstrated that interpreters tend to omit the coercive force of leading questions.[34] Interpreters either omitted the tag portion of the question completely, or re-worded the question and reduced its controlling features. Cross-examination is often called the attorney's greatest tool. Attorneys spend hours crafting cross-examination questions to draw out inconsistencies and create inferences that the witness is not worthy of credence. When conducting cross-examination through an interpreter, that tool is blunted.

One issue in ASL interpreting concerns leading when certain nouns are used which have no one-sign-equivalent, such as the words "sports," "fruit," "alcohol," "drugs," or "seafood." ASL employs a listing strategy to convey the equivalent of these words. The signer will provide examples of different members of the class represented by the noun. The interpreter has a measure of discretion in determining which items to include. For "sports," the interpreter might sign BASEBALL, FOOTBALL, BASKETBALL, DIFFERENT+++.[35] In the legal setting, "weapon" is one such noun that is represented in ASL by listing examples of different types of weapons. Attorneys are concerned that if the list includes the actual weapon at issue, the interpreter is leading the witness by supplying the answer. However, if the question was "did you see Mr. Defendant with a weapon?" and if the interpreter does *not* include the specific item at issue in the list, the response will be "No" even if the witness did see the specific weapon. Unless certain modifications are made to the interpretation, the interpretation will cause an untruthful answer.

ASL has strategies to convey the word "weapon" without constricting the witness to a limited number of choices by using the signs VARIOUS or DIFFERENT+++ at the end of the list. In this manner if the interpreter is unsure of the specific weapon used, and it is not included in the list, the deaf person understands that the final sign includes similar items not specifically mentioned. The witness is free to select a choice not included in the list. Further, interpreters and attorneys should not be overly concerned about the inadvertent leading of a deaf witness. When a witness poses communicative challenges, the rules of evidence permit leading questions to be used even on direct examination with the judge's permission. [36] Courts always have the inherent discretion to regulate the mode of the examination. As long as the interpreters are trained, certified professionals, they should be accorded the trust to make appropriate language choices in the most equivalent manner.

c.   Not Widgets: Register & Credibility

Register is mentioned expressly in the tenet on accuracy in the NCSC Code because it is a critical tool for gauging credibility. Courts want, and deserve, an accurate representation of the witness; they do not want the interpreter making the witness sound better or worse than they actually are. If a witness says "smack," the interpreter should not say "heroin" unless there is no lower register term or phrase with the equivalent meaning. In one case in which the author was involved as a table interpreter, a young deaf witness used a sign that meant "oral sex." The proceedings interpreter, who had a medical background, used the English term "fellatio" in the interpretation. The defendant's attorney on cross-examination implied that the young witness was far more experienced in sexual matters than proper for his age because of his knowledge of such high register terms for sex. The impression given to the jury was inaccurate and merely a reflection of the interpreter's limited choice of terminology.

In a world of perfect linguistic correspondence, the meaning, form and the register would all be maintained in exactly the manner issued in the source language. Of the three, however, the form is the least critical because of the danger that a literal interpretation will be incomprehensible. Arguably on cross-examination, form is vital to the attorney. However even a perfectly executed formed-based interpretation will thwart the cross-examiner's goal if it is incomprehensibly literal. The realistic standard should be that the interpretation is effective when the equivalent meaning is rendered in the appropriate register.

D. English-Like-Signing With or Without Voice

Contributing to the court's confusion about ASL and the verbatim interpretation issue is that signs can be uttered in English word order which results in a rendition that shares some similarities with English (primarily word order). This phenomenon has been called, among other things, signed English or English-like signing.[37] English-like signing can be done with or without voice. When English-like signing is used with voice, word-for-word interpreting seems possible because the signer appears to be using ASL and English at the same time. Signing and talking at the same time has been termed **simultaneous communication**. Research has shown that when voice is added to the signed product, the signer tends to omit signs. [38] The signed portion, but not normally the speech, tends to be slurred and incoherent. The meaning that is typically conveyed non-manually by mouth movements, eyebrow movements and eye gaze is replaced with signs leaving the signer's affect flat. The signer also tends to use semantically incorrect signs to conform to the structure and usage of spoken English. For example, the word "meat" is often used in English in its figurative sense, to mean something of substance. English signers often sign MEAT when they hear the term "substantive." To a deaf person not familiar with the figurative sense in English having a foodstuff appear in an otherwise normal sentence is anomalous. Another example comes from an interpreter who was signing in English and interpreting a sentencing hearing and signed the following: YOU + WRITTEN-SENTENCE + HOUSE + APPROPRIATE for the English statement "You are hereby sentenced to the House of Corrections."

When interpreters sign and talk at the same time, they give the erroneous impression that since the languages can be used at the same time, the grammar of the two languages is the same. Logically, then, the interpreter should also be able to interpret effectively in a word-for-word manner. Courts would like nothing more than for the interpreter to be able to engage in lexical substitution of this kind. However, signing in English word order is no more effective for deaf people who use ASL than an interpreter who speaks German words in English word order is effective for a German audience.

E. Cultural Factors Affecting Accuracy

When the cultural experiences of the two language communities are very different, it is more difficult to find lexical equivalents.[39] Different language communities value different things. Members of a culture not only speak a common language, but share common experiences which create a bond of uniqueness among them. Languages develop rich ways of talking about those things that are important to the users. Although decried as a myth, it is popularly believed that Alaskan native people have many ways to discuss snow because of its import in their climate.[40] However, people from northern climes may have limited ways of discussing things like tropical fruit. Some indigenous people of Latin America, on the other hand, have many varied words for specific types of bananas, yet no one generic word for the fruit banana.[41] In Mexico, users of Amuzgo have two words for "love" one which is used when speaking to higher status people and a different word for listeners of a lower status than the speaker.[42] The volume and density of lexical items in any language reflects the social structure and the things within the culture that are valued.

Deaf Americans are no different. They are united by the shared experience of facing barriers to accessing information so easily available to people who can hear. In the past, deaf people formed close communities fostered by a segregated educational system.

The segregated state schools for the deaf did not engender negative connotations as might be expected; rather, the schools represent a cherished institution for identifying other cultural members, transmitting American Sign Language and the sharing of information. Deaf people created a visual language informed by the experience of being considered different, broken and even pitied by the majority culture. Not surprisingly, ASL has hundreds of rich ways to speak of the concept of communication, whether it be sign or spoken, because communication is the unifying experiential bond in the deaf community. Both the deaf lawyer and the deaf janitor will board the wrong flight if the gate change announcement is only made over the PA system.

On the other hand, ASL has relatively few specific legal signs because the legal system has not traditionally been easily accessible to deaf people. Disputes within the community are typically handled in a mediation-based, collective manner in which pardons are issued liberally and excommunication is rare. Conflict resolution in the deaf community has been likened to First Nation sentencing circles which "are community based tribunals that are composed of the tribal leaders, the victim, the defendant, friends and family."[43]

Interpretation is complex because people share not only different languages, but also different experiences, values and cultures. In the field of translation, experts warn that "[a] translator is not simply dealing with concepts in a system in one language, but rather concepts in systems in two languages. Each language will fence off and label a particular area of reality or experience differently."[44] In choosing the culturally appropriate equivalent from a range of options, the interpreter must master a range of tools.

F. Linguistic Factors Affecting Accuracy

Interpreters are always searching for strategies to infuse their interpretations with accuracy. In looking at equivalents for lexical units referring to things or events, interpreters look at the form and the function of the specific item. For example, a pencil has a cylindrical form, is usually made of wood and has a pointed graphite tip.[45] A pencil's function is to write. A quill pen has the same function, but the form is different. Always, the interpreter looks for exact counterparts to both form and function in the target language. If both form and function occur in one lexical item in the target language, then a word-for-word equivalent exists. If not, then the interpreter has several choices.

When there are shared concepts in both languages, but not word-for-word equivalents, a descriptive phrase or analogy is often used. The interpreter can use a descriptive phrase or analogy to explain the form of the item, explain the function of it, or explain both the form and the function. In the quill pen example, the interpreter could analogize to a pencil if the target language did not have a lexical item representing the pen. A descriptive phrase for the word "glutton" is "one who eats too much" or the term "anchor" which can be described as "heavy iron weights used to keep a boat still."[46] In ASL, no equivalent exists for the legal word "custody." An effective descriptive phrase could be rendered "CHILD + LIVE + MOTHER + FATHER + WHICH."

Translators also use a technique of substituting terms to match a specific form or function depending on which is critical to the meaning of the utterance. Consider the word "bread" in two different cultures – Culture A and Culture B. The bread's physical form is the same in both. However, in Culture A, bread is eaten daily as a staple. In Culture B, it is eaten only rarely at ceremonious occasions.[47] The form may be the same, but the function is different. If the speaker's intent is to speak of the ceremonial bread, the concept will not be fully communicated in Culture A, without additional information. Translators have the flexibility to find another ceremonial food in Culture A and substitute that word for "bread" even though the substituted word – "wine" perhaps – was not included in the original source language. Interpreters, particularly in court, are hesitant to incorporate these strategies wholesale into their work, though it may happen more frequently than interpreters will admit. Without making the additional meaning explicit in some manner, the interpretation would not be equivalent.

Court interpreters are wary of this practice because of the heightened attention to literalness in court. In one case, the source language in Greek was "large man" and the interpretation was rendered as "Defendant Murphy" because in context it was clear the witness was referring to this particular person.[48] The accuracy of the interpretation was challenged on appeal for the meaning-based substitution. The interpretation was deemed satisfactory. Interpreters are affected by knowing that their interpretation will be subjected to this level of scrutiny. As a result, interpreters are hesitant to stray too far from the form of the source language, even when there are alternative target language structures that would make the overall interpretation more robust. Interpreters must determine how to incorporate the additional meaning of terms that are not fully equivalent in the target language or risk the participants not appreciating the complete message because of a meager interpretation.

The cultural rules regarding attention-getting strategies illustrate the incongruence of form/function in ASL and present an illustration of appropriate cultural substitution. In English, people who can hear will call out a person's name to get his or her attention. In ASL, names are not used for this function. Rather, to get someone's attention who is the room, the person will employ a visual or physical method. The person will wave, flash the lights, tap the person on the shoulder or knee, or rap on a flat surface to create a vibration that can be felt by the other person. The function of names in ASL is normally to distinguish or discuss a third party who is not present during a conversation.

Hence, when faced with the English source language "Roger yelled for Camilla," the ASL interpreter could substitute a visual equivalent of the attention-getting strategy, assuming Camilla is deaf. Culturally, a verbatim interpretation of vocally calling for Camilla would be incorrect in ASL. At the very least it would imply that Camilla could hear. Likewise if the statement had been signed in a culturally appropriate manner, the interpretation would be incorrect if the spoken English was rendered as "Roger waved at Camilla."

Finally, grammatical differences between the source and the target language often preclude a verbatim interpretation. In one spoken language, the statement "there was a man who went down to the river one evening to fish" is represented literally as "one-person fish-hook throwing-in sun going-down he-went" in another spoken language.[49] In the Denya language of Cameroon, the literal sentence: "you-are-if poor, you are people eyes open. In gathering your speech person he-put-not head there" would be interpreted as: "If you are poor, you are worthless in people's eyes. In a gathering, nobody pays attention to what you say."[50] A verbatim version of these perfectly grammatical source language statements makes no sense, makes the speaker appear inarticulate and skews the listener's impression of the speaker.

In ASL, the grammatical patterns are as varied and complex as in other languages. ASL often uses a sentence structure called topic – comment because the topic is placed first in the sentence, and then a description or comment concerning the topic is produced. A verbatim representation of the sentence: "The boy was shocked upon seeing the blood on the floor" could be signed BLOOD-ON-FLOOR + BOY-SEE + SHOCK. A verbatim interpretation of the sentence in spoken English would sound unnatural, be hard to understand and give the impression of an inarticulate speaker.

G. Understandable to the Deaf Person Standard

In *Bednarski,* the court pointed out an important point about ASL interpreting. Many times the ASL interpreter's oath and/or statute requires the interpreter to interpret in a manner *understandable to the deaf person.* As illustrated, interpreting verbatim is not normally effective for a deaf person who uses ASL, or to a person who can hear listening to a verbatim version of ASL. The "understandable to the deaf person" standard should supplant any requirement that ASL interpreters provide a verbatim interpretation. *Bednarski* warned that any 'paraphrase' of a witness' testimony given by the interpreter would have "violated the provision of the [interpreter's] act which requires an interpreter to make an oath or affirmation that the interpreter 'will make a true interpretation in an understandable manner to the deaf person for whom the [interpreter] is appointed.'"[51] Recognizing that a literal interpretation is not possible in ASL, the court stated, "due to the conceptual nature of sign language, a verbatim translation of oral testimony (or vice versa) may not be possible. However, the very fact of the unavoidable translation difficulty renders the need for accurate and skillful interpretation even more critical."[52]

The court in *Bednarski* discussed the ASL interpreter's ethical duty of accuracy: "Above all, the interpreter's foremost desire should be to give a verbatim translation of the terminology used in legal proceedings. It is in his Code of Ethics. He is sworn to it by oath. The deaf (sic) have a right to it."[53] Actually, the court only got it half right. The ethical requirement calling for accuracy does not demand a literal interpretation. Interpreter ethics do require accuracy which is what interpreters swear to in their oath and which is also what the court in *Bednarski* most likely intended by the statement.

The key lies in creating a partnership of trust and collaboration with the stakeholders in the court interpreting process. If courts are truly concerned about accuracy of interpretation, then only interpreters who have the appropriate skills, education, certification and experience to interpret accurately should be hired. Likewise, interpreters should take the initiative to obtain certification, training and mentoring to provide effective interpretation before accepting court assignments carte blanche. To lessen its own linguistic handicap, the court should still require the oath, and should ensure that it is equipped with a monitoring mechanism. The litigants should have table interpreters monitoring for accuracy, and the proceedings should be preserved on videotape. In this manner, a court can bypass the need for an instructional fiction and can create a linguistic environment in which deaf people are truly present at the same proceedings as those who can hear.

II. Competency-Based Appeals

In addition to challenges based upon the accuracy of the interpretation, appeals are often taken based on the interpreter's competency which refers to more than having adequate skills to interpret.[54] Competency means whether the interpreter is free of any bias or other impediment which might skew the interpretation. Competency deals with whether the interpreter is able to abide by the ethical rules and knows and can follow standard protocol governing the work. On appeal, the court looks to whether the whole of the interpretation was understandable, comprehensible and intelligible even in light of the interpreter deficiencies. [55] If the interpretation fell below this standard, the defendant must also show that he or she was prejudiced, or denied a fair trial, by the inadequate interpretation.[56] Normally, these issues are raised at the outset and the opportunity is given to the parties to *voir dire* the interpreter to draw out any bias or skill-related issues.[57] Sometimes, the difficulty with the interpreter's competency cannot be anticipated and only arises during the course of the proceedings. Almost always, this occurs during interpreted witness testimony.

A. Mode-Based Issues

NES or deaf witness testimony should be interpreted in the consecutive mode because it is more accurate than the simultaneous mode. However, a Texas appeal alleged that the interpreter's *inability* to interpret simultaneously was indicative of general incompetence.[58] During witness testimony, the interpreter asked the attorneys to pause long enough to permit a consecutive rendition of the message. The defendant objected that the interpreter was not competent because he could not keep up with the speech.[59] The trial court agreed. On appeal, this misconception was corrected. The appeals court recognized that if the interpreting process is forced into a simultaneous mode when the grammars of the languages are quite different (in this case Chinese and English), even a competent interpreter can produce an inaccurate translation.[60] The judge had used the interpreter's ability to keep up with the pace as the standard of competency, and this was inappropriate.

Consecutive interpreting is more accurate because the interpreter controls the flow of the source language input and has time to arrange the target language in the most naturally-occurring equivalent structure. In the Texas case, the court dictated the working conditions of interpreters. Yet no record was made by the interpreter to inform the court of the standard practice of consecutive interpreting. Interpreters are not as powerless as they feel when ordered to submit to substandard conditions. Interpreters who refuse to work under unacceptable conditions face severe sanctions. Interpreters should, before refusing to work if that is necessary, make a complete and accurate statement regarding the reasons the court's order is inappropriate. This gives the court an opportunity to change its mind or come up with an alternative course of action. If the court insists upon its order, then the interpreter has a difficult decision to make. The decision whether to face contempt charges is one that only the individual interpreter can make after an assessment of all of the facts and circumstances. That decision is one that deserves no second-guessing.

One other federal criminal case illustrates the fundamental misunderstanding of interpreters and their proper role constraints. In this case, the NES defendant was proceeding without an attorney, and was unable to form correct cross-examination questions. Instead, the defendant would argue and make statements. Frustrated, the court ordered the interpreter to translate only properly formed questions and not the defendant's diatribes.[61] Essentially, the court ordered the interpreter to provide a summary interpretation by editing out all commentary and only interpreting questions. On appeal, the court was reprimanded for requiring the interpreter to provide a summary instead of a fully equivalent interpretation. The summary mode violated the requirements of the Federal Court Interpreter's Act. Clearly when the interpretation is forced into the wrong mode, accuracy suffers. The interpreter did object to the burden placed upon her; however, because she was unable to state the objection in a persuasive manner, the court saw no alternative other than to require her to evaluate and edit the defendant's statements. On appeal, the court was reversed for this decision.

There are other ethical rules and standards of protocol which, if ignored, will cause the interpretation to be less effective. One of the most critical issues that interpreters do not attend to with sufficient regard is the duty to adequately prepare for a matter he or she is interpreting.

B. Preparation-Based Ethical Issues

Mode is not the only factor that can create an inaccurate interpretation from an otherwise competent interpreter. Court interpreters are ethically obligated to prepare for assignments. According to the NCSC Code, "interpreters are encouraged to make inquiries as to the nature of a case whenever possible before accepting an assignment. This enables interpreters to match more closely their professional qualifications, skills, and experience to potential assignments and more accurately assess their ability to satisfy those assignments competently."[62] The ability to comply with other portions of the Code depends on successfully undertaking preparation activities. For example, an interpreter cannot effectively make the disclosures of potential or actual conflicts of interest required by Canon 3 if the interpreter has not adequately inquired as to the nature of the case and the parties involved. Additionally, Canon 8 requires interpreters to refrain from accepting assignments if they feel unable to perform competently due to the nature of the case, among other things. If the interpreter has not undertaken the effort to inquire regarding the nature of the case, he or she will be in violation of this tenet. The interpreter who arrives at an assignment and finds himself or herself unable to continue for what ever reason also wastes valuable court time and resources if the case cannot go forward.

Highly skilled interpreters may find themselves thrust into situations in which their ability to function competently is compromised because they are unfamiliar with the linguistic or procedural terrain. The NCSC Code recognizes that "[e]ven competent and experienced interpreters may encounter cases where routine proceedings suddenly involve technical and specialized terminology unfamiliar to the interpreter (e.g., the unscheduled testimony of an expert witness.). When such instances occur, interpreters should request a brief recess to familiarize themselves with the subject matter."[63] The Code contemplates that even an experienced, *prepared* and competent interpreter faced with unexpected testimony can be taken by surprise. If the unexpected content creates an untenable internal conflict for the interpreter he or she has the latitude to withdraw from the assignment and should feel no compunction about doing so.

At times then, the interpreter is not at fault for the lack of preparation. Requesting a recess to explore the nature of the new materials is an appropriate remedy. However, interpreters need to make sure that the lack of preparation is not through neglect of their pretrial obligation to obtain as much information about the assignment as possible. ASL interpreters simply cannot accurately render an interpretation without having read the case files, spoken with the deaf person, and seen the physical evidence prior to interpreting. ASL is a visual language heavily dependent upon the ability to depict objects, concepts and relationships in space and in context cohesively. Without a good understanding of the facts of the case and some familiarity with the law, interpreters will make errors.

Many misinterpretations are a direct result of the interpreter not being adequately prepared. In community interpreting, rarely will an ASL interpreter walk into an assignment without some information, and they often require a great deal of information prior to interpreting.[64] In community settings, interpreters feel comfortable asserting their needs. In legal settings, the need for preparation is even more intensified due to the unique style, register, vocabulary, procedures and nature of the assignment. Without preparation, the interpreter will lack the context to provide an interpretation that rises to the level of understandable and intelligible. At a minimum, interpreters must be aware of the duty to prepare and know how to prepare. Interpreters must know that without the essential preparatory work, they will not be true to the oath.

Although legal work requires extensive preparation, many court interpreters do not adequately prepare prior to a court assignment.[65] By and large, interpreters wait until the day of a proceeding to begin to gather information about a case. Interpreters often protest that the person who hired them will not provide the necessary preparation materials. This complaint misplaces the burden to prepare. The responsibility to negotiate the conditions adequate to effective interpreting rests squarely on the interpreter's shoulders. This duty cannot be delegated. If unable or unwilling, the assignment should be left to those who are. Inadequate preparation hurts deaf people, hurts the prospect for justice, and hurts those interpreters who later attempt to institute adequate preparation strategies. The oath and the interpreter's ethics require interpreters to treat their preparation obligations in court the same as in the classroom.

The duty to prepare encompasses more than preparing for a specific assignment. The interpreter has a duty to learn the legal system, as was discussed in Chapter 1. The interpreter should observe proceedings, read widely on legal topics and engage in discussion and interaction with other legal interpreters and deaf people. The more the interpreter knows about the overall court system, the more energy can be directed to preparing for the unique aspects of the specific assignment.

Attorneys are understandably hesitant to share information with interpreters. Attorneys do not understand the need for preparation materials and worry that the privilege may be waived if they share the information with third parties. Attorneys may be laboring under the impression that interpreting is no more difficult than court reporting; therefore, no more preparation is required. Interpreters need to be confident in approaching attorneys well in advance of a proceeding to obtain the information needed in order to effectively interpret the case. If interpreters face resistance, they can call on the court for assistance. At the very least, the court's file, which contains no privileged information, should be inspected by the interpreter prior to the assignment.

Along with the duty to understand the nature of the case, interpreters have a corresponding duty to assist the parties understand the interpreting process. Given the expectations that the deaf community has about the role of the interpreter, it is critical that time is spent with the deaf person beforehand. The interpreter must meet the deaf person, ensure that there will be no language difficulties and instruct the deaf person on how court interpreting differs from community interpreting. At times, the interpreter must also educate the court by providing guidance regarding the interpreting process. This is particularly true if the matter involves any unusual interpreting issues, such as when qualified deaf interpreters (CDIs) will be retained to work with the interpreters who can hear. Essentially, the court interpreter, as expert and officer of the court, must actively coordinate certain preparation activities to ensure that the integrity of the proceedings is not compromised by interpreting issues.

Spoken language interpreting associations are in accord. NAJIT has drafted guidelines for courts when working with certain language communities which have little experience in court and a small pool of trained interpreters. The guidelines have a wider application than simply for rare languages and represent the items that every interpreter needs to know prior to stepping into a court assignment. NAJIT suggests that courts provide, among other items, the following information to interpreters:[66]

Preparation Checklist

- Case name, names of the parties in the case, docket number.
- Charges in complaint or indictment, potential minimum and maximum penalties.
- Purpose of the proceeding plus relevant vocabulary including local acronyms or rules referred to by number.
- Description of likely arguments, based on type of proceeding and what is known about the case.
- Description of the courtroom, positions of the courtroom players, use of electronic equipment and what is expected of the interpreter.
- Pretrial conference with the consumer to ensure adequate communication compatibility.
- Pretrial legal conference to resolve any issues related to communication.

Figure 1 Preparation Checklist

Preparation for a case should not be confused with interpreting the attorney's preparation of the witnesses. Interpreters should not rehearse testimony with either side prior to interpreting a matter. A number of appeals have been based upon using a table interpreter for the proceedings function who has prepared privately with one of the parties. Ethically, as has been discussed in earlier chapters, if an interpreter works privately for either side of a case, he or she is precluded from then interpreting the proceedings.[67]

Interpreters should not delegate their duty to be adequately prepared for an assignment. Interpreters should not take assignments if preparation materials are withheld. Interpreters who accept work in substandard conditions lower the bar for their peers. Eventually as more interpreters receive training, and see their colleagues successfully obtaining preparation materials, adequate preparation will become a standard working condition for court interpreters.

C. Skills-Based Issues

At times, courts suffer abysmal interpreting services which reinforces the general suspicion of the overall quality of interpreters. William Hewitt has fittingly stated that "[w]hen poor interpretation occurs, the English speaking members of the court and the non-English speaking litigants or witnesses virtually *do not attend the same trial.*"[68] Inadequate interpreting skill strikes the very heart of the NES person's ability to understand and participate in the proceedings.

Almost all of the appeals involving a challenge to the accuracy of the interpretation can be discussed as raising skills-based issues. Several of these appeals illustrate how ineffective interpreting contributes to the court's mistrust of interpreters. In a federal change of plea hearing in Oregon, the interpreter interpreted "manslaughter" as "something less than murder."[69] The defendant claimed that the interpretation was deficient and that he did not understand the nature of the crime to which he entered a plea of guilty. The seriousness of the error prompted the court to vacate the plea on appeal. The statutory distinctions between the various degrees of crimes are difficult at times for attorneys to grasp. While finding the interpretation grossly inadequate, the court recognized that interpreters are not expected to have the same legal training as lawyers; however, the general import of technical terms must be imparted. As a part of the interpreter's preparation, care must be taken to review the charges in the case in order to arrive at an effective interpretation. In a guilty plea, the defendant must know not only the elements of the crime for which he or she was originally charged with but also the elements of the crime to which he or she is pleading. The information is available to interpreters by reviewing the charges and understanding the plea which can and should be obtained prior to interpreting.

In another federal criminal case, the interpretation was so appalling that the prosecutor personally replaced the interpreter; however, the replacement interpreter was no better.[70] The second interpreter made repeated errors and blamed the witness for the errors stating "he says a lot of mumbo-jumbo that doesn't mean a lot of things."[71] The interpreter also made indiscreet statements on a break that may have been overheard by the jury which were derogatory about the witness. This interpreter was replaced and the jury was instructed to disregard her improper remarks.

The appeal was based in part upon the prosecutor replacing the interpreter on his own. Only the court has the power to appoint and remove an interpreter as we have discussed. The accuracy of the interpretation was another ground for appeal. The court determined that the interpretation did not meet the standard for competent interpreting; however, the conviction was not reversed because the court found that the defendant had not been prejudiced by the interpreter's inadequate interpretation.

The interpreter was chastised for making inappropriate remarks about the character of the NES person. There is never a good reason for blaming the NES person for an interpreter's inadequate interpretation. If the interpreter does not understand a specific item, he or she should seek permission to inquire of the witness. If the interpreter is struggling generally with the NES's language, then the only responsible course is to ask to be removed on the assignment and assist in locating a capable interpreter. Interpreters need to be very careful that indiscreet remarks do not compromise the case. The interpreter's conduct, comments, and facial expression can influence the jury negatively and create an issue for appeal.

In one early Illinois case, the appeal was based on both accuracy and bias issues. The sole witness to a crime needed an interpreter.[72] Without the witness' testimony, the state's case was much weaker. As a result, it was critical that the interpretation was accurate. During trial, both counsel repeatedly brought mistranslations to the court's attention. Even though the judge and the attorneys did not understand Spanish, they could plainly see that the quality of the interpretation was inferior. In addition, the interpreter held repeated private conversations with the witness even after the judge admonished her. Because of the cumulative effect of the mistranslations and protocol errors, the interpretation did not rise to the standard of understandable, comprehensible and intelligent.[73] As a result, the court held that the defendant was denied his constitutional right to confront witnesses and the conviction was reversed.

In another more recent Florida case, the defendant was on trial for murder.[74] Again, there was only one witness to the crime. The witness testified through an interpreter about statements made by the defendant, concerning the victim, at the scene of the crime. The interpreter added a statement which could be considered a racial slur to the defendant's response which was not present in the original testimony. The defense moved for a mistrial which was denied. On appeal, the severity of the error compelled the court to reverse the conviction. Because the prosecution had little other evidence connecting the defendant to the crime, the use of the racial slur in front of the jury fell below the standard of competent interpreting and prejudiced the defendant. In this respect, the court stated that "because the evidence of guilt was not overwhelming, the error cannot be harmless."[75]

Attorneys should also beware because the adequacy of their representation can be challenged due to the inaccurate skills of the interpreter. In Iowa, a court found that the attorney had provided ineffective assistance because he had failed to challenge an inadequate interpretation. [76] The court explained "inaccurate and incomplete translations of attorney-client communications by an interpreter are an example of deficient conduct by an intermediary giving rise to an ineffective assistance of trial counsel claim."[77] The attorney owes a duty of competent representation to the client, which can be breached by the use of an unskilled interpreter.[78] The premise is fundamental that in order to give competent legal advice, the attorney's words must be accurately conveyed. The attorney has no way to know if the interpretation is deficient.[79] Counsel should be proactive and vigilant in ensuring that the most effective interpretation is provided to the NES client by working with credentialed, trained and experienced interpreters.

D Bias-Based Issues

Prior to modern statutes requiring professional interpreters to be provided for NES litigants, courts typically relied upon whoever was available for language assistance. This created fertile grounds for appeal. Though standards have improved, many early cases permitted family members, friends and even other litigants to interpret in court.[80] Often, the cases concerned the use of a family member who allegedly could not be neutral because of the nature of the relationship. Litigants have a right to flesh out and challenge any bias that the interpreter might harbor in favor of or any prejudice against either party. When the objection to a biased interpreter is overruled, the issue is preserved as a ground for appeal.

Bias exists when the interpreter either subjectively cannot be neutral or when the relationship creates the appearance to others that the interpreter cannot be neutral. In legal settings, these appearances take on added importance, even though the interpreter may feel as if the interpretation will not be affected by the relationship. Courts frequently state that "the interpreter should be one who has no interest in the outcome of the case because of the danger that a primary witness' message will be distorted through interpretation."[81] In one case in which a co-defendant was being used to interpret a change of plea, the court stated that "an interpreter should be a neutral and detached individual whose abilities are first screened by the court and who is sworn to make a true, literal and complete bilateral translation. The use of an unqualified, un-sworn interpreter, who was the co-defendant with the accused and also has a substantial interest in the outcome of the proceedings, renders the [proceeding, here a plea] itself questionable."[82] When an adverse party is used to interpret, the basic unfairness is obvious.

Courts have used family members to interpret even when the family member/interpreter was involved as a witness and planned to testify against the person for whom they were interpreting.[83] Family members are often used because they appear to be the only people who can understand the NES or deaf person.[84] In a somewhat amusing early case, an appeal was taken because the plaintiff's daughter had interpreted.[85] The problem was not the familial relationship; rather the daughter's evil was that she was very attractive and "by her demeanor on the witness stand gave the plaintiff an undue advantage!"[86] Normally, however, the fear is that the relationship will cause the interpreter to change the interpretation either in support of or to the detriment of the NES person.

At times, permitting an interested interpreter, such as a co-defendant, is more worrisome. One court permitted a "friend" of the victim to interpret for the accused at trial.[87] The same "friend" had interpreted the victim's report to the police of the crime. As it turned out, the "friend" had also witnessed the crime and would be called to testify. The defense theory was that the "friend" had actually perpetrated the crime. Because the interpreter had a motive to skew the interpretation and was a participant in the proceedings, it was inappropriate to also serve as the proceedings interpreter. The defendant's conviction was reversed on appeal.

a. Disclosure Conflicts

The conflicts provisions in the NCSC Code recognize that there are different kinds of relationships which may interfere or be seen as interfering with the interpreter's ability to be impartial. The Code has certain disclosure rules which require the interpreter personally to analyze the nature of the relationship to determine whether it would interfere or be seen as having the potential to interfere with the interpretation. In those cases, the interpreter *can accept* the assignment, but must disclose the prior contact to the court and let the court decide if the appearance of impropriety is too great.[88]

The nature of the contact, not the fact of contact, must be carefully and objectively analyzed. If in the view of a neutral outsider, the nature of the relationship might entice the interpreter to slant the interpretation, then a disclosure conflict exists. The interpreter ethically must disclose the relationship to the presiding official on the record and have a determination made. Interpreters must disclose the nature of the relationship, whether private or professional, with the deaf person in order for the court to make an informed decision regarding the potential for bias or prejudice.[89]

If the interpreter does not disclose the prior contact and it is later discovered, their motivation is questioned and their credibility suffers. Being the sole holder of information which can compromise the effectiveness of the legal process is a position interpreters must avoid. Interpreters, not trained in the law, are in charge of one of the most critical parts of the trial – the witness' testimony. In the past, interpreters have, unwittingly or by design, wreaked havoc on the process. These disclosure rules in the ethics code serve a screening function for courts.

b. Decline Conflicts

The NCSC Code creates another category of conflicts of interest for which an interpreter should decline the assignment and should not serve as a proceedings interpreter.[90] When these relationships exist, the conflict analysis has already been done for the interpreter. Regardless of the interpreter's feelings of neutrality, the drafters of the code have determined that the appearance of impropriety is too great to permit the interpreter to work the proceedings. In those cases, the interpreter does not have to disclose anything on the record because the interpreter does not accept the assignment in the first place. Listed among those conflicts of interest are when the interpreter is a family member or close friend of the litigants. Other *per se* conflicts prohibited by Canon 3 were discussed in Chapter 5. In general, these prohibitions attempt to insulate the legal process from the effects of an interested or biased interpreter.

The deaf community is quite small and many interpreters know the deaf person for whom they interpret in court. ASL interpreters generally have a deep connection to the community and empathize with deaf people who have been subjected to discrimination and oppression. At times, even trained interpreters succumb to over-identification which jeopardizes the ability to remain objective and places the interpretation at risk. The desire to equalize an inherently oppressive environment needs to be carefully self-monitored. Equalization can best be attained by providing an effective and understandable interpretation and by attaining a thorough understanding of the legal system.

The bond between ASL interpreters and the deaf community can best be explained historically. Traditionally, the community of interpreters came from family members, church members or professionals in deaf education. Interpreters were to some extent peripheral members of the community, had a vested interest in its welfare, and often acted out of pure charity. Though much has changed in the past fifty years, ASL interpreters still enter the field in one of two ways: ASL interpreters are either born into the community by virtue of having deaf family members, or they learn ASL as a second language, generally, though not always, as an adult. When born into the community, there is a natural tie or bond that exists and a feeling of protectiveness. For this reason, when interpreters are related to those whom they are asked to interpret for in court, interpreters are prohibited from accepting the assignment.[91]

When learning the language later in life, an ASL student is encouraged, and in many cases required, to interact socially in the community to develop language skills, cultural fluency and lasting community connections. As a result, ASL interpreters who are not born into the community often know, sometimes quite well, those whom they work for in court. If an ASL interpreter could only work with deaf people whom they do not know in court, the pool of available interpreters would be nearly non-existent. These interpreters are not conflicted out of interpreting because of the familial relationship; however, the nature of the contact may be quite intense, and if it approaches a familial relationship, the interpreter should decline the assignment. If the relationship does not approach that degree of intensity, the interpreter must disclose its existence on the record for the court's consideration. A disclosure can be as simple as "Your Honor, the interpreter has a prior professional contact with the defendant which she does not believe will impair her ability to interpret neutrally and impartially in the proceedings."

Luckily, today, in many places, courts have access to professional interpreters and do not have to rely exclusively upon *ad hoc* interpreting services for NES litigants. In the past, justice was dependent upon whatever resources were immediately available. In modern times, courts are more careful about locating an impartial interpreter. Additionally, today courts can rely on trained interpreters to disclose contacts which would or could be viewed as impairing their ability to work neutrally and impartially.

III. Protocol-Based Appeals

A. Private Negotiations Prohibited

In ASL community interpreting, a fairly common strategy is to verify with the deaf person, during the act of interpreting, that the person understands the interpretation. If the interpreter receives feedback that the deaf person does not understand, the interpreter is able to make adjustments to the signing style, or restructure the interpretation to ensure comprehension. Interpreters accomplish this verification by signing directly and discreetly to the deaf person. A related issue is when the deaf person is signing, and the interpreter misunderstands a term or needs a clarification of an unfamiliar sign. In community interpreting, traditionally, the interpreter inquires directly of the deaf person for a repetition or a clarification when it is for minor adjustments to accuracy. The other participants are often unaware of the real time process of negotiating subtle contours of meaning. For longer transactions, interpreters generally stop the communication and inform the participants of the nature of the interaction. In court, however, this practice is prohibited and has served as a ground for appeal repeatedly in interpreted cases.

Courts prohibit private conversations because they cannot monitor the content or the nature of the conversation. Conferring privately with a testifying witness is simply not tolerated in court for anyone, for any amount of information. Research in the field of ASL interpreting confirms that attorneys and judges dislike and distrust *any* conferencing even between interpreters to which they are not privy.[92] When the content is linguistically inaccessible to the court, private conversations inspire immediate legal consternation. One judge ruled that "extraneous conversations between the witness and the interpreter should not be permitted. If such conversations do occur for some reason, they should be translated into English for the judge and counsel to hear."[93] In an Ohio appeal to vacate a guilty plea, the defendant had been asked whether anyone had promised him anything to enter into the plea agreement.[94] The transcript indicated that the interpreter engaged in a long colloquy with the defendant before interpreting his response as "no." On appeal, the defendant claimed that he did not understand the interpreter's explanation of whether anything had been promised him. The defendant also accused his attorney of ineffective assistance because the attorney did not ask the court to order a recording of the interpreter's extensive private conversations. Though the argument was unsuccessful, the interpreter's inappropriate conduct created the ground for appeal.

Given the poor track record of interpreters in court, the concerns about private negotiations are reasonable. In a Nebraska case, the bilingual judge found the interpretation so poor that he repeatedly stopped the proceedings to correct the errors in the interpretation.[95] Eventually, the judge ordered the testimony to *proceed without the interpreter* because of the magnitude of the errors. The interpreter held private conversations with the NES witness and even answered questions directed to him. The court on review stated:

> It is rather difficult to be compelled to examine an important witness through an interpreter. The interpreter should be absolutely impersonal [with] the counsel asking a question the same as if the witness could understand it and the interpreter repeating the question with no added remarks of his own, and giving back the witness' answer in her own words. There should be no extraneous conversations between counsel and the interpreter.[96]

Most matters are not presided over by a bilingual judge. Most monolingual judges and attorneys then will be under the assumption that once told to interpret accurately, the interpreter will interpret accurately. The best the attorneys can do is object to the behavior, seek to have the interpreter instructed or the conversations recorded, and preserve their objections for appeal.

Interpreters who hold private conversations or answer questions put to witnesses destroy the fairness of the legal process. [97] Likewise, interpreters who guess at an interpretation rather than admit to struggling to understand a deaf person do a disservice to the community and the legal system. Some courts recognize that these protocol errors both violate the rules of evidence and occur far more frequently than courts are willing to admit. One court, in a sexual assault trial, stated: "[I]t is obvious that if [the interpreter] undertakes – *as is too often done* – to expound things to the witness in his own fashion, or to have any conversation with him beyond strict translation, no one can tell how far the testimony is reliably genuine, or how far it consists of what is admissible."[98] In this case, the errors of the interpreter reached constitutional proportions: "[The] inadequate translation of the complainant's cross-examination denied defendant his constitutional right to confront the witness against him."[99] Reliability is the hallmark of admissible evidence. An unscrupulous, unskilled, unprepared or under-educated interpreter possesses the ability to color the trustworthiness of the evidence. The court is simply not in a position to know how the interpreter may have manipulated the evidence; and therefore, has little tolerance for the practice of private negotiations.

Attorneys' trepidation about examining witnesses through interpreters is based in experience. The damage caused by an unrestrained interpreter during cross-examination was displayed in a 1990 Virginia case.[100] The defendant appealed because of the protracted private conversations between the interpreter and the witness and because of the interpreter's brazen commandeering of the attorney's role. During cross-examination, the following exchange was one of several similar exchanges that took place:

Counsel:	Do you remember me coming into your store?
Witness	(through interpreter): Yes I can.
Counsel:	I have never been to your store, tell me where it is.
Interpreter:	I didn't ask her that, I asked her if the attorney came into the store after today, would you remember him.[101]

Counsel immediately moved for a mistrial. There is no conceivable linguistic reason to justify this wholesale substitution of form, meaning and intent of the interpretation. The notion that interpreters cannot be trusted and must be carefully supervised is strengthened by this conduct. Courts do not like being excluded. An interpreter who holds extended conversations with a witness in a language the court does not understand tries the patience of even the most accommodating judge. Best court interpreting practices require the interpreter to seek permission from the presiding official prior to engaging in any private negotiations with the NES person. The interpreter can achieve the necessary latitude to construct an effective interpretation by getting the attention of the court and asking, "May the interpreter have a moment to inquire of the witness?"

B. Active Involvement Prohibited

Interpreters are ethically prohibited from becoming involved in a case they are interpreting by taking an active part in the proceeding. Canon 7 of the NCSC Code states: "Interpreters shall limit themselves to interpreting or translating, and shall not give legal advice, express personal opinions to individuals for whom they are interpreting, or engage in any other activities which may be construed to constitute a service other than interpreting or translating while serving as an interpreter."[102] The rule is equally applicable to the interpreter who volunteers to perform the additional roles and to those instances when the interpreter is asked by the court or attorneys to perform some role other than interpreting for the proceeding.

1. When Asked to Testify

Under Canon 7 falls the common practice of seeking the interpreter's opinion sometimes in the form of testimony about various issues. Typically the interpreter is the only person in the room who knows the foreign language. It is quite natural for the court to look to the interpreter, its expert, to provide guidance and assistance in language-related matters. Depending upon the scope of the requested involvement, however, these questions place the interpreter in a position of violating the ethical code by taking an active part in the proceedings.

When the proceedings interpreter is asked to *testify* during a proceeding, the request is inappropriate for a host of reasons. First, the interpreter is actively involved in the proceeding which constitutes an ethical violation. Second, if there is only one court interpreter, the deaf person will be left without interpreting services while the interpreter is functioning as a witness. Third, assuming only one court interpreter, the interpreter will have to sign and talk at the same time to ensure the deaf person's linguistic presence. The use of spoken English and signed communication at the same time actually excludes the deaf person from full participation. The spoken English tends to be more grammatically accurate while the signed communication is usually incomplete and less intelligible.[103] While the people who can hear are fairly included, the deaf person usually is not. Fourth, if there are two court interpreters, the interpreter who is not testifying will be interpreting alone and without supervision for accuracy. <u>Fifth,</u> the practice of participating in a role other than interpreting while also interpreting creates perception and credibility problems. If the interpreter's opinion is discredited or perhaps inarticulate, he or she loses professional stature. If the interpreter's opinion is accepted, the interpreter's status may be raised in the eyes of the jury or other participants. <u>Sixth,</u> it is a conflict to take on more than one role. Just as an attorney or a judge may not become a witness in a matter he or she is handling, an interpreter should not become involved in a matter he or she is interpreting.[104] <u>Seventh,</u> once assumed, the mantle of expert witness becomes hard to lay aside and return to the ostensibly less prestigious role of simply interpreting.

Courts look to interpreters because they are the logical choice in matters related to language and interpretation in court. The most serious violation occurs when proceedings interpreters are required to testify to the quality of another's interpretation.[105] The court interpreter should resist the entreaty and firmly suggest that the parties retain a qualified expert to give an opinion on the linguistic features of the other's interpretation. An interpreter's refusal to provide testimony as to the quality of an officer's rendition of the *Miranda* warnings has been upheld on appeal.[106] The proper protocol is for the proceedings interpreter to approach the bench, object to the request and indicate that it presents a conflict of interest to act as a witness for the defense and also function as the court's interpreter.

2.   When Asked About Comprehension

At other times, judges want to know from the interpreter if the deaf person is following the proceedings. Interpreters often react defensively when asked for their opinion with respect to such matters. An interpreter may be receiving all of the signals normally associated with comprehension, yet comprehension is easy to fake and difficult to accurately gauge. Interpreters find it particularly difficult when asked for an opinion regarding the deaf person's actual level of understanding. No interpreter can say the defendant understands 25% -- 50% -- 75% of the communication with any confidence. Any attempt to state a specific level of comprehension will be outside the interpreter's expertise and most likely inaccurate. Further, simply because the interpreter may doubt that the person is understanding, does not mean the interpreter has the facility to explain the reasons why. If the court insists, experts exist who can provide that information to the parties through proper testing. The interpreter can serve as a gateway in helping identify experts to provide those diagnostics. If the interpreter also holds the credentials to perform the testing, then the interpreter should remove herself or himself from the case as the proceedings interpreter before taking on that role.

Several cases have recognized that the expectation that the working interpreter will give an opinion on the NES person's comprehension level is outside of the scope of the interpreter's practice, while others have permitted the inquiry. A Michigan court held that it was an improper delegation of judicial authority to ask the interpreter to determine the defendant's level of understanding even though interpreter was also a lawyer. [107] However, in Washington state, the court permitted a certified court interpreter to testify about the defendant's ability to comprehend trial proceedings.[108] Best practices are unambiguous on the point: Interpreter ethics command that the interpreter refrain from taking an active role in a case in which he or she is also functioning as the proceeding interpreter.

3. When Asked About Interpreting-Related Issues

At times, the request for information or the need to take an active part in the proceeding is not so intrusive as to interfere with the interpreting process. Here interpreters must use their discretion. Ethical codes provide the interpreter some leeway in intervening in a proceeding, without being asked, in several distinct instances. Interpreters are permitted ethically to interject as a last resort when communication is breaking down, if reporting an impediment to their work or if a term or phrase needs explaining, among other permitted intrusions.[109] If there is an issue related to interpretation which needs to be addressed for the proceedings to continue, then it is most logical for the interpreter to address the issue, privately at the bench or in chambers, in order for the court to make an educated decision. Participating in this manner, like participating in preparatory meetings with the court to inform them of the interpreter's role, is not a violation of the ethics. Rather, it is part of the court interpreter's duty as an expert to ensure that the court understands how to work with interpreters in a manner which will ensure the appropriate working conditions. However, interpreters must use discretion in assessing whether the participation is inappropriate or not. No right answer exists for determining the proper course of action. Most importantly, interpreters must inform the deaf person of this difference in the role.

4. Other Types of Prohibited Participation

Interpreters have, at times, contributed to the court's paranoia about their unchecked power. Giving legal advice seems particularly tempting even for experienced interpreters. Interpreters are connected to the community and often have a desire to help. Frankly, laypeople do not always realize that in explaining procedures and concepts to a deaf consumer, they are, in fact, giving legal advice. Consider the example of the deaf person contesting a traffic ticket and the interpreter knows from experience in court that if the officer does not show up and if the deaf person maintains their innocence, the ticket will be dismissed. Many interpreters find it impossible to resist sharing this information. Whether the source is a desire to help or otherwise, the practice constitutes giving legal advice and it is unethical and illegal.

Sometimes, the conduct is more egregious. In one criminal case, the court interpreter privately had offered his services to the defendant's family as an investigator.[110] The interpreter was hired and paid for his services. The same interpreter interpreted the proceedings. On appeal, the court stated:

> [The interpreter] abused his powers as an officer of the court by acting outside the scope of his duties as a court-appointed interpreter. He falsely held himself out to be a private investigator, accepting money from Martin Ledezma to 'investigate' Jose and Gonzalo's cases. [The interpreter] interfered with the attorney-client relationship by directly answering Jose's questions concerning the case instead of communicating the inquiries to trial counsel. In addition, [the

interpreter] provided extensive legal advice to Jose, telling him the prosecution's case was 'weak' because it did not have sufficient evidence for a conviction. [The interpreter] also convinced Jose he could arrange for Jose's deportation to Mexico, claiming he had a special relationship with the court.[111]

Such conduct "may, in essence, deprive defendants of their constitutional right to an interpreter."[112] Self-awareness is a critical skill for interpreters to hone. Interpreters must be able to look at their behavior and see themselves as others do. The ability to be critically self-aware will reduce the possibility that interpreter-related conduct will serve as the basis for an appeal or reversal.

Obviously, the legal system's mistrust of interpreters has a reasonable basis grounded in experience. Until relatively recent times, courts have failed to implement quality control standards for language interpreters. Many courts still rely on uncertified and inexperienced interpreters. The NES person's ability to understand and participate in the proceedings is directly proportional to the quality of the interpretation provided. Courts need a system of checks in place better than simply instructing the interpreter to interpret accurately. Otherwise, judges have no way to know how often the interpretation is effective. The fiction that the court interpreter is accurately interpreting, standing alone, is not a panacea.

In sum, though courts have had experiences with poor interpretation in the past, it is the wrong approach to artificially impose upon the interpreter a requirement of verbatim interpretation. Courts and deaf people are entitled to an accurate interpretation by experienced and competent practitioners. Courts must understand that languages do not always share the same concepts and even when they do, they may well have various and differing ways of expressing those concepts.

Much trouble can be avoided if the court would raise the bar of interpreting services and hire only trained and qualified court interpreters. When the courts listen to practitioners who advise them on the requirements for effective interpreting, the proper staffing for the various functions in court and other important issues, the level of participation and ultimately, justice will rise for deaf people. Courts can protect the participants by ensuring that the proceedings are recorded to preserve the original source language testimony and the interpretation. Courts provide an additional layer of protection by retaining qualified monitor interpreters when the details of the case indicate. Finally, although courts must do their part, interpreters, attorneys and consumers of court interpreter services must also take responsibility to increase the level of professionalism and to enhance the quality of services provided in court.

Appendix A:
Glossary

ASL

A visual language used by deaf people in the United States and Canada as their primary means of communication which is "a system of arbitrary symbols by means of which persons in a culture carry on the total activity of that culture." Taken in part from William C. Stokoe, Jr., (2005) 10th Anniversary Classics. Sign Language Structure: An Outline of the Visual Communication systems of the American Deaf. *Journal of Deaf Studies and Deaf Education* vol. 10 no. 1 Oxford University Press.

CI

According to the RID, Certificate of Interpretation ("CI") "[h]olders ... are recognized as fully certified in Interpretation and have demonstrated the ability to interpret between American Sign Language (ASL) and spoken English in both sign-to-voice and voice-to-sign. The interpreter's ability to transliterate is not considered in this certification. Holders of the CI are recommended for a broad range of interpretation assignments. This test is currently available"

CT

According to the RID, Certificate of Transliteration "[h]olders ... are recognized as fully certified in Transliteration and have demonstrated the ability to transliterate between English-based sign language and spoken English in both sign-to-voice and voice-to-sign. The transliterator's ability to interpret is not considered in this certification. Holders of the CT are recommended for a broad range of transliteration assignments. This test is currently available."

CSC

According to the RID, Comprehensive Skills Certificate ("CSC") "[h]olders ... have demonstrated the ability to interpret between American Sign Language and spoken English and to transliterate between spoken English and a English-based sign language. Holders of this certificate are recommended for a broad range of interpreting and transliterating assignments. The CSC examination was offered until 1987. This test is no longer offered."

CONDUIT MODEL OF INTERPRETING

An outdated model of interpreting in which the interpreter was considered to be an invisible tool simply to convey information. The purpose of the model was to approximate a natural two-party communicative event for the deaf and hearing participants. In order to do this, the parties took the position that the interpreter was invisible. The interpreter could not participate in any manner in the interaction even if communication was breaking down. Over the years, the interpreting field has matured as trust has developed with deaf people who work with interpreters. Nevertheless, a sometimes uneasy partnership exists in which interpreters and deaf people continually negotiate and redefine the nature of the interpreter's role.

CONTACT LANGUAGE VARIETIES/CONTACT SIGNING:

According to Valli and Lucas, who are credited for first applying the sociolinguistic concept of contact language varieties to signing, "Contact signing is also a unique phenomenon. Contact signing results from the contact between English and ASL and has features of both. This is what has traditionally been called Pidgin Sign English (PSE) in the American Deaf community. We have done a lot of research on this kind of signing. We don't use the term pidgin because this kind of signing does not seem to have the linguistic features of what linguists call pidgins, and the social situations in which contact signing is used are not like the ones in which spoken language pidgins come about,. .. . [In the deaf community] its linguistic features include English word order, the use of prepositions, constructions with *that,* English expressions, and mouthing of English words, as well as ASL non-manual

signals, body and eye gaze shifting, and ASL use of space."
Valli & Lucas (2000) p.188.

COUNSEL TABLE INTERPRETER

The designation for the ASL interpreter who sits at counsel table and interprets all privileged communications between the deaf party and counsel. The interpreter has adjunct duties to monitor the proceedings interpreter for accuracy and make adjustments as necessary through a variety of strategies. The table interpreter serves as an expert to the litigation team to which he or she is identified.

COURT INTERPRETER

The generic term used to refer to the interpreter who performs the proceedings function. The term "court interpreter" is used both by ASL interpreters and in the spoken language interpreting community.

DEAF

The designation for those people who do not have natural access to spoken communication through auditory means. In the United States, and parts of Canada, a segment of the universe of people encompassed by the term "deaf" have formed a community that shares a visual language (American Sign Language).

DEFENSE INTERPRETER

A term formerly used by sign language interpreters to refer to the interpreter who performs the access to counsel function. A term used by spoken language interpreters to mean the interpreter who interprets all the proceedings for the non-English speaking person and who also interprets the access to counsel function.

EEOC

The United States Equal Employment Opportunity Commission is the federal administrative agency responsible for receiving, investigating and attempting to resolve, both informally and formally, complaints of employment discrimination by people in protected categories. It can be accessed at www.EEOC.gov.

ELECTRONIC INTERPRETING EQUIPMENT

Interpreting equipment used by spoken language interpreters in which the interpreter speaks into a receiver and the NES participants hear the interpretation through individual headsets. The interpreter can be located anywhere in the room within the reception distance of the equipment.

ELEMENTS

According to Law.com the definition of an element is "n. 1) an essential requirement to a cause of action (the right to bring a lawsuit to enforce a particular right). Each cause of action (negligence, breach of contract, trespass, assault, etc.) is made up of a basic set of elements which must be alleged and proved. Each charge of a criminal offense requires allegation and proof of its elements. 2) essential requirement of a zoning general plan."

EXOTIC LANGUAGES

Used by courts and spoken language interpreters to refer to low incidence languages which usually do not have interpretation tests developed.

FEED INTERPRETER

The designation for the member of the interpreter team who is actively watching the working interpreter and making adjustments for accuracy of the interpretation either by signing small units of information to the interpreter who is signing or by whispering short segments to the interpreter who is speaking for the deaf person. *See also Off Mic Interpreter*

FICTION

Law.com defines a fiction as "n. a presumption of fact assumed by a court for convenience, consistency or to achieve justice."

GLOSSING

A term used by interpreters of ASL to refer to literal or word for word translations of particular signs. The gloss spoken in English for the sign does not accurately represent the entire meaning of the sign. According to Metzger, "because ASL is not a written language and, perhaps even more important, because of the existence of multiple articulators (including fingers hands, arms, shoulders, neck, head, mouth, cheeks, eyes, and eyebrows), written transcription can lose more of the original than it captures." Metzger (1999) p. 44. Glosses are simply English labels which serve to permit ASL – English bilinguals to discuss ASL in spoken English. When spoken in English, glossed ASL sounds ungrammatical and nonsensical since it is simply a shorthand way of referring to signs by using a spoken language. ASL Glosses in this text is represented in capital letters.

HARD OF HEARING

A term used to refer to a segment of society which can to varying degrees access spoken language through auditory means. At times, hard of hearing people are fully self-identified members of the deaf community. In other instances, probably the majority, hard of hearing people simply lost some of their ability to hear after a lifetime of living as a person who can hear. In that case, the person usually does not know sign language or associate with other deaf people.

HEARING PEOPLE

A term commonly used by deaf people to refer to the wider population who can hear, who do not use sign language and typically do not interact with deaf people or other users of ASL.

INTERPRETING

Interpretation involves rendering a message in one language to the equivalent message in a different language orally or through signs.

LEGAL AUTHORITY

That body of literature consisting primarily of case law, statutes, court rules, professional articles and research in the field of law which guides courts in making determinations. Binding authority is the rule of law that must be followed in a particular jurisdiction and consists primarily of case law and statutes. Persuasive authority is other literature or cases or statutes from outside the jurisdiction which the court may use for enlightenment or to assist in making a determination but that the court is not bound to follow. The authority of an interpreter working with a deaf defendant and an attorney in a criminal case may be the Sixth Amendment of the Constitution or a state statutory provision requiring interpreters to be provided for defendants and counsel. On the other hand, in a state civil matter, the authority may be either the Americans with Disabilities Act or the state interpreting statute requiring interpreters for civil participants. In a federal court setting where the Americans with Disabilities Act does not apply, the authority for an interpreter may be the Federal Court Interpreting Act, or the United States Administrative Office of the Courts' internal regulation agreeing to provide ASL interpreters in federal matters.

MCSC

According to the RID, the Master Comprehensive Skills Certificate ("MCSC") "examination was designed with the intent of testing for a higher standard of performance than the CSC. Holders of this certificate were required to hold the CSC prior to taking this exam. Holders of this certificate are recommended for a broad range of interpreting and transliterating assignments. This certificate is no longer offered."

MENS REA

Law.com defines *mens rea* as "(menz ray-ah) n. Latin for a "guilty mind," or criminal intent in committing the act."

MOUTHING

The practice by sign language interpreters of forming the English word on their mouth without voice to facilitate speech reading. Mouthing replaces naturally occurring ASL mouth movements which tend to serve an adverbial purpose in modifying ASL signs.

NAJIT

The National Association of Judiciary Interpreters and Translators is a professional association consisting primarily of spoken language interpreters. NAJIT can be accessed at www.najit.org.

NCSC

The National Center for State Courts can be accessed at www.ncsconline.org. According to the NCSC "The mission of NCSC is to improve the administration of justice through leadership and service to state courts, and courts around the world. Through original research, consulting services, publications, and national educational programs, NCSC offers solutions that enhance court operations with the latest technology; collects and interprets the latest data on court operations nationwide; and provides information on proven "best practices" for improving court operations. NCSC disseminates information to state court leaders on key national policy issues, and helps advocate their policies with Congress as well as supporting several prestigious national organizations." The NCSC maintains a program specifically geared towards improving the nation's court interpreting service delivery models.

NES

An acronym for non-English speaker or speaking person who is typically dependent upon an interpreter to understand and participate fully in a court proceeding.

OFF-MIC/ ON-MIC INTERPRETER

Terms coined by spoken language interpreters to indicate the interpreter who is not actually providing the simultaneous or consecutive interpretation. In a team of two proceedings interpreters, the interpreter who is physically working is the on-mic interpreter and the interpreter who is mentally processing, monitoring for accuracy and providing support to the working interpreter is called the off-mic interpreter.

ASL interpreters have used inconsistent terminology for this interpreter including terms such as the "feed" interpreter, the "monitor" interpreter, the "off" interpreter or the "back up" interpreter. *See also Feed Interpreter.*

PER SE

Law.com defines *per se* as follows: "(purr say) adj. Latin for "by itself," meaning inherently. Thus, a published writing which falsely accuses another of having a sexually transmitted disease or being a convicted felon is "libel per se," without further explanation of the meaning of the statement."

In the court interpreting context, a per se ethical conflict is one in which the drafters of the code have defined certain contexts, such as interpreting for the police, that constitute an automatic (per se) conflict for which the police interpreter should not then interpret for the court in the same proceeding.

PIDGIN LANGUAGES

Valli & Lucas describe a pidgin as: "[u]sually a pidgin is the result of language contact between the adult users of mutually unintelligible languages. The language contact occurs for very specific purposes, like trade. These adult users are usually not trying to learn each other's language, but rather a third language that will help them improve their social and economic status. . . . When children are born in these situations and learn the pidgin as their native language, they begin to change it and make it more complex. The result is what linguists call a *creole*." Valli & Lucas (2000) p. 186.

PLAIN ERROR

The standard by which errors in a trial that were not brought to the attention of the trial court will be judged on appeal.

If the error is not plain, obvious and egregious, the appellate court will not reverse the matter. The logic is that the trial court could have taken notice of and remedied a plain error even in the absence of an objection from counsel. Any other type of error that is not plain, requires a contemporaneous objection from counsel to preserve for appellate review.

PRAGMATIC EQUIVALENCE

Pragmatics refers to the supremacy of meaning and intention over form and syntax. What people mean derives more from the words used, but is affected by the parties' relationship, history, context, audience and any other events in context which create inferences. According to Morris, "[p]ragmatics is thus centrally concerned with meaning in context, and hence speaker/listener intentions. Speaker intention lies at the heart of modern speech-act theory. ... To achieve effective [pragmatic equivalence] in a judicial setting ... in speech-act terms there must be equivalence not only of propositional content (referential equivalence), but also, and sometimes primarily, of illocutionary force (pragmatic equivalence), in order to achieve the same perlocutionary effect on L2 as on L1 listeners. From a pragmatics viewpoint, what the speaker means by the utterance (speaker intention) outweighs the individual or combined significance of the words." Morris, R. (1993) pp. 77-78. (internal citations omitted).

PRECEDENT

Law.com defines precedent as "n. a prior reported opinion of an appeals court which establishes the legal rule (authority) in the future on the same legal question decided in the prior judgment. Thus, "the rule in *Fishbeck v. Gladfelter* is precedent for the issue before the court in this case." The doctrine that a lower court must follow a precedent is called stare decisis."

PRESUMPTION

According to the online dictionary service provided by www. law.com, a presumption is a noun meaning "a rule of law which permits a court to assume a fact is true until such time as there is a preponderance (greater weight) of evidence which disproves or outweighs (rebuts) the presumption. Each presumption is based upon a particular set of apparent facts paired with established laws, logic, reasoning or individual rights. A presumption is rebuttable in that it can be refuted by factual evidence. One can present facts to persuade the judge that the presumption is not true. Examples: a child born of a husband and wife living together is presumed to be the natural child of the husband unless there is conclusive proof it is not; a person who has disappeared and not been heard from for seven years is presumed to be dead, but the presumption could be rebutted if he/she is found alive; an accused person is presumed innocent until proven guilty. These are sometimes called rebuttable presumptions to distinguish them from absolute, conclusive or irrebuttable presumptions in which rules of law and logic dictate that there is no possible way the presumption can be disproved. However, if a fact is absolute it is not truly a presumption at all, but a certainty."

PROCEEDINGS INTERPRETER

The ASL interpreter who performs the function of interpreting all the proceedings, including all deaf witness testimony. The ASL proceedings interpreter does not interpret privileged communications or preparation of witnesses with counsel. Spoken language proceedings interpreters sit at counsel table and interpret the additional function of privileged communications, though there are reasons suggesting that if the interpreter's role includes the full panoply of interpreting preparation activities for the litigation team, this spoken language interpreter should refrain from interpreting for the witnesses whom she or he assisted in preparing. *See also Court Interpreter.*

PRO SE

Law.com defines *pro se* as "(proh say) prep. Latin for "for himself." A party to a lawsuit who represents himself (acting *in propria persona*) is appearing in the case *"pro se.""*

QUALITY ASSURANCE CREDENTIALS

State administered systems whereby pre-RID certified interpreters are given diagnostic evaluations and rated into levels of interpreting skill. Normally, at the lower levels, these interpreters are not prepared for typical community interpreting with a variety of deaf people, but are generally only authorized to work in one-on-one settings with supervision from a more experienced interpreter. Some states provide more extensive regimes of testing. Texas and Kansas both have systems that have upper levels which equate to or surpass the skill required for an RID certified interpreters, and their systems are used in lieu of, not in preparation for, the RID certification systems.

QUALIFIED

See Voir Dire

REBUTTABLE PRESUMPTION

According to www.law.com, a rebuttable presumption is a noun. The dictionary states "since a presumption is an assumption of fact accepted by the court until disproved, all presumptions are rebuttable. Thus rebuttable presumption is a redundancy." *See also Presumption.*

RECORD INTERPRETING

Also called witness interpreting, though record interpreting is actually broader than witness interpreting. At any time the interpreter is voice interpreting for a deaf person, and the interpreter's voice is what is taken down by the court reporter, then the interpreter is functioning in the record interpreting mode.

REPORTED CASES/OPINIONS

Not all cases decided by appellate courts are printed in the law books and published for use by practitioners. Those cases that are chosen by the court for publication are termed "reported cases" or "reported opinions." The cases are published in bound volumes called reporters. Only reported opinions can be cited by attorneys and relied upon as binding precedent.

Unpublished or unreported opinions are not binding on a court and in some jurisdictions may not be cited as authority.

RID

The Registry of Interpreters for the Deaf is the national professional membership organization for sign language interpreters which also serves as the certifying body for sign language interpreters.

SC: L CERTIFICATION

According to the RID, "Specialist certificate: Legal. This certificate is awarded to interpreters who hold a valid RID generalist certificates. Once the interpreter holds a generalist certificate indicating they have demonstrated a minimal level of skill in interpreting non-legal settings, the RID suggests that the interpreter have at least five (5) years general interpreting experience prior to sitting for the legal examination. In addition, other eligibility requirements must be met to sit for the test depending on the combination of one's educational and experiential background." Source: www.rid.org

SIGHTLINE

Refers to the physical positioning of two parties when using sign language. The parties must be facing each other and where it is visually comfortable to see each other. In court, the interpreter stands in the well facing the deaf person whether the person is a party, witness or juror.

SIMULTANEOUS COMMUNICATION

Refers to the generally discredited ability to speak English and sign at the same time. Research has shown that when voice is added to the signed English product, the signer tends to omit signs. ASL and signed English are different in structure, semantics and to a large degree lexicon.

Further, each signer using a manual representation of English will vary in the amount of English word order used and the amount of ASL in the signed rendition. Some signers will use ASL signs to represent the concepts in the order they appear in the spoken English utterance. If there is no counterpart to an English word, there is no sign produced though the word may be represented on the mouth to facilitate speech reading. Some signers will use contrived signs for the English words that have no ASL counterparts in conjunction with mouthing. Over the years, the educational system has created signing systems to represent words and parts of words that do not have counterparts in ASL. For example, ASL does not use helping verbs. These English-based systems have created separate signs for the various helping verbs. Another difference is that ASL represents past tense by a time-indicator sign at the beginning of the utterance. All subsequent information is assumed to be in the past tense until another time-indicator sign is used. English indicates tense by suffixes affixed to the verb. The English-based signing systems have created signs to represent the various suffixes. Some signers will use some or all of these contrived signs when they sign in English word order with voice.

SOLE HOLDER

When a proceedings interpreter, by virtue of their linguistic skill and training, has information helpful to the tribunal and which will enable the proceedings to be conducted more smoothly. When the interpreter is the sole holder of information, the duty to act is triggered. Generally, the interpreter would ask to approach the bench and be heard on the point.

SOURCE LANGUAGE

The language of the original message.

TARGET LANGUAGE

The language of the resulting interpretation.

TEXTUAL SUPPORT

A phrase which means that the interpreter is relying on literature in the field of law, ethical codes, case law, statutes, professional literature or standard practices other than the individual interpreter's own idiosyncratic opinion and that the interpreter can point to the support or the text they are relying upon when faced with a challenge to their position.

TRANSLATION

Translation involves rendering a message from one language to the equivalent message in another language when both the source language and the target language are in the written form.

VIDEO RELAY SERVICE (VRS)

A federally mandated telecommunication communication system based upon video streaming technology sent over the internet and used by deaf people and those who can hear to communicate over the telephone/internet though an interpreter. The deaf party has a video camera attached to a high speed internet connection. The deaf party uses the video technology to call an interpreter service who is equipped with the same equipment and a telephone line. The interpreter places a call and interprets between the person on the voice line and the deaf person on the monitor.

VOICING/VOICE INTERPRETING

The term in ASL interpreting when the source language is ASL and the target language is spoken English.

WITNESS INTERPRETER

The denomination for the proceedings interpreter working with a non-English speaking or deaf witness.

VOIR DIRE

Though the term is generally used to refer to the questioning of potential jurors regarding their ability to serve impartially on a jury, it is also used in reference to questioning experts and other witnesses to determine competency to testify. In regards to interpreters, the *voir dire* process refers to questioning them to ensure they have the skills, training and experience necessary to interpret the proceedings accurately and that they do not have any conflicts of interest which would affect their ability to interpret neutrally and impartially.

WORD-FOR-WORD INTERPRETING

A misnomer for most language interpretation where there are usually few lexical equivalents which can simply be substituted for words in another language. The import of the direction to interpret in a word-for-word manner normally is a direction to interpret accurately.

Appendix B: References[1]

Berk-Seligson, Susan. (1999). The impact of court interpreting on the coerciveness of cross examination questions. *Forensic Linguistic: The International Journal of Speech, Language and the Law. Vol. 6. No. 1.* 30-57.

Cokely, Dennis. (1992). *Interpretation: A sociolinguistic model.* Burtonsville, MD: Linstok Press, Inc.

Dery, Leslie, V. *Disinterring the "Good" and "Bad Immigrant": A Deconstruction of the State Court Interpreter Laws for Non-English-Speaking Criminal Defendants,* 45 U. Kan. L. Rev. (1997).

Eclavea, Romulado P. Annotation, *Admissibility of Testimony Concerning Extrajudicial Statements Made to, or in the Presence of, Witnesses Through Interpreters,* 12 A.L.R.4th 1016 (1980).

Edwards, Alicia B. (1995). *The practice of court interpreting.* Amsterdam: Benjamins Translation Library.

Federal Procedure, Lawyers Edition (2004). Vol 12A, § 33:420. St. Paul, MN West Group.

Fleming, Thomas, M. Annotation, *Right of Accused to Have Evidence or Court Proceedings Interpreted Because Accused or Other Participant in Proceedings is Not Proficient in the Language Used,* 32 A.L.R.5th §65 (1995).

Grabau, Hon. Charles M., & Llewellyn, Joseph Gibbons. *Protecting the Rights of Linguistic Minorities: Challenges to Court Interpretation,* 2 New Eng. L.Rev. 30 (Winter 1996).

---

[1] Legal sources such as cases, periodicals and annotations or treatises are cited using the Blue Book: a uniform system of citation. Non-legal materials and books are cited according to APA format. The Blue Book system has been modified to comport with APA's Last-name-first alphabetical conventions.

Harrison, David B. Annotation, *Disqualification of Attorney Because Member of His Firm Is or Ought to be Witness in the Case – Modern Cases*, 5 A.L.R.4ᵗʰ 574 (2005).

Hatim, Basil & Mason, Ian. (1997). *The translator as communicator.* London: Routledge.

Hewitt, William E. (1995). *Court interpretation: Model guides for policy and practice in the state courts.* Wiliamsburg, VA: National Center for State Courts.

Hovland, Debra L. *Errors in Interpretation: Why Plain Error Is Not Plain,* 11 Law and Inequality: A Journal of Theory and Practice 473 (1993).

Imwinkelried, Edward L. (1980). *Evidentiary Foundations.* New York: Michie Publishing Co.

Johnson, Robert E., Liddell, Scott K., & Erting, Carol J. (1989). *Unlocking the curriculum: Principles for achieving access in deaf education* (Working paper 89-3).   Washington, DC: Gallaudet University. Gallaudet Research Institute.

Larson, Mildred L. (1998). *Meaning-based translation: A guide to cross-language equivalence.* London: University Press of America, Inc.

Manson, Harold Craig. *Jury Selection: The Courts, the Constitution, and the Deaf,* 11 Pac. L.J. 967 (1980).

McCormick on Evidence. (1992). *Practitioner's series.* (4ᵗʰ ed., Vol. 1, Ch. 8) St. Paul, Minn: West Publishing Co.

Md. R. Civ. P., Title 16, *Courts, Judges and Attorneys,* Chapter 18 Miscellaneous Appendices 1-2. (2005).

Metzger, Melanie. (1999). *Sign language interpreting: Deconstructing the myth of neutrality.* Washington, D.C. Gallaudet University Press.

Mikkleson, Holly. (2000). *Introduction to court interpreting, translation practices explained series.* Manchester UK: St. Jerome.

Mindess, Anna. (1999). *Reading between the signs: Intercultural communication for sign language interpreters.* Yarmouth, ME: Intercultural Press.

Morris, Ruth. (1993). *Images of the interpreter: A study of language-switching in the legal process.* Unpublished Ph.D. thesis, Lancaster University.

Morris, Ruth & Colin, Joan. (1996). *Interpreters & the legal process.* Winchester UK: Waterside Press.

Pullum, Geoffrey. (1991). *The Great Eskimo Vocabulary Hoax and Other Irreverent Essays on the Study of Language.* University of Chicago Press.

Quigley, Stephen P. (1965). *Interpreting for deaf people* (Ed.), Washington, DC: U.S. Department of Health, Education and Welfare Social and Rehabilitation Service, Rehabilitation Services Administration.

Ramirez, Deborah. *Excluded Voices: The Disenfranchisement of Ethnic Groups from Jury Service,* 1993 Wis.L.Rev. 761.

Reagan, Helen. *Considerations in Litigating a Civil Case with Non-English Speaking Litigants,* 65 Am. Jur. Trials 1. (1997 & Supp. 2004).

Russell, Debra L. (2002). *Interpreting in legal contexts: Consecutive and simultaneous interpretation.* Burtonsville, Md: Linstock Press.

Stokoe, William C. Jr. (2005). Sign language structure: An outline of the visual communication systems of the American deaf. *Journal of Deaf Studies and Deaf Education.*10(1) Oxford University Press.

Taylor, Marty M. (1993). *Interpretation skills: American Sign Language to English.* Edmonton, Alberta, Canada: Interpreting Consolidated.

Taylor, Marty M. (2002). *Interpretation skills: English to American Sign Language.* Edmonton, Alberta, Canada: Interpreting Consolidated.

Valli, Clayton & Lucas, Ceil. (2000). *Linguistics of American Sign Language: An introduction.* (3ʳᵈ ed.) Washington, DC: Gallaudet University Press.

5 Wigmore on Evidence §§ 1421-22 (1940).

Wright, Edward, T. (1990). *Evidence: How and when to use the rules to win cases.* Englewood Cliffs, NJ: Prentice-Hall.

Wright & Miller. (1990). *Federal Practice & Procedure* §6056. St. Paul, MN: West Publishing Co.

Endnotes Chapter One

[1] For an excellent presentation regarding court interpreting in other countries Mikkleson (2000) has written a text that presents a cogent description of interpreting practice and procedures in countries other than the United States.

This text will provide case law for the reader's use with the caveat that **reported opinions** must be used carefully. Most states will not have opinions on each point discussed because ASL interpreting is relatively rare in court compared to spoken language interpreting. Nevertheless, it is beneficial for ASL interpreters to explore cases involving spoken language interpreting issues. However, some significant differences exist between spoken language interpreting and sign language interpreting. It is important to keep in mind that cases must be followed only by lower courts in the same jurisdiction. The law also changes over time and cases are binding only until they are overruled or changed by the legislature. At the same time, interpreters seeking to establish their own working conditions can use these cases, by analogy, to support their arguments for specific working conditions. It behooves the interpreter to remember, as lawyers know, that cases supporting a contrary position can always be found. This text presents cases which can be used to support specific working conditions, but not all cases in every jurisdiction are discussed. When general rules and court practices do exist on a particular topic, those practices and rules are noted in the discussion. As should be plain, this text does not attempt to give legal advice. For specific legal questions, the reader is advised to seek an opinion from a duly licensed attorney in his or her state.

[2] *United States v. Miller,* 806 F.2d 223, 224 (10th Cir. 1986).

[3] *Id.* at 224.

[4] The Conference of Legal Sign Language Interpreters, Inc., held its first national training in 2003 in the Atlanta area. The conference, Iron Sharpens Iron, is designed to bring together working legal interpreters who have already been trained on the basic obligations of court interpreting and provide a source of training on cutting edge topics in legal interpreter education. The conference was attended by over 200 certified and trained legal interpreters.

[5] The Distance Opportunities for Interpreter Training Center created an eighteen (18) month legal interpreter educational program through the online distance education format and philosophy. The program provides procedural, substantive, ethical and skills components for participants

who work in cohorts with established facilitators, attorneys and program staff.

6   *See* Taylor, M. (1993) p.6.

7   *Garcia v. State,* 2004 WL 574554 *7 (Tex. Crim. App.)(unpublished decision).

8   *Id.*

9   Taylor, M. (1993) p. 6.

10 Even worse, as many ASL interpreters know, administrators develop relationships with certain interpreters who are either always available for last minute assignments or who they are friendly with and tend to call first for an assignment. In Maryland, the Administrative Office of the Courts has tried to implement a system, with little success, where interpreters holding the highest level of certification are contacted first for an assignment. The effectiveness of this system is difficult to determine and it requires staff awareness of the differences in the variety of certifications, among other things. With high staff turnover, and the relatively low demand for ASL interpreting, it is difficult to ensure that the staff will have any real understanding of the levels of skill represented by interpreters.

11 *Tamayo-Reyes v. Keeney,* 926 F.2d 1492 (9th Cir. Or.1991).

12 *Id.* at 1494.

13 *See also United States v. Aleman,* 417 F.Supp. 117 (S.D. Tex. 1976)(holding that the interpreter improperly added elements to the crime in the interpretation making it inaccurate).

14 *Atkins v. Social Security Administration,* 2000 WL 1090767 (E.E.O.C.).

15 *Id.* at *2.

16 *Id.* at *5.

17 *Id.* The interpreter was obviously not RID certified since RID does not currently maintain a system in which skills are measured by levels and in which certain levels are restricted to certain interpreting content or with supervision. Unless otherwise noted as a specialist certificate, all of RID certifications are generalist certificates indicating that the holder is qualified in a variety of settings as evidenced by a skills examination. In order to obtain the specialist certificates in sign language interpreting, one must already hold a valid generalist certificate. Certain states do have their own "quality assurance" instruments which are generally given to interpreters who do not yet possess the skills or abilities to attain RID certification. Some states, such as Texas, have extensive testing systems. Texas ranks interpreters at 5 levels and the top 2

levels are said to require more skill than is necessary to pass the RID generalist examination. Texas maintains that its level 3 is equivalent to an RID certified interpreter holding the CI and CT credentials. Quality assurance ratings that fall below the rigorous requirements of the RID examinations are not appropriate credentials for court interpreters. Interpreters must not misrepresent to courts that holders of a quality assurance rating have demonstrated the equivalent skill of an RID certified interpreter. The author has seen misrepresentations of this type in court. The author has seen interpreter's business documents stating that the person was certified when the interpreter only had a quality assurance rating. The author has been told by an interpreter holding only a CT from the RID that she was "court certified" because she was on the court's list of approved interpreters. Courts do not know the differences between quality assurance credentials and nationally certified by the RID, and interpreters must be vigilant in accurately representing their skills and credentials.

[18] *Id.*

[19] The NCSC Code is discussed more fully in later chapters.

[20] *See* information presented at www.rid.org. (Last accessed January 2, 2006).

[21] *Id.*

[22] *Id.*

[23] *Id.*

[24] For a number of years now the RID has required interpreters to undertake continuing education in order to maintain their credentials. Interpreters holding specialty certificates like the Legal Specialist Certificate are required to have at least twenty (20) contact hours per cycle in their specialty area.

Endnotes Chapter Two

[1] The Sixth Amendment to the United States Constitution reads: "In all criminal prosecutions, the accused shall enjoy the right to a speedy and public trial, by an impartial jury of the State and district wherein the crime shall have been committed, which district shall have been previously ascertained by law, and to be informed of the nature and cause of the accusation; to be confronted with the witnesses against him; to have compulsory process for obtaining witnesses in his favor, and to have the Assistance of Counsel for his defense." U.S. Const. Amend. VI.

[2] *United States v. Carrion,* 488 F.2d 12 (1st Cir. 1974).

[3] The Fourteenth Amendment to the United States Constitution reads: "No State shall make or enforce any law which shall abridge the privileges or immunities of citizens of the United States; nor shall any State deprive any person of life, liberty, or property, without due process of law; nor deny to any person within its jurisdiction the equal protection of the laws." U.S. Const. Amend. XIV.

[4] Cal. Const. art. 1, § 14; N.M. Const. art. 2, § 14.

[5] Dery, L. (1997) p.837.

[6] In the 1984 case *People v. Rivera,* 480 N.Y.S.2d 426 (1984), the court was reversed on appeal because the defendant's earlier felony convictions had been obtained without an ASL interpreter. Nevertheless, the prosecution wanted to use those earlier convictions to increase his sentence. At the first felony trial, ironically, Rivera had been provided with a Spanish interpreter who worked the entire proceeding never realizing he was deaf. The interpreter testified that when he indicated he could not hear, she would raise her voice and use gestures. With the assistance of prominent experts in the field of sign language interpreting, the court determined that Mr. Rivera was deaf and he had been deprived of his constitutional rights during the two previous un-interpreted trials. The court stated the holding as: "I hold that Rivera's New Jersey conviction was obtained in violation of his constitutional rights as guaranteed by the Sixth Amendment and the due process clause of the Fourteenth Amendment." *Id.* at 528; *see also Salazar v. State,* 93 S.W.3d 339 (Tex App. Texarkana 2002)(holding that the Texas statute which required a judge to provide an interpreter for a deaf person implements the constitutional right of confrontation).

[7] *State v. Guzman*, 555 N.E.2d 259 (NY 1990); *State v. Marcham*, 770 P.2d 356 (Az.1988). The analysis tends to focus on the individual characteristics of the deaf people and their ability to use signed English. The more English-like signing, the more likely the person would be permitted (pre-ADA) to serve on a jury. Most statutes have an English competency requirement because it is believed that those who sit in judgment of others should share the common values of the community. The logic, whether valid or not, suggests that those who have not learned the language of this country probably do not share American values. In popular culture, this is frequently termed 'a jury of one's peers.' The only state that the author is aware of which provides interpreters for NES jurors is New Mexico. New Mexico may have based that decision on the fact that it has a state constitutional right to an interpreter.

[8] Section 504 of the Rehabilitation Act of 1973, as amended, 29 U.S.C. § 794 (2002). The Rehabilitation Act prohibits discrimination against people with disabilities in programs and/or services funded by the federal government. Section 504 states that "no qualified individual with a disability in the United States shall be excluded from, denied the benefits of, or be subjected to discrimination under" any federally funded programs, services or activities. According the to Department of Justice website "over 20 Implementing Regulations for federally assisted programs [exist to enforce section 504 at the federal level], including: 34 CFR Part 104 (Department of Education); 45 CFR Part 84 (Department of Health and Human Services); and 28 CFR §§ 42.501 et seq." http://www.usdoj.gov/crt/ada/cguide.htm#anchor66738. (Last accessed November 25, 2005). Additionally, the site indicates that there are "over 95 Implementing Regulations for federally conducted programs, including: 28 CFR Part 39 (Department of Justice)." *Id.*

[9] Americans with Disabilities Act of 1990, 42 U.S.C. §§ 12101 et seq. Implementing Regulations for the ADA include: 29 CFR Parts 1630, 1602 (Title I, EEOC); 28 CFR Part 35 (Title II, Department of Justice); 49 CFR Parts 27, 37, 38 (Title II, III, Department of Transportation); 28 CFR Part 36 (Title III, Department of Justice); 47 CFR §§ 64.601 et seq. (Title IV, FCC). *See* http://www.usdoj.gov/crt/ada/cguide. htm#anchor66738. (Last accessed November 25, 2005).

[10] *See* www.nad.org. Internal citations omitted. (Last accessed November 25, 2005).

[11] Manson, H. (1980) p. 975 n.60, *citing* Bible Mark 9:17-26, stating "[t]his idea arose from the common tendency to equate intelligence with language skills...."

[12] *See People v. Rodriguez*, 546 N.Y.S.2d 769, 771-72 (1989).

[13] *United States ex rel. Negron v. New York*, 434 F.2d 386 (2d Cir. 1970).

[14] Federal Court Interpreting Act, 28 U.S.C. § 1827, *et seq.*

[15] *Negron,* 434 F.2d 386, 388 (2d Cir. 1970).

[16] *Id.*

[17] *Id.* at 389-90.

[18] *United States ex rel Negron v. New York*, 310 F.Supp. 1304, 1307 (E.D.N.Y. 1970).

[19] *See infra* Chapter 4 explaining the various functions that court interpreters are retained to provide.

[20] *Negron,* 310 F.Supp. at 1309.

[21] *Negron,* 464 F2d at 389 (Internal citations omitted).

[22] *Id.* 391-92. Courts also rely on *Dusky v. United States*, 362 U.S. 402 (1962), to establish linguistic presence is required to effectively receive assistance of counsel.

[23] 28 U.S.C. §1827 *et seq.* (1996).

[24] 28 U.S.C. § 1827(b)(1)(1996).

[25] *Id.* at §1827(b)(3)(1996).

[26] Interim Regulations of the Director of the Administrative Office of the Untied States Courts Implementing the Court Interpreters Amendments Act of 1988 at §§ 8-9. Available from United States Administrative Office of the Courts, Washington, D.C. 20544.

[27] *Id.* at §8.

[28] *Id.*

[29] *Id.*

[30] *Id.* at §9.

[31] Section 5 of the Interim Regulations indicates that ASL interpreters holding the SC: L are considered certified by the Director. Section 8(c) states that interpreters of languages certified by the director cannot be considered professionally qualified. This insures that interpreters of certified languages have incentive to obtain certification since they cannot work at the professionally qualified level. ASL interpreters would have difficulty qualifying for professionally qualified status in any event because the RID does not have by-laws with the requirements listed in §8(ii)(A).

[32] *Id.* at § 5.

[33] Annual Report of the Director of the United States Administrative Office of the Courts (2004) available at http://www.uscourts.gov/library/annual_managetech.html (last accessed October 9, 2005).

[34] In 2004, 212,233 legal events in federal courts were interpreted in Spanish. *Id.*

[35] *Id.* at §1827(d)(2)(1996).

[36] *Id.*

[37] *Id.* at §1827(e)(2) (1996).

[38] *Id.* at §1827(f)(1)(1996).

[39] *Id.* at §1827(k)(1996).

[40] 28 U.S.C. §1828(1996).

[41] 28 U.S.C. §1827(d)(1)(1996).

[42] There are several internet list-services for discussing issues related to spoken language legal interpreting including a lively one administered by the National Association of Judiciary Interpreters and Translators, www.najit.org. (Last accessed January 3, 2006). ASL court interpreters can join a yahoo group list-serve administered by Arthur Smith and Pasch McCombs by visiting Mr. McCombs' website dedicated to court interpreters. www.pcisd.org (Last accessed January 3, 2006).

[43] States can provide additional protection for NES individuals in expanded settings. The District of Columbia passed a language access statute in 2004 which provided for interpretation and language services in a wide variety of government settings. See D.C. Law 15-167, the "Language Access Act of 2004."

[44] The NAD keeps track of the number of states with interpreting statutes on its website. According to the NAD, 38 states have statutes that regulate legal interpreting. (Last accessed November 25, 2005).

[45] D.C. Code § 2-1901 *et seq.*,(2001) provides an example of a statute that provides for all three purposes: to assist hearing-impaired (sic) and non-English speaking persons as they participate in proceedings of the D.C. Court System, the Council of the District of Columbia, and the District's Administrative Agencies.

[46] D.C. Code § 2-1901 *et seq.*(2001).

[47] *Id.*

[48] *Id.*

[49] T.C.A. § 24-1-211, *as amended,* (2001). See also California Evidence Code, Division 6, Chapter 4, § 754 regarding interpreters and their qualifications. California became involved in certifying interpreters and have listed their Judicial Council as the overseer of the court interpreting program. *See* California Government Code, Title 8, Chapter 2, Article IV: Court Interpreter Services §68566 for the definition of Certified court interpreter.

[50] *Id.*

[51] The states are posted on the NCSC website and include Alaska, Arkansas, California, Colorado, Connecticut, Delaware, Florida, Georgia, Hawaii, Idaho, Iowa, Illinois/Cook County, Indiana, Kentucky, Maryland, Massachusetts, Michigan, Minnesota, Missouri, Nebraska, Nevada, New Jersey, New Mexico, North Carolina, Ohio, Oregon, Pennsylvania, South Carolina, Tennessee, Texas, Utah, Virginia, Washington and Wisconsin.

[52] See www.ncsconline.org.

[53] Maryland Rules of Procedure, Title 16, "Courts, Judges and Attorneys" Chapter 18 Miscellaneous Appendices 1-2. Michie Publishing Co. 2005.

Endnoted Chapter Three

[1] *See generally*, McCormick on Evidence. (1992) p. 269.

[2] *State v. Aquino-Cervantes,* 945 P.2d 767 (Wash. 1997).

[3] In England, under what is known as the *Atard* Rule, police interpreters are automatically placed on the prosecution's witness list and thereby disqualified from interpreting any associated proceedings. *See generally* Morris & Colin (1996).

[4] Schedulers should also be aware that nine times out of ten, a case will settle. In that case, the trial never happens so it makes better sense to send the highly qualified person to the law enforcement assignment. The person still will be conflicted out from interpreting any of the pretrial proceedings in the case because of their prior law enforcement work.

[5] Imwinkelried, E. (1980) p. 204.

[6] Wright, E. (1990) p. 77.

[7] *See State v. Aquino-Cervantes,* 945 P.2d 767 (Wash.Ct.App.Div. 2 1997).

[8] *See United States v. Beltran,* 761 F.2d 1, 9-10 (9th Cir. 1991)(stating that translator is normally an agent of defendant).

[9] In July 2005, the members of the RID enacted a new code of professional conduct. The first tenet relates to confidentiality and reads, in pertinent part:

1.0 CONFIDENTIALITY

Tenet: Interpreters adhere to standards of confidential communication.

Guiding Principle: Interpreters hold a position of trust in their role as linguistic and cultural facilitators of communication. Confidentiality is highly valued by consumers and is essential to protecting all involved. Each interpreting situation (e.g., elementary, secondary, and post-secondary education, legal, medical, mental health) has a standard of confidentiality. Under the reasonable interpreter standard, professional interpreters are expected to know the general requirements and applicability of various levels of confidentiality. Exceptions to confidentiality include, for example, federal and state laws requiring mandatory reporting of abuse or threats of suicide, or responding to subpoenas.

The RID can be contacted at www.rid.org. (Last accessed November 26, 2005).

[10] Federal Rules of Evidence 801(c).

[11] *Englebretson v. Industrial,* 170 Cal. 793, 798 (1915).

[12] The hearsay rule can run afoul of the Sixth Amendment right to confront witnesses against the accused in a criminal context. If the maker of the statement is not present, but the repeater is permitted to repeat the testimony in court, the defendant is not permitted to confront and cross-examine witnesses. In the case of interpreted statements, the *Nazemian* court stated

> In *Ohio v. Roberts,* 448 U.S. 56, 100 S.Ct. 2531, 65 L.Ed.2d 597 (1980), the Supreme Court set out a two-pronged test for evaluating alleged confrontation clause violations. Where a defendant claims that an out-of-court statement was received into evidence in violation of the confrontation clause, the record must show that the government produced the declarant or presented facts showing that the person was unavailable. Secondly, the government must prove the declarant's statements are trustworthy. . . . If the [interpreted] statements are properly viewed as Nazemian's own, then there would be no confrontation clause issue since Nazemian cannot claim that she was denied the opportunity to confront herself.

Nazemian, 948 F.2d at 525-26.

A 2004 Supreme Court case, *Crawford v. Washington,* No. 02-9410 ___ S.Ct. ___, (decided March 8, 2004), has brought the issue of testimonial hearsay and the Confrontation Clause back into the limelight and has reaffirmed the Confrontation Clause's superiority over the hearsay rules in criminal trials. Until *Crawford,* prosecutors were permitted by statute in many states to present reliable out-of-court testimonial evidence against the defendant without calling the witness to the stand. For example, in domestic violence cases, the victim's statement to a police officer in an interview could be repeated by the officer in court against the defendant. Likewise, in cases with child victims, the child's out-of-court statement in an interview could be presented in court against the defendant without producing the child to testify. *Crawford* prohibits these practices and reasserts the defendant's right to confront the witnesses against him and not merely to confront repeaters of the accuser's statements.

[13] Federal Rules of Evidence 602.

[14] The Federal Rules of Evidence permit certain hearsay statements upon a showing that the maker of the statement is unavailable. Federal Rules 804(a)(1-5) define unavailability of a witness as one who cannot be placed on the stand because of a valid privilege, who refuses to testify,

who persists in claiming the inability to remember, is unable to be present because of death or illness, or whose presence could not be obtained by subpoena.

[15] 5 Wigmore on Evidence (1940) §§ 1421-22.

[16] Federal Rule of Evidence 801(d) states, in pertinent part:

> (d) *Statements which are not hearsay.* A statement is not hearsay if-

> (2) *Admission by party-opponent.* The statement is offered against a party and is (A) his own statement, in either his individual or a representative capacity or (B) a statement of which he has manifested his adoption or belief in its truth, or (C) a statement by a person authorized by him to make a statement concerning the subject, or (D) a statement by his agent or servant concerning a matter within the scope of his agency or employment, made during the existence of the relationship, or (E) a statement by a coconspirator of a party during the course and in furtherance of the conspiracy.

> Interpreted statements fall under Federal Rule of Evidence 801(d)(2).

[17] *See State v. Garcia-Trujillo,* 948 P.2d 390, 393 (Wash. Ct.App.Div.1 1997)(stating that in the absence of a finding of agency, only the interpreter had personal knowledge of the source language statements and only the interpreter could repeat those statements).

[18] A different case would apply if the defense attorney called the same interpreter to testify. In that case, the defense attorney is generally attempting to suppress a confession by attacking the interpretation of the *Miranda* warnings by claiming that the interpretation was deficient and the client did not "knowingly" waive his or her constitutional rights.

[19] Federal Rule of Evidence 804(b)(3) states that "a statement which was at the time of its making so far contrary to the declarant's pecuniary or proprietary interest, or so far tended to subject the declarant to civil or criminal liability, or to render invalid a claim by the declarant against another, that a reasonable person in the declarant's position would not have made the statement unless believing it to be true. A statement tending to expose the declarant to criminal liability and offered to exculpate the accused is not admissible unless corroborating circumstances clearly indicate the trustworthiness of the statement." In common parlance, this exception is known as a confession or a statement against interest.

[20] The Fifth Amendment to the United States Constitution reads, in pertinent part, "No person . . . shall be compelled in any criminal case to be a witness against himself. . . ." Amendment V.

[21] *See in chronological order People v. Lee Fat*, 54 Cal. 527, 531 (1880*); People v. Ah Yute*, 56 Cal. 119, 121 (1880); *People v. John*, 137 Cal. 220, 222 (1902); *People v . Luis*, 158 Cal. 185, 192 (1910). These early cases wrestled with, among other issues, whether an interpreter in a court proceeding could repeat the witness' testimony and in later cases began to draw the distinction between in-court interpretation under oath and unsworn out-of-court interpretation. *See also, State v. Fong Loon*, 29 Idaho 248 (1916); *Territory v. Big Knot on Head*, 6 Mont. 242 (1886); *State v. Noyes*, 36 Conn. 80 (1869); *Boyd v. State*, 78 Tex. Crim. 28 (1915); *Turner v. State*, 89 Tex. Crim. 615 (1921)(and cases collected in *Statements to Witnesses through Interpreters*, 122 ALR4th 1016 (1980) at § 4.).

[22] *People v. Gelabert,* 39 Cal. 663, 664 (1874).

[23] *See United States v. Lopez,* 937 F.2d 716, 724 (2d Cir. 1991)(holding that statements could be considered admissible as statements by a co-conspirator since evidence demonstrated that interpreter was herself a co-conspirator); *State v. Letterman*, 616 P.2d 505 (Or. App. 1980)(admitting an interpreted statement without analysis other than saying that it was reliable and trustworthy); *United States v. Abell*, 586 F.Supp. 1414 (D.Maine 1984)(using the present sense impression exception because the interpreter was voicing the source language statement at or near the time it was being made).

[24] Interestingly, this is the view that interpreters hold in community interpreting. Interpreters view themselves as extensions of the deaf person and the person who can hear involved in the interaction. In the past, interpreters have gone so far as to explain their role as functioning as a machine, invisible to the parties, simply a transparent communication apparatus. *See* Chapter 6. Most interpreters now recognize that their very presence in the communicative transaction has an effect on the event, and interpreters normally attempt to minimize that effect. Still, most interpreters would probably agree that when interpretation is done well, the interpreted statements should be considered the statements of the deaf party. Likewise, the signed statements should be considered the statements of the person who can hear. If the interpretation is not effective, for reasons of skill or bias, most interpreters have not thought in terms of the statements not being attributed to the deaf person, but they would likely agree that the deaf person should not be held accountable for poorly interpreted statements.

[25] Federal Rule of Evidence 801(d)(2) states, in pertinent part, that a statement is *not hearsay* if it is an: "Admission by party-opponent. The statement is offered against a party and is . . . or (C) a statement by a person authorized by the party to make a statement concerning the subject, or (D) a statement by the party's agent or servant concerning a matter within the scope of the agency or employment, made during the existence of the relationship. . . ." This rule demonstrates an instance of courts making up the law and removing an entire category of statements that by any analysis meet the definition of classic hearsay. The rationale behind this fiction is that the statements are normally reliable and necessary.

[26] Early agency cases include: *Schutter v. Williams*, 1 Ohio Dec. Rep. 47 (1844); *Sullivan v. Kuykendall*, 82 Ky. 483 (1885); *Miller v. Lathrop*, 50 Minn. 91 (1892)(and cases collected in *Statements to Witnesses through Interpreters*, 122 ALR4th 1016 (1980) at § 4.).

[27] *Massachusetts v. Vose*, 157 Mass. 393 (1892).

[28] *Id.* (Emphasis added).

[29] 948 F.2d 522 (9th Cir. 1991).

[30] *Id.* at 525 n. 3.

[31] *Id.* at 527.

[32] *Id.* Ms. Nazemian could only have pointed out specific misinterpretations if she had hired an expert interpreter to assist her in reviewing the equivalence of the interpreted statements. While similar to the function of the table interpreter discussed in Chapter 5, this expert interpreter would have provided testimony as an expert witness on the adequacy of the "friend's" interpretation. This function of providing expert witness services, not as a table interpreter but as an independent witness, is becoming more and more common and an area that ASL interpreters are starting to address in advanced training.

[33] *Id.* at 528, *citing* Weinstein & M. Berger, *Evidence* ¶ 801(d)(2)(c)[01] at 801-217 n. 34 (1988)(Internal citations omitted).

[34] *Chao v. State*, 478 So.2d 30 (Fla. 1985).

[35] *Id.* at 30.

[36] *United States v. Lopez*, 937 F.2d 716 (2d Cir. 1991).

[37] *Garcia-Trujillo*, 948 P.2d 390 (Wash. Ct. App. Div. 1 1997).

[38] *Id.* at 205.

[39] *Id.* at 206 n.1; *see also State v. Huynh*, 49 Wash.App. 192, 742 P.2d 160 (1988), *rev. denied*, 109 Wash.2d 1024 (1988); *State v. Lopez*, 29 Wash. App. 836, 631 P.2d 420 (1981).

[40] *Garcia-Trujillo*, 948 P.2d at 393.

[41] It should be noted that even in Washington, if enough other circumstantial evidence exists in the record, interpreted evidence may come in regardless of whether the interpreter was an agent or not. In *State v. Bernal,* 93 Wash. App. 1052 (Wash.App. Div. 1 1999)(unpublished opinion), the defendant challenged repeated statements as hearsay. The Court held that "the record contains sufficient circumstantial evidence of the translation's reliability to support the admission of the witness testimony, exhibits, and medical report, despite their hearsay character." *Id.* The Court explained that Washington's prohibition on interpreted evidence is triggered *when the interpretation is the only evidence available.* It stated that the court did not err because "both Rosa and the interpreter testified at trial and were available for cross-examination . Rosa acknowledged that she had used the interpreter to communicate much of the information reported by the hospital personnel, including the identification of Pedro as her assailant. There is no evidence to suggest that the interpreter had an interest in the case or a motive to misrepresent Rosa's statements." *Id.* Even though acknowledging that the *Nazemian* analysis had not been adopted in Washington state, the court undertook the analysis anyway.

See also, *People v. Wing Choi Lo,* 150 Misc.2d 980, 570 N.Y.S.2d 776 (1991)(holding that out-of-court statements to an officer could not be attributed to the defendant because the interpreter, a police officer, was clearly an agent of the interrogator and not someone selected by the defendant to speak for him);

[42] *United States v. Felix-Jerez,* 667 F.2d 1297 (9th Cir. 1982).

[43] *Id.* at 1298-99.

[44] *Id.* at 1300 n.1.

[45] *Gomez v. Texas,* Trial Court Case No. 256-99 *7 (1999). The Court stated that " a growing majority of jurisdictions allow admission of translated testimony in *appropriate circumstances assuring its reliability,* on the theory that the interpreter serves as an agent of, or a language conduit for, the declarant. *See, e.g., United States v. Cordero,* 18 F.3d 1248, 1252 (5th Cir. 1994) (stating that *except in unusual circumstances,* an interpreter is no more than a language conduit and therefore his translation does not create an additional level of hearsay); *United States v. Da Silva,* 725 F.2d 828, 831 (2d Cir.1983) (holding that translator may *in some circumstances* be viewed as an agent of defendant; thus, translation attributable to defendant as her own admission); *People v. Gutierrez,* 916 P.2d 598, 600-01 (Colo. Ct. App. 1995) (discussing both agency and language conduit theories); and *State v. Robles,* 458 N.W.2d 818, 821-22 (Wis. Ct. App. 1990), *aff'd,* 470 N.W.2d 900 (1991)

(applying and discussing agency theory). The key language in these cases is italicized and demonstrates that the interpreter must testify to the circumstances of the interpretation in order to assure its reliability.

[46] It should be noted that the words "jointly chosen" or "jointly constituted" have specific legal meaning. The terms do not mean that the parties conferred necessarily on who the interpreter should be, though if they did that would be a strong factor indicating agency. Generally it means that nothing in the surrounding circumstances indicated that the interpreter should not be trusted or that there were problems with the accuracy of the interpretation. The surrounding circumstances are explored by subpoenaing the interpreter to testify. The law has never given the non-English speaker the right to the interpreter of choice or the best interpreter, just an interpretation that is fair.

[47] *Id.* at 2-3.

[48] *Id.* at 5, *citing, Durbin v.Hardin,* 775 S.W.2d 798, 808 (Tex. App.—Dallas 1989, writ denied).

[49] *Id. See also People v. Sanchez,* 125 Misc. 2d 394, 479 N.Y.S.2d 602 (1984)(holding that a confession through an interpreter who was not called to testify was inadmissible hearsay); *Green v. Philadelphia Gas Works,* 333 F.Supp. 1398, *aff'd,* 478 F.2d 313 (3rd Cir. 1971)(holding statements by a decedent through an interpreter to a fire marshal inadmissible hearsay when the interpreter was not called to testify).

[50] *Gomez,* No 256-99 at *7.

[51] The Texas statute is reproduced below, in relevant part:

HUMAN RESOURCES CODE

CHAPTER 82.

CONFIDENTIALITY OF INTERPRETED, TRANSLITERATED, OR RELAYED CONVERSATIONS

§ 82.002. CONFIDENTIALITY OF CONVERSATIONS.

A qualified interpreter or relay agent who is employed to interpret, transliterate, or relay a conversation between a person who can hear and a person who is hearing impaired or speech impaired is a conduit for the conversation and may not disclose or be compelled to disclose, through reporting or testimony or by subpoena, the contents of the conversation.

Added by Acts 1991, 72nd Leg., ch. 333, § 1, eff. Sept. 1, 1991.

§ 82.003. CRIMINAL PENALTY.

(a) A qualified interpreter or relay agent who is employed to interpret, transliterate, or relay a conversation between a person who can hear and a person who is hearing impaired or speech impaired commits an offense if the qualified interpreter or relay agent discloses the contents of the conversation, unless the qualified interpreter or relay agent obtains the consent of each party to the conversation.

(b) An offense under this section is a Class C misdemeanor.

Added by Acts 1991, 72nd Leg., ch. 333, § 1, eff. Sept. 1, 1991.

[52] *People v. Villagomez,* 313 Ill. App.3d 799, 809, 730 N.E.2d 1173, 1182 (1st Dist. 2000).

[53] *Martinez-Gaytan,* 213 F.3d 890, 892-93 (5th Cir. 2000) (Emphasis added).

[54] *People v. Torres,* 164 Cal.App.3d 266 (1985)(failure to have interpreter testify to authenticate translation error but not prejudicial enough in this case to reverse the conviction); *People v. Johnson,* 46 Cal.App.3d 701, 704 (1975)(holding that failure to call the original translator to the witness stand denied the defendant a meaningful opportunity to cross-examine the individual who translated the material as to his qualification and the accuracy of the translation).

[55] *United States v. Ushakow,* 474 F.2d 1244, 1245 (9th Cir. 1973). *See also United States v. Cordero,* 18 F.3d 1248, 1252 (5th Cir. 1994)(stating that interpreter is normally no more than a language conduit); *United States v. Koskerides,* 877 F.2d 1129, 1135 (2d Cir. 1989)(stating interpreter is a language conduit therefore no hearsay issue); *United States v. DaSilva,* 725 F.2d 828 (2d Cir. 1983)(stating that the NES person's conscious reliance on the translation amounted to authorization for purposes of the hearsay rule).

[56] 28 C.F.R. § 35.160(b)(2). Of course, the CFR can be read to mean that the deaf person should be consulted about whether they would prefer one type of accommodation (writing) over another (interpreting) and not necessarily an intra-accommodation choice (which interpreter would you prefer – an officer-interpreter or a certified trained interpreter).

[57] *See United States v. Beltran,* 761 F.2d 1 (1st Cir. 1985); *United States v. Alvarez,* 755 F.2d 830 (11th Cir. 1985); *United States v. DaSilva,* 725 F.2d 828 (2d Cir. 1983).

[58] See for example § 754.5 of the California Evidence Code which states: "[w]henever an *otherwise valid privilege exists* between an individual who is deaf or hearing impaired and another person, that privilege is not waived merely because an interpreter was used to facilitate their communication." (Emphasis added). In the case of a law enforcement setting, there is never an otherwise valid privilege between and officer and a deaf suspect, so this privilege statute would not apply.

[59] Texas Statute § 21.008. Privilege of Interpreter for the Deaf states "If a deaf person communicates through an interpreter to a person under circumstances in which the communication would be privileged and the

deaf person could not be required to testify about the communication, the privilege applies to the interpreter as well." Acts 1985, 69th Leg., ch. 959, § 1, eff. Sept. 1, 1985. Many other states incorporate this provision into the interpreting statutes.

The other Texas interpreter privilege statute, *supra note 50,* Human Resources Code, Chapter 82, makes it a class C misdemeanor for a Texas certified interpreter to disclose, even by subpoena, mandatory reporting of child or vulnerable adult abuse or testimony regarding the contents of a communication. Though counsel should still be able to call non-certified signers who are used in law enforcement and other settings, this statute is objectionable because even certified interpreters need to be examined for agency issues.

[60] Colorado RID Evidence Seminar presented by Carla M. Mathers. June 7-8, 2003. In-class communication.

[61] *State v. Randolph,* 698 S.W.2d 535 (Mo. 1985).

[62] *Id.* at 538.

[63] *Id.* at 538-39.

Endnotes Chapter Four

[1] For the proposition that an interpreter is an officer of the court bound by the court interpreter's code of conduct, *see State v. Alvarez*, 797 N.E.2d 1043, 1046 (Ohio 2003)(stating that the interpreter works under the direction of the court, not the direction of the defendant or other witness); *Ledezma v. State*, 626 N.W.2d 134, 149 (IA 2001)(holding that unethical interpreter acted outside the scope of his duties and abused his power as an officer of the court); *State v. Gonzales-Morales*, 979 P.2d 826 (Wash. 1999); *Commonwealth v. Kauffman*, 1961 WL 6184 *8 (Pa. O. & T.).

[2] *State v. Burris*, 643 P.2d 8, 14 (Ariz. App. 1988) ("[T]he position of the court interpreter was no more than that of an expert witness."); s*ee also People v. Braley*, 879 P.2d 410 (Colo. App. 1993). The Federal Rules of Evidence are used in all trials conducted in the United States District Courts. Many states have either adopted the federal rules or adopted them with some modification. States often will look to the federal rules for guidance in determining specific evidentiary issues even if the state has not specifically adopted the rules. All states will have some form of rules, though they may be spread out in various cases and not collected in one resource, which govern the admissibility of evidence.

[3] Massachusetts Trial Court, Administrative Office of the Trial Court, Office of Court Interpreter Services, Code of Professional Conduct for Court Interpreters of the Trial Court. Some states where interpreters are employed either on staff or where a regular pool of contractors is used have the interpreters sign a written oath which is kept on file in the court administrator's office and which relieves the interpreter of the obligation to take an oath prior to each proceeding. In these states, there is a strong argument that the interpreter serves as an officer of the court because the process of taking an oath only once is more similar to how attorneys take the oath. *See* discussion presented Chapter 6.

[4] *See e.g., United States v. Taren-Palma*, 997 F.2d 525, 532 (9th Cir. 1993), *cert. denied*, 511 U.S. 1071 (1994); *Denton v. State*, 945 S.W.2d 793 (Tenn. Crim. App. 1996); *United States v. Armijo*, 5 F.3d 1229, 1235 (9th Cir. 1993); *People v. Best*, 580 N.Y.S.2d 55 (1992); *State v. Puente-Gomez*, 827 P.2d 715 (Idaho App. 1992); *People v. Carreon*, 198 Cal. Rptr. 843, 854-55 (Ct. App. 1984); *United States v. Perez*, 651 F.2d 268 (5th Cir. 1981).

[5] Rule 702 titled "Testimony by Experts" states "[i]f scientific, technical, or other specialized knowledge will assist the trier of fact to understand

the evidence or to determine a fact in issue, a witness qualified as an expert by knowledge, skill, experience, training, or education, may testify thereto in the form of an opinion or otherwise." Federal Rules of Evidence Rule 702. *See also Malekar v. State,* 26 Md. App. 498, 508 (1975), which suggests that "to the extent to which someone translates words spoken in a foreign tongue into English, the rendering of an opinion is inherent in the situation. . . . the need for an expert opinion in this regard was self-evident."

[6] *See Choi v. State,* 497 S.E.2d 563 (Ga. 1998)(determining the interpreter was qualified because during *voir dire* the interpreter testified she was a native speaker, fluent in the language, had studied by English and Korean, understood the witness's Korean, belonged to an interpreter association and had interpreted four previous times for the county court system); *State v. Mendoza,* 891 P.2d 939 (Ariz. App. Div. 1 1995)(holding interpreter's qualifications are subject to proper inquiry by the parties); *People v. Braley,* 879 P.2d 410 (Colo. 1993)(holding that competency of interpreter can be attacked on direct or cross-examination or by independent testimony).

[7] In fact, most court interpreter ethics codes specifically prohibit the interpreter from taking an active part in a proceeding in which they are interpreting. The NCSC Model Code of Professional Responsibility, Canon 7 -- Scope of Practice states: "Interpreters shall limit themselves to interpreting or translating, and shall not give legal advice, express personal opinions to individuals for whom they are interpreting, or engage in any other activities which may be construed to constitute a service other than interpreting or translating while serving as an interpreter." Hewitt, W. (1995).

[8] The Ninth Circuit Court of Appeals, Criminal Jury Instructions (2000) to bilingual jurors reads as follows:

1.13 JURY TO BE GUIDED BY OFFICIAL ENGLISH TRANSLATION/INTERPRETATION

Languages other than English may be used during this trial.

The evidence you are to consider is only that provided through the official court [interpreters] [translators]. Although some of you may know the non-English language used, it is important that all jurors consider the same evidence. Therefore, you must base your decision on the evidence presented in the English [interpretation] [translation]. You must disregard any different meaning of the non-English words.

[9] The National Association of the Deaf ("NAD") maintains a chart on its website that lists the court interpreting and generic interpreting statutes in each state. The information can be accessed at www.nad.

org (last accessed November 23, 2005). *See also, Denton v. State,* 945 S.W.2d 793 (Tenn. Crim. App. 1996)(finding that if interpreter was appointed and qualified in accordance with the statutory procedures, a rebuttable presumption arises that interpreter is qualified to interpret trial proceedings); *People v. Harley,* 632 N.Y.S.2d 39 (N.Y. 1995)(stating that interpreter's identification as a 'certified sign language interpreter' and taking the oath may have been insufficient and additional inquiry may have been required to determine whether interpreter had satisfied the statutory credential requirements).

[10] *Ko v. United States,* 722 A.2d 830 (D.C. 1998).

[11] D.C. Code § 31-2704 (2001).

[12] *See also Gonzalez v. United States,* 697 A.2d 819 (D.C. 1997)(holding failure to verify that the interpreter was able to accurately communicate with the defendant was an error).

[13] Some ethical codes for interpreters require the interpreters to be sworn prior to the attorneys introducing themselves for the record. In reality, it is more common for the case to be called, the parties and attorneys identified for the record and then the interpreter's credentials and disclosures are placed on the record prior to taking the oath.

[14] *See also State v. Rodriguez,* 682 A.2d 764 (N.J.Super. Law 1996)(indicating that interpreter must be examined during *voir dire* not only for the interpreter's ability to interpret accurately but also to ensure that the interpreter does not have any bias for or against any party or witness).

[15] 675 P.2d 848, 856 (Kan. 1984).

[16] *Id.*

[17] *Id* at 858; *See also, National Labor Relations Board v. Bakers of Paris, Inc.,* 929 F.2d 1427, 1441 (9th Cir. 1991)(concluding that due process was not denied to the defendants because they had the opportunity to *voir dire* the interpreters and to point out any potential biases and the demeanor of the interpreters).

[18] The questions were extracted from The Courtroom Interpreter: A User's Guide and Checklist, an article published by Judge Lynn W. Davis, in the Utah Bar Journal 9 (February 1996): 26. Judge Davis in turn credited two sources: (1) Heather K. Van Nuys and Joanne I. Moore, "Using an Interpreter in Court," Washington State Bar News, May 1987: 13, and (2) a document entitled "Recommended Procedures for Finding Certified Court Interpreters and Voir Dire Procedures to Establish the Qualifications of a Non-certified Interpreter," circulated for review by The California Judicial Council. The Guide is available online from the NCSC at www.ncsconline.org (last accessed November 23, 2005).

[19] Though the NES person may be able to tell by listening that the interpreter is not fluent in the foreign language; the NES person cannot, unless they are bilingual, gauge the effectiveness of the interpretation from and to English. Likewise, a deaf person without access to the spoken English cannot gauge whether an interpreter, even one who signs well, is actually interpreting effectively.

[20] *People v Aranda,* 186 Cal. App.3d 230, 237, 230 Cal. Rptr. 498, 501-02 (2d Dist. 1986)(citations omitted internally)(emphasis added).

[21] In *Denton v. State,* 945 S.W.2d 793 (Tenn. Crim. App. 1996), the court spoke of a rebuttable presumption that an appointed and sworn interpreter would interpret accurately. Because the presumption can be rebutted, it may be that Texas courts following *Denton* would permit a challenge to the interpretation mid-trial.

[22] Only the Court can replace the working interpreter. In an interesting case, *United States v Anguloa,* 598 F.2d 1182, (9th Cir. 1979), the prosecutor replaced the working interpreter because his language monitor pointed out serious mistranslations by the assigned interpreters. Even though all of the participants knew that the interpreters were not qualified, the court held it was the judge's responsibility under Federal Rule of Criminal Procedure 28 to replace interpreters. Though used as a basis for appeal, the appellate court found that the error was harmless and the conviction was affirmed. This case and its implications are discussed more thoroughly in Chapter 6.

[23] The deaf party will have the assistance of an interpreter at the table. The table interpreter's role permits identification with the deaf person and the litigation team. Interpreters have a reputation for being aloof and distant to the community they serve. A negative by-product of conferring status as an officer of the court is that the status may reinforce the perception held by deaf people that interpreters are no longer stakeholders in the deaf community. The table interpreter, who can and should function like a community interpreter, has a great responsibility to rectify what can be seen as a regression for interpreters as allies of a linguistic minority culture. It is hoped that what the officer of the court status brings to the interpreter in terms of being able to provide a more accurate interpretation will be able to offset lasting damage. Further, many of the conflicts that are rectified by the status arise when there are hostile deaf parties. In those instances, separating the court's interpreters from identification with the parties reduces the tension and mistrust that exists when adverse deaf parties have to share the same interpreter.

[24] (Emphasis added). According to the drafters, "[t]he model code presents key concepts and precepts, which over the years have emerged in statutes,

rules, case law, and professional experience. Like the Model Court Interpreter Act (Chapter 10), it has been prepared in consultation with an advisory group of individuals who have special expertise in court interpretation. The advisory group included the judges, lawyers, court administrators, and state and federally certified professional interpreters who are named in the acknowledgements for this publication.

Purposes of the Model Code

The purposes of the Model Code are threefold:

1. to articulate a core set of principles, which are recommended for incorporation in similar codes that may be adopted in the several states or local jurisdictions;

2. to serve as a reference, which may be consulted or cited by interpreters, judges, and court managers where no other authoritative standards have been adopted, and

3. to serve as a basis for education and training of interpreters and other legal professionals.

Research has shown that courts must often rely on interpretation services of bilingual individuals who have received no specific training about the requirements, role and responsibilities of a court interpreter. Research has also shown that many judges and attorneys are also unaware of the professional responsibilities of the interpreter and how these translate into highly demanding technical skill requirements. At the very least, anyone serving as a court interpreter should be required to understand and abide by the precepts set out in this Model Code. Judges and attorneys should also become familiar with the code and expect conduct from interpreters that is consistent with it." Hewitt, William E. (1995) pp. 197-98.

[25] *Id.*

[26] As of 2005, thirty-four (34) states were members of the NCSC consortium administered by its court interpreting project. Member states may then enact the code or not as they choose. Maryland, for example, has enacted the interpreter's ethical code as an appendix to the Rules of Procedure. *See* Maryland Rules of Civil Procedure, Appendix. Md. Code Conduct for Ct. Interp. (Michie 2004). States can modify the Code as well. Again, Maryland adopted the code after adding an enforcement provision that allows removal of an interpreter from the approved roster upon certain violations of the ethical code.

[27] *See also* Grabau, Charles M., & Gibbons, Llewellyn J., (1996) p. 232 for the proposition that "the court interpreter is an impartial officer of the court directly under the control and supervision of the trial judge."

[28] *Paucher v. Enterprise Coal Mining Co,*183 Iowa 86, 87 (1918).

[29] Grabau, Charles M., & Gibbons, Llewellyn J., (1996) p. 262 n.6.

[30] *Kley v. Abell,* 483 S.W.2d 625, 628 (Mo. App. 1972).

[31] (Internal citations omitted. Emphasis added). *Id.*

[32] Some courts will maintain contracts with interpreting services or with state agencies who will procure the interpreting services. In that case, it behooves legal interpreters to develop good relationships with those scheduling intermediaries and to train them with respect to the terms and conditions necessary to work in court effectively.

[33] Wright & Miller, (1990) §6056.

[34] *United States v. Bennett,* 848 F.2d 1134 (11th Cir. 1998).

[35] *Id.* at 1141.

[36] *State v. Gonzalez-Gongora,* 673 S.W.22d 811, 816 (Mo. App. 1984)(Emphasis added).

[37] This text tends to talk of the interpreter in the singular; however, the reader should keep in mind that standard practice in ASL interpreting will typically require two interpreters as the proceedings team. Outside of the legal setting, ASL interpreters have done remarkably well in establishing team interpreting working conditions and most do not work alone for any but the most mundane assignment. Spoken language interpreters both in and out of court typically work alone and are just beginning to advocate for better working conditions. Courts have been accustomed to the standards set by spoken language interpreters because the majority of interpreted proceedings are for Spanish speakers. As a result, all interpreters face stiff resistance in convincing the court to hire a team of proceedings interpreters. Best practice suggests a team be provided for proceedings over an hour in duration or in complex proceedings of any length, particularly if record interpreting is involved. *See also Commonwealth v. Pirela,* 726 A.2d 1026, 1033 (Pa.. 1999)(the basis of an ineffective assistance of counsel claim was that counsel failed to ask for a second interpreter to be appointed at trial).

[38] As noted earlier, these interpreters are typically called defense interpreters because it is in the criminal context that courts are required to provide spoken language interpreting services. They are also properly termed proceedings interpreters and sometimes they are called court interpreters which even further clouds the terminology issue. In the case of deaf Americans, the courts are statutorily required to provide access to both civil and criminal matters. ASL table interpreters for deaf civil plaintiffs then cannot logically be called defense interpreters. Wright & Miller clarified that interpreters seated next to the party are more properly termed "party" interpreters because they are not limited to

working with NES defendants but can work with plaintiffs on the civil side as well.

39 ASL interpreters call the interpreter performing this function a proceedings interpreter or a court interpreter.

40 In the context of a spoken language interpreter, a proceedings interpreter may be defined as an officer of the court who interprets all the proceedings (including all English-speaking witnesses) and all privileged communications between the attorney and the client during a proceeding. In the case where there are NES witnesses and at least one NES party, then a separate spoken language proceedings interpreting team should interpret for the witness testimony in order for the NES party to have full access to counsel during witness testimony. The issue of borrowing the spoken language table interpreter to work for NES witnesses is dealt with in section V of this chapter and often a source of controversy. Again, interpreters have the ability and obligation to establish their own working conditions and therefore should understand both optimal conditions and typical conditions.

41 For further discussion and cases on the monitor and table interpreting function see Chapter 5.

42 The commentary to Canon 3 of the NCSC Code sets forth the basic principles regarding conflicts of interest, and lists several situations in which an interpreter should not serve. The Commentary addresses *per se* conflicts of interest which prohibit the interpreter from taking the assignment. The Commentary states, in pertinent part: "The following are circumstances that are presumed to create actual or apparent conflicts of interest for interpreters where interpreters should not serve: . . . 2. The interpreter has served in an investigative capacity for any party involved in the case . . . ." Hewitt, W. (1995) pp. 202-03. The duties of the table interpreter extend to the investigative portions of the pre-trial preparation for example by interpreting the attorney's preparatory sessions with the client and other witnesses. As a direct result of interpreting these sessions, the interpreter is privy to the attorney's strategy, trial theories, plans, and will have previewed the witness' testimony.

43 *See People v. Carreon,* 198 Cal.Rptr. 843 (Cal.App. 5 Dist. 1984). Generally, these conversations during the heat of a trial are short and limited to assisting counsel in examination of a witness, pointing out discrepancies in testimony or suggesting lines of questioning for specific witnesses. An ASL interpreter can, even though seated beside the deaf person, effectively interpret these short communications without difficulty.

44 Reagan, H. (Supp. 2004) §14.

[45] *Id.*

[46] *See People v. Rivera*, 390 N.E.2d 1259 (1st Dist. Ill. 1979)(challenging the court interpreter for a witness when that interpreter had interpreted the preparation for the witness. The court stated that the challenger must make a specific showing of bias to violate due process).

[47] This is the traditional practice of spoken language interpreters; however, it should be limited to in-court privileged communications interpreting to avoid the issues just discussed about bias and rehearsing testimony. Many spoken language interpreters maintain that they are able to interpret neutrally and impartially all parts of a case without interference from information learned in prior settings. As a result, many do not consider it improper to interpret private work and then interpret for the witness' testimony.

[48] Spoken language interpreters face a similar borrowing issue when there are NES co-defendants who are required to share the same interpreter for the proceedings and for access to counsel work even if no NES witnesses are present. This issue is addressed in section V.A.2 of this chapter.

[49] The Sixth Amendment states, "In all criminal prosecutions, the accused shall enjoy the right to a speedy and public trial, by an impartial jury of the State and district wherein the crime shall have been committed, which district shall have been previously ascertained by law, and to be informed of the nature and cause of the accusation; to be confronted with the witnesses against him; to have compulsory process for obtaining witnesses in his favor, and to have the Assistance of Counsel for his defense." U.S. Const. Amend. VI.

[50] For further discussion and cases on the constitutional right to be present see Chapter 5.

[51] 35 Cal. 3d 785, 787, 677 P.2d 1198 (Cal. 1984).

[52] *Id.* at 790.

[53] This rationale could be applied equally to other state interpreting statutes which contain the "throughout the proceedings" language.

[54] *Id.*

[55] 35 Cal.3d at 790.

[56] 161 Cal.App.3d 905 (1984).

[57] *See United States v Joshi*, 896 F.2d 1303, 29 Fed Rules Evid. Serv. 1114, (11th Cir. 1990), *cert. denied*, 498 U.S. 986, 112 L. Ed. 2d 534, 111 S. Ct. 523, for the proposition that the defendant was not denied the right to a fair trial because the interpreter was located at the back of the room and interpreting through electronic equipment and was not available for immediate consultation with counsel, in part, because a second

interpreter was appointed for counsel table privileged communications interpreting. The court noted that even in the absence of a second interpreter, no reversible error would occur because the trial court permitted ample opportunity for the defendant to confer with counsel with the interpreter present.

58 *Rioz,* 161 Cal.App.3d at 908.

59 To avoid the cacophony of simultaneous whispered interpreting in a case with several co-defendants, arrangements could be made to have one team of spoken language proceedings interpreter use with the fm system and interpret all of the proceedings and all NES witness testimony, as ASL interpreters do. The remaining interpreters at the table would monitor and be available for privileged communications.

60 *Dang v. United States* 741 A.2d 1039 (D.C. 1999).

61 *Id.* at 1044.

62 *Id.*

63 D.C. Code § 31-702(b)(2001)(Emphasis added).

64 *Rioz,* 161 Cal. App.3d at 912-13.

65 *Id.* at 913.

66 Adverse parties can share *proceedings interpreters* without these concerns arising because the interpreter is an officer of the court not affiliated with either side and is only interpreting the proceedings. The proceedings interpreter stands in a different relation to the parties than the interpreter who has been assisting in private consultations and strategy sessions. In the case of spoken language interpreters, one interpreting team can interpret the proceedings for several co-parties through the use of electronic fm interpreting equipment. In the case of ASL interpreting, the proceedings interpreter in the middle of the courtroom can easily be seen by deaf people at either counsel table.

67 210 Cal.Rptr. 609 (Cal.App. 5 Dist. 1985).

68 *Id.* at 611.

69 *Resendes,* 210 Cal.Rptr. at 612, *citing, Carreon,* 198 Cal. Rptr. at 843.(Emphasis added).

70 *Resendes,* 210 Cal.Rptr. at 612.

71 28 U.S.C.A. §§ 1828 (1996), *See United States v. Johnson,* No. 98 CR 845 (Feb. 26, 2001); *United States v. Yee Soon Shin,* 953 F.2d 559, 561 (9th Cir. 1992); *United States v. Lim,* 794 F.2d 469, 471 (9th Cir. 1986); *United States ex rel. Navarro v. Johnson,* 365 F.Supp. 676 (E.D. Pa. 1973).

72 *United States v. Sanchez,* 928 F.2d 1450, 1455 (6th Cir. 1991).

73 *United States ex rel Navarro v. Johnson,* 365 F.Supp. 676 (E.D.Pa. 1973).

74 *Id.* at 683.

75 *Navarro*, 365 F.Supp. at 682-83 n.3 (Internal citations omitted)(Emphasis added).

76 *Bednarski v. Bednarski,* 366 N.W.2d 69 (Mich. App. 1985).

77 *Id.* at 70.

78 *Id.* at 71.

79 *Id.* By way of explanation, the "third interpreter for the Court" refers to making deaf witness testimony accessible to the Court through the witness interpreting function.

80 *State v. Alvarez,* 797 N.E.2d 1043, 1046 (Ohio 2003); In *Oznua v. State,* 703 N.E.2d 1093 (Ind. App. 1998), the interpreters had met the prosecution's witnesses as a part of their pretrial preparation for the case. On appeal it was argued that the meeting created the appearance that the interpreter was interested in the defendant's conviction and aligned with the prosecution. The court rejected the contention since the purpose of the meeting was to become acquainted with the witness' specific Spanish dialect. The court may have held differently if the interpreter had actually practiced the prosecution witness' testimony. Since the interpreter's behavior will be carefully scrutinized, even if the appeals are unsuccessful, the better practice is to avoid even the appearance of partiality and refrain from pretrial contact that is not geared toward preparing to actually interpret the case. For other cases appealed based upon an interpreter's prior work for one side or the other s*ee National Labor Relations Board v. Bakers of Paris, Inc.,* 929 F.2d 1427, 1439-40 (9th Cir. 1991)(appealed on the grounds that the proceedings interpreters were the same interpreters who prepared the Labor Board's case in private and that the interpreters had social relationships with some of the witnesses);

81 *See* endnote 95 and accompanying text.

82 Grice's Maxims of Communication are discussed in many works on sociolinguistics. *See generally* Hatim & Mason. (1997) p. 117-19.

83 *See* note 42 and accompanying text.

84 (Emphasis added). Hewitt, W. (1995) p. 203.

85 For further discussion on the implications for law enforcement interpreters being called to testify with respect to their prior work in a subsequent hearing, *see* Chapter 3.

86 *United States v. Sun Myung Moon,* 718 F.2d 1210 (2nd Cir. 1983); *Commonwealth v. Salim,* 503 N.E.2d 1267 (Mass. 1987)(challenging interpreter's pretrial discussions with witnesses); *People v Rivera,* 72 Ill App 3d 1027, 28 Ill Dec 669, 390 NE2d 1259 (Ill. 1st Dist. 1979)(rejecting a challenge to interpreters who had been used to prepare the state's

witnesses); *Gonzales v. State,* 372 A.2d 191 (Del. Sup. 1977)(arresting officer appointed as the court interpreter); *Chee v. United States,* 449 F.2d 747 (9ᵗʰ Cir. 1971). *See also* Chapter 5 and the discussion regarding the other duties assigned to table interpreters which militate against the interpreter functioning as a proceedings interpreter.

[87] *Ko v. United States,* 722 A.2d 830 (D.C. 1998).

[88] *Id.* at 833 n.6.

[89] *Id.* at 833.

[90] *Dang v. United States,* 741 A.2d 1039 (D.C. 1999).

[91] *Bednarski*, 366 N.W.2d at 71, n.2. The citation in *Bendarski* was taken from one of the first professional publications in the ASL interpreting field which was edited by Stephen P. Quigley called *Interpreting for Deaf People,* and created with funding from the Department of Health, Education and Welfare Social and Rehabilitation Service, Rehabilitation Services Administration, Washington, D.C.

[92] Senate Bill 371, *amending* Title 8 of the Government Code §71812.5.

[93] Superior Court Rule 109.

[94] *State v. Roldan,* 855 A.2d 455, 448 (N.H. 2004). In *State v. Izaguirre,*272 N.J. Super 51, 639 A.2d 343 (1994), the defendant objected to the use of his personal interpreter for a psychiatric interview conducted by the state. He also contended that it was unfair to use this interpreter at trial to interpret the proceedings for him because he felt constrained in his freedom to speak with counsel through an agent of the state. Though declining to reverse the defendant's conviction, the Court agreed that it is better to use separate interpreters when possible for adversarial parties' pre-trial events.

[95] It should be noted that many spoken language interpreters feel no compunction about interpreting for all aspects of a case. Many feel that the restraints discussed herein are an affront to their professional integrity and ability to interpret neutrally. Some spoken language interpreter educators even recommend interpreting at prior proceedings as a method of previewing the story and preparing for trial. The late Alicia B. Edwards, (1995) pp. 85-86 wrote:

> On the witness stand, is is (sic) especially helpful to know beforehand what the witness might say, what the general drift of his remarks will be. If you have interpreted for the witness at grand jury, you will have an idea, or if you have been at the jail with him and his attorney, you will also know. Wise trial attorneys try to use the same interpreter for trial that they used

at grand jury or at the jail, because then the story has the best chance of being fully and faithfully transmitted.

Edwards went on to suggest that the interpreter seek to have a private meeting with the witnesses to preview the content of the testimony. *Id.* at 85. To be clear, these practices run afoul of many of the statutes, cases and codes presented here.

[96] Canon 7 of the NCSC Code regarding scope of practice states: "Interpreters shall limit themselves to interpreting or translating, and shall not give legal advice, express personal opinions to individuals for whom they are interpreting, or engage in any other activities which may be construed to constitute a service other than interpreting or translating while serving as an interpreter." Attorneys face similar ethical rules prohibiting an attorney from becoming a witness in a case he or she is handling.

[97] *State v. Van Pham* 675 P.2d 848 (Kan. 1984).

[98] *Id.* at 861 (Emphasis added).

[99] *Id.*

[100] Regan, H. (Supp. 2004) §14.

[101] See section E.1 for a discussion of when an ASL table interpreter should be hired regardless of the nature of the cases.

[102] The positioning for ASL interpreters will change when and if there is a deaf witness on the stand testifying. In that case, the interpreters tend to stand side by side facing the witness stand (in the absence of a deaf party at the table). If a deaf party is at the table, and a deaf witness on the stand, the interpreters still stand together with their back to the judge and in a position where both the deaf party and the deaf witness can see the interpreters. In the absence of any unusual language differences between the deaf witness and the deaf party and as long as adequate sightlines can be maintained, no further proceedings/witness interpreters need to be retained.

Endnotes Chapter Five

[1] Hoveland, D. (1993) p. 481.

[2] A leading legal text states: "The competency of an interpreter may be demonstrated through the interpreter's trial testimony that the interpreter had no trouble communicating with the party and that the party had no apparent problem understanding the interpreter." 12A Federal Procedure, Lawyers Edition § 33:420 (2004).

[3] As mentioned in the previous chapters, when this text speaks in singular of the "proceedings interpreter" it is done for convenience and readability. The typical case for ASL interpreters is to work in teams of two certified hearing interpreters ("CHIs") when working an assignment of particular complexity, which involves witness testimony, or is of lengthy duration. Spoken language interpreters are advocating for similar working conditions but given the volume of spoken language cases compared to ASL cases, there is little chance that they will have much success in essentially convincing the courts to double their interpreting budgets.

[4] Though it may seem odd to think of whispering in ASL, it is common for fluent users to manipulate the signing space to serve the same function of keeping a signed conversation private. People tend to sign lower, down near the lap or the legs, sign smaller, shield their communications by turning their body and sign more cryptically to avoid chance comprehension of their message. These tools are employed by the table interpreter to indicate to other bilinguals in the room, particularly the proceedings interpreters, that the communications are privileged and should not be viewed or interpreted.

[5] *People v. Carreon,* 198 Cal. Rptr. 843 (Cal.App.5 Dist. 1984)(Emphasis added).

[6] *Id.* at 855 (Emphasis added).

[7] *Id.*

[8] *Id.*

[9] *Id.*

[10] *United States v. Desist,* 384 F.2d 889 (2d Cir.), *aff'd,* 394 U.S. 244 (1969). Even today in many non-criminal legal settings there is no obligation to provide spoken language interpreters and NES people may have to hire their own interpreter. For example, in most civil matters, courts are not obligated to provide interpreting services to non-English speakers though some do as a matter of fairness. In federal courts in

all civil matters except those that are brought by the government, there is no duty for the courts to provide spoken language interpreters. Deaf people are fortunate in the regard that access to interpreting services has been provided statutorily since the 1970s at the state and federal level.

[11] 434 F.2d 386 (2d Cir. 1970).

[12] Inconsistent use of terminology is always an issue as a field develops and matures. The reasons why the terms have evolved were discussed in Chapter 4. Currently, in order to distinguish the ASL interpreter's function from that of a spoken language interpreter, the interpreter is described by their physical location (at the table) or the function of the interpreter is described (the interpreter who interprets privileged conversations and monitors the working proceedings interpreters for accuracy).

[13] *Paucher v. Enterprise Coal Mining Co.,* 183 Iowa 86, 88-89 (1918).

[14] *See* www.aiic.net. (last accessed January 20, 2006), emagazine containing book review by Ruth Morris September 2000 edition of AIIC *quoting* Francesca Gaiba, (1998) *The Origins of Simultaneous Interpretation: The Nuremberg Trial.*

[15] *See* Chapter 4.

[16] *Id.*

[17] Many of the cases discussing the right to access to counsel during the time the proceedings spoken language interpreter is borrowed by the court for NES witness testimony have been discussed in detail in Chapter 4.

[18] U.S. Const. Amend. VI.

[19] A copy of the settlement agreement is available electronically at www. usdoj.gov. (last accessed November 26, 2005). After the settlement, the Monroe County Bar Association created a pool of monies to assist all solo practitioners in hiring interpreters for office conferences and counsel table work.

[20] 287 U.S. 45, 69 (1932); *See also People v. Carreon,* 198 Cal.Rptr. 843 (1984).

[21] *Holmes v. State,* 494 So.2d 230, 231 (Fla. 1986).

[22] *Id.*

[23] *See Shook v. State,* 2000 WL 877008 *2 (N.D. Miss.)(stating that a defendant's right to effective assistance of counsel is impaired when he cannot cooperate in an active manner with his attorney), *citing Riggins v. Nevada,* 504 U.S. 127, 144, 112 S.Ct. 1810, 1819, 118 L.Ed.2d 479 (1992).

[24] *Holmes,* 494 So.2d at 232.

[25] It should be noted that not all people who cannot hear use ASL or are members of the deaf community. There is a segment of deaf people who use their speech and lipreading skills to communicate. There are segments of the larger universe of deaf people who are late-defended due to accident, injury or age-related factors. There are also some deaf people who could hear, speak and understand English and who became deaf during adulthood who learned ASL and attempted to gain entry into the culture. In those cases, which are not the subject of this text, other accommodations for legal interpreting such as using real time captioning or oral interpreters may ensure linguistic competency.

[26] *People v Aranda,* 186 Cal. App.3d 230, 236, 230 Cal. Rptr. 498, 501 (2d Dist. 1986).

[27] *Id.* (emphasis added).

[28] *United States v. Cirrincione,* 780 F.2d 620, 633 (7th Cir. 1985).

[29] *Id.* at 634.

[30] For an interesting discussion on the interpreter's duty when it becomes clear that cognitive difficulties exist, *see* Morris & Colin. (1996) p. 34.

[31] *Negron,* 434 F.2d at 390.

[32] *See* Chapter 4 for cases and discussion; *see also People v. Tomas,* 484 N.E.2d 341, *cert. denied,* 475 U.S. 1067 (Il. 1985)(holding no federal right to separate interpreters).

[33] See Chapter 4 for cases and discussion.

[34] *See United States v. Huang,* 960 F.2d 1128 (2d Cir. 1992); *Mariscal v. State,* 687 N.E.2d 378 (Ind. Ct. App. 1997)(denying interpreter to non-English speaking criminal defendant violates due process clause of Fourteenth Amendment; interpreter enables non-English speaking defendant to understand trial and provides means of communication between defendant and his attorney); *People v. DeArmas,* 483 NYS2d 121 (2d Dept 1984)(reversing because the court refused to permit the witness interpreter to be used at counsel table for private conversations).

[35] *Sin v. Fischer,* 2002 WL 1751351 (S.D.N.Y.).

[36] *Id.* at *2 (Emphasis added).

[37] *Negron,* 310 F.Supp. at 1308 n.3.

[38] While proceedings interpreters should work in teams to prevent fatigue and to maintain the ability of the defendant to be fully present and receive an accurate interpretation, ASL table interpreters typically work alone during a proceeding given the relatively small amount of communication they interpret between counsel and client during the proceedings.

[39] *People v. Mata Aguilar,* 35 Cal. 3d 785, 787, 793 n.10, 677 P.2d 1198 (Cal. 1984).

[40] *People v Aranda,* 186 Cal. App.3d 230, 236, 230 Cal. Rptr. 498, 501 (2d Dist. 1986).

[41] 830 F.2d 1084 (10th Cir. 1987).

[42] *Id.* at 1088.

[43] *Id.* at 1088, n.7.

[44] *Lujan v. United States,* 209 F.2d 190 (10th Cir. 1953).

[45] The case does not mention how much time was spent in attempting to locate a suitable replacement or the resources that the court was willing to expend to bring in a replacement. However in another case, *United States v. You,* 382 F.3d 958, 962 (9th Cir. 2004), the court recessed for *twenty-four minutes* in order for the government to locate a suitable replacement interpreter. Not surprisingly, none was found.

[46] *Lujan,* 209 F.2d at 192.

[47] *Id.*

[48] Hewitt, W. (1995) p. 201.

[49] *Hernandez,* 111 S.Ct. 1859 (1991). The Ninth Circuit Court of Appeals, Criminal Jury Instructions (2000) to bilingual jurors reads as follows:
1.13 JURY TO BE GUIDED BY OFFICIAL ENGLISH TRANSLATION/INTERPRETATION
Languages other than English may be used during this trial.
The evidence you are to consider is only that provided through the official court [interpreters] [translators]. Although some of you may know the non-English language used, it is important that all jurors consider the same evidence. Therefore, you must base your decision on the evidence presented in the English [interpretation] [translation]. You must disregard any different meaning of the non-English words.

[50] Rameriz , R. (1993) p. 771.

[51] *Id.* at 776.

[52] *Prokop v. State,* 28 NW2d 200 (Neb. 1947).

[53] *Id.* at 201.

[54] *United States v. Kramer,* 741 F.Supp. 893 (S.D. Fla. 1990).

[55] *Id.* at 895.

[56] *Santana v. New York City Transit Authority,* 505 N.Y.S.2d 775 (Sup.Ct. 1986).

[57] *Id.* at 777.

[58] *Id.* at 778.

[59] *United States v. Perez,* 658 F.2d 654, 662 (9th Cir. 1981).

[60] *Id.*

[61] *Dias v. State,* 743 A.2d 1166, 1176 (Del. 1999).

[62] *Id.* at 1175.

[63] *Id.*

[64] *United States v. Chang Guo You,* 382 F.3d 958 (9th Cir. 2004).

[65] *See State v. Burris,* 643 P.2d 8 (Az. 1982)(stating that the parties have the right to cross examine both the proceedings interpreter and the defense interpreter with respect to the extent of the alleged interpreting errors).

[66] Hewitt, W. (1995) pp. 206-07.

[67] *State v. Mitjans,* 408 N.W.2d 824, 832 (Minn.1987).

[68] *Id.*at 831-32.

[69] *State v. Her,* 510 N.W.2d 222, 223 (Minn. 1994).

[70] *Id.*

[71] *Santos v. Ashcroft,* 2004 WL 1447831 *1 (9th Cir.).

[72] *See* Chapter 6, note 54 for an explanation of written English representation of ASL signs.

[73] Russell, D. (2002) pp. 52-54.

[74] In a rather serious custody trial the author was conducting, the interpretation for the deaf mother who was fighting for custody of her children was generally accurate. However, the manner in which the interpreter spoke was rhythmic, lyrical and presented in a sing-song manner. The deaf witness appeared nonchalant about important issues such as her proposed parenting plan if she was awarded custody. The manner in which the interpretation was produced affected the believability of her testimony.

[75] As a final caveat, the table interpreter should *never* directly communicate with any deaf witness who is testifying on the stand.

[76] *Valladares v. United States,* 871 F.2d 1564, 1566 (11th Cir. 1989).

[77] *State v. Casipe,* 5 Haw. App. 210, 214, 686 P.2d 28, 32 (1984); *State v. Her,* 510 N.W.2d 218, 222 (Minn. 1994)(holding that there was no clear standard for whether the testimony was understandable, comprehensible and intelligible, though the interpretation was adequate); *same United States v. Gomez,* 908 F.2d 809 (11th Cir. 1990)(holding the translation error did not render the trial fundamentally unfair so as to require a reversal); *People v. Koch,* 618 N.E.2d 647 (1 Dist. N.Y. 1993).

[78] *United States v. Cirrincion,* 780 F.2d 620, 633-34 (7th Cir. 1985).

[79] *Kley v. Abel,* 483 S.W.2d 625, 628 (Mo. App. 1972); *see also Denton v. State,* 945 S.W.2d 793 (Tenn. Crim. App. 1996)(finding a rebuttable

presumption that the court-appointed interpreter will interpret accurately and the presumption can be rebutted any time a challenge is made to the interpretation).

[80] *State v. Casipe*, 5 Haw. App. 210, 686 P.2d 28 (1984); *State v. Van Pham*, 234 Kan. 649, 675 P.2d 848, 860 (1984); California Evidence Code §664.

[81] Hovland, D. (1992) p. 501.

[82] *Id.*

[83] *State v. Her*, 510 N.W.2d 222 (Minn. 1994).

[84] Reagan, H. (2004 Supp.) at §37. Several years ago, the author was observing an interpreted trial where the court ordered the interpreters to sit in the jury box at a right angle to the deaf party who was ordered to sit in the audience.

[85] 675 P.2d 848, 856, 858 (Kan. 1984).

[86] *Id.* at 862.

[87] Federal Rule of Evidence 103 Rulings on Evidence states "(c) *Hearing of jury.* In jury cases, proceedings shall be conducted, to the extent practicable, so as to prevent inadmissible evidence from being suggested to the jury by any means, such as making statements or offers of proof or asking questions in the hearing of the jury."

[88] Once, the author was interpreting for a witness and being monitored by an interpreter for the state in a criminal matter. The monitoring interpreter chose to stand at the end of the jury box between the jury and the audience. During deaf witness testimony, the author mispronounced a name. The monitoring interpreter yelled across the jury box to correct the pronunciation of the word. If the officer of the court mantle is to be meaningful, interpreters must strive to maintain the integrity of the proceedings in the *least disruptive manner.*

[89] *See also State v. Van Pham*, 675 P.2d 848, 860 (Kan. 1984)(stating that merely because an interpreter has had some problems in translating, [that is] not sufficient to rebut this presumption); *United States v. Urena*, 27 F.3d 1487, *cert. denied*, 130 L.Ed.2d 364 (10th Cir. Kan. 1994)(minor errors are permitted).

[90] Federal Rule of Evidence 103 states in pertinent part "Error may not be predicated upon a ruling which admits or excludes evidence unless a substantial right of the party is affected, and in case the ruling is one admitting evidence, a *timely objection or motion to strike appears of record,* stating the specific ground of objection. . . ."

91 *Denton v. State,* 945 S.W.2d 793 (Tex. 1997), *citing,* Leo Bearman, Jr., Esq., *Competency and Impeachment of Witnesses* 57 Tenn. L. Rev. 89 (1985).

92 *U.S. v Joshi,* 896 F2d 1303 (11ᵗʰ Cir. 1990).

93 *State v. Her,* 510 N.W.2d 218 (Minn. 1994).

94 The case received great public attention because a local reporter attended the trial and noted many of the errors in the news reports.

95 *United States v. Guerra,* 334 F.2d 138, 142 (2d Cir. 1964).

96 *Id.*

97 *Kan v. State,* 4 S.W.2d 38 (Tex. 1999).

98 *Denton,* 945 S.W.2d at 800.

99 *Van Pham,* 675 P.2d at 858.

100 *See Nioum v. Commonwealth,* 128 Ky. 945, 946-47 (1908)(holding that since there was no side by side translation pointing out where the errors were and submitted to the appellate court, the court had no way to independently determine the severity of any alleged errors); *accord Claycomb v. State,* 211 P.2d 429 (Okla. 1923).

101 For videotape case references in general see, *Hernandez v. State* (1984, Fla App D4) 444 So 2d 1165; *State v Auria* (1991, Ohio App, Erie Co) 1991 Ohio App LEXIS 6104, *motion granted,* 65 Ohio St 3d 1434, 600 NE2d 677, *cause dismissed* 65 Ohio St 3d 1461, 602 NE2d 1170. *State v. Avria,* 65 Ohio St.3d 1434, 600 N.E.2d 677, *cause dismissed* 65 Ohio St. 3d 1461, 602 N.E.2d 1170. Two prior cases had the original record preserved for later post-conviction review by a linguist.

102 28 U.S.C. § 1827(d)(2)(1996). *See also, United States v. Ojeda-Rios,* 714 F. Supp. 600 (D.P.R. 1989), in which the defendant claimed that he had a right to have his case conducted in Spanish. Because Mr. Ojeda-Rios was proceeding without an attorney, the Court permitted him to conduct his opening and closing statements in his mother tongue. The Spanish would be interpreted simultaneously into English for the court reporter and taped for review in case of an error. The court stated "should any objection to the English translation be raised, it may then be verified and corrected, if necessary." Id.

103 *People v. Mendes,* 219 P.2d 1 (Cal. 1950).

104 *Id.* at 4.

105 *Guerra,* 334 F.2d at 143. This rationale is frequently articulated by appellate courts to avoid reversing a conviction based upon interpreted errors. *See also People v. Koch,* 618 N.E.2d 647 (1 Dist. 1993)(stating that minor testimonial inconsistencies arising from linguistic misunderstandings do not warrant reversal of conviction).

[106] *Id.*

[107] *See generally* Russell, D. (2002); Taylor, M. (1993); Cokely, D. (1992).

[108] *United States v. Anguloa,* 598 F.2d 1182 (9th Cir. 1979).

[109] *Id.* at 1184.

[110] *Id.* at 1185.

[111] *Id.*

[112] *Id.* at 1185 n.3, *citing,* H.R.Rep. No. 95-1687, 95th Cong., 2d Sess. 4, *reprinted in* [1978] 4 U.S.Code Cong. & Admin. News, pp. 4652, 4655.

[113] 470 U.S. 68, 76 (1985).

[114] *Id.* at 77.

[115] *People v. Cardenas,* 62 P.3d 621 (Colo. 2003); *Rey v. State,* 897 S.W.2d 333 (Tex. Crim. App. 1995); *State v. Gonzalez,* 752 S.W.2d 695 (Tex. 1988).

[116] Reagan, H. (2004) at § 2.

[117] *Id.*

[118] *Id.* at §1.

[119] *See* cases collected Fleming, T. (1995) §65.

[120] 675 P.2d 848, 860 (Kan. 1984).

[121] *Id.* at 861.

[122] *Id.*

[123] *United States v. Sun Myung Moon,* 718 F.2d 1210 (2nd Cir.), cert den, 466 U.S. 971 (1983).

[124] *Id.*

[125] *People v. Mata Aguilar,* 35 Cal. 3d 785, 677 P.2d 1198 (Cal. 1984).

[126] *Id.* at 793.

[127] 210 Cal.Rptr. 609, 612-13 (Cal App. 5 Dist. 1985) (Emphasis added).

[128] *Id.* at 613.

[129] Ramirez, D. (1993) p. 781.

[130] *Id.* at 781-82.

[131] *See* settlement agreement between United States Department of Justice and Greg Tirone, Esquire available at www.usdoj.gov. (last accessed November 25, 2005).

[132] The Justice Department stated in its analysis of the regulations "the Department has already recognized that imposition of the cost of courtroom interpreter services is impermissible under section 504. Accordingly, recouping the costs of interpreter services by assessing

them as part of court costs would also be prohibited." *Cited at* <u>www. nad.org</u>. (last accessed November 25, 2005).

[133] *Commonwealth v. Belete,* 37 Mass. App. Ct. 424, 640 N.E.2d 511 (1994).

[134] *Id.* at 427.

[135] *Matter of Appointment of an Interpreter in State v. Tai V. Le,* 517 N.WS.2d 144 (Wisc. 1994).

Endnotes Chapter Six

1 *State in the Interest of R.R.,* 398 A.2d 76, 85-86 (NJ 1979).

2 *State v. Watson,* 190 So.2d 161, 167 (Fla.1966).

3 *Commonwealth v. Festa,* 341 N.E.2d 276, 283 (Mass. 1979).

4 Morris, R. (1993) p. 203.

5 *People v. Rivera,* 2004 WL 1276711 *12 (S.D.N.Y.)(Emphasis added).

6 *Id.*

7 Taylor, M. (2002) p.2.

8 Metzger, M. (1999) p. 22.

9 Even though the conduit model of interpreting was discredited in the 80s, it has enjoyed resurgence with the advent of video relay interpreting ("VRS") as regulated by the Federal Communications Commission ("FCC"). The FCC's regulations were originally designed to govern telephone relay operators who type messages to deaf people on special equipment. Relay operators must know how to type quickly, but otherwise fluency in ASL is unnecessary. Section 401 of Title IV, found in Section 225, of the Communications Act of 1934, as amended, requires that Telephone Relay Service be offered and defines Telephone Relay Service as:

    [T]elephone transmission services that provide the ability for an individual who has a hearing impairment or speech impairment to engage in communication by wire or radio with a hearing individual in a manner that is *functionally equivalent* to the ability of an individual who does not have a hearing impairment or speech impairment to communicate using voice communication services by wire or radio.

    Though admirable as a goal, defining the interpreter this way does not guarantee an accurate product. With respect to the FCC and VRS services, it remains to be seen whether the droves of highly qualified interpreters who were initially attracted to the decent pay and working conditions will have much of a shelf life after working with VRS on a long term basis.

10 *United States v. Torres,* 793 F.2d 436, 443 n.10 (1ˢᵗ Cir. 1986).

11 *Id. See also State in Interest of R.R., Jr.,* 398 A.2d 76, 86 (N.J. 1979).

12 *United States v. Anguloa,* 598 F.2d 1182, 1186 (9ᵗʰ Cir. 1979).

13 The RID Code of Professional Conduct lists under its second principle of professionalism, the interpreter's obligation to render the message faithfully conveying the content and the spirit of what is being

communicated, using language most readily understood by consumers, and correcting errors discretely and expeditiously.

[14] Hewitt, W. (1995) p. 200.

[15] *Id.*

[16] National Association of Judiciary Interpreters and Translators, Code of Ethics ad Professional Responsibility, Canon 1 Accuracy. Available at www.najit.org (last accessed December 21, 2005).

[17] Hewitt, W. (1995) p. 200 (Emphasis added).

[18] *Stubblefield v. Commonwealth,* 392 S.E.2d 197 (Va. 1990).

[19] *Id.* at 200-01. (Emphasis added). *See also State v. Alvarez,* 797 N.E.2d 1043, 1044-45 (Ohio 2003).

[20] *United States v. Long,* 301 F.3d 1095, 1105 (9th Cir. 2002).

[21] This fear is illustrated by a joke in interpreter circles which has a judge admonishing an interpreter to start interpreting since he had been speaking for awhile. The interpreter faced the court and stated, "Your honor, I will interpret when you say something important."

[22] National Association of Judiciary Interpreters & Translators. Position Paper: Summary Interpreting in Legal Settings. Available online at www.najit.org (last accessed December 21, 2005).

[23] *United States v. Torres,* 793 F.2d 436 (1st Cir. 1986).

[24] *Id.* at 439.

[25] *Id.* at 439-40.

[26] *Id.* at 443.

[27] *Commonwealth v. Festa,* 341 N.E.2d 276, 283 (Mass. 1979).

[28] Larson, M. (1998) p. 10.

[29] Hewitt, W. (1995) p. 201.

[30] Larson, M. (1998) p. 61-62.

[31] *Id.* at 62.

[32] *Id.* at 110.

[33] *Ortega v. State,* 659 S.W.2d 35, 36-37 (Tex. 1983). According to the case, "ya cstuvo ya me lo heche," which was translated to mean "That's it, I've done him in." Rubio was expected to testify appellant said to him "ya estuvo lo marcho," which was translated to mean "That's it, He's gone." The interpreter stated, "That's it, literally it would be he marched him."

[34] Berk-Seligson, S. (1999) p. 39.

[35] ASL transcription conventions include the following. All capital letters are used for English representations for signs. When two English words are joined by a minus sign, the two glosses are represented by one

sign, or are signed together without pausing. Fingerspelled words are indicated by capital letters separated by hyphens. Pauses are indicated by spaces. When an English word is followed by a + it means the sign is repeated once for each + symbol.

[36] FRE 611. *See also State in the Interest of R.R.,* 398 A.2d 76 (NJ 1979)(permitting leading questions when a witness is young or has difficulty communicating).

[37] ASL and signed English are different in structure, semantics and, to a large degree, lexicon. Further, each signer using a manual representation of English will vary in the amount of English word order used and the amount of ASL in the signed rendition. Some signers will use ASL signs to represent the concepts in the order they appear in the spoken English utterance. If there is no counterpart to an English word, there is no sign produced though the word may be represented on the mouth to facilitate speech reading. This is called **mouthing** by interpreters. Some signers will use contrived signs for the English words that have no ASL counterparts in conjunction with mouthing. Over the years, the educational system has created signing systems to represent words and parts of words that do not have counterparts in ASL. For example, ASL does not use helping verbs. These English-based systems have created separate signs for the various helping verbs. Another difference is that ASL represents past tense by a time-indicator sign at the beginning of the utterance. All subsequent information is assumed to be in the past tense until another time-indicator sign is used. English indicates tense by suffixes affixed to the verb. The English-based signing systems have created signs to represent the various suffixes. Some signers will use some or all of these contrived signs with or without mouthing when they sign in English word order. Linguists have, for years, attempted to describe the "wintry mix" that results when signers attempt to sign in English word order. Currently, in vogue is the term *language contact.* For the purposes of this text, I describe it as English-like signing or signing in English word order.

[38] *See* Johnson, Lidell & Erting (1989).

[39] Lawson, M. (1998) p.169.

[40] *See* Pullum, G. (1991).

[41] Lawson, M. (1998) p. 174.

[42] *Id.* at 164.

[43] Mindess, A. (1999) p. 49.

[44] Larson, M. (1998) p.104.

[45] *Id.* at 181.

46 *Id.* at 171, 180.

47 *Id.* at p. 181.

48 *People v. Murphy,* 114 N.E. 609 (Ill. 1916).

49 Larson, M. (1998) p. 177. Examples from spoken languages follow the transcription conventions used in the source text.

50 *Id.* at 178.

51 *Bednarski v. Bednarski,* 366 N.W.2d 69, 71 (Mich. App. 1985).

52 *Id.*

53 *Id.* at 71 n. 4, *citing,* Quigley, S. (1965) p. 56.

54 In *Garcia v. State,* 887 S.W.2d 862 (Tex. 1994), the Texas Court held that while the appointment and qualifications of an interpreter (competency) are legal questions that can be reviewed on appeal, the *accuracy* of a translation is a non-appealable jury question. It is not grounds for appeal that the jury did not believe a particular witness. In Texas, if there are differing views of the accuracy of the interpretation, both views are presented to the jury who determines which to believe. The accuracy of interpretation, similar to witness credibility, is determined by the jury and is not a proper subject for appeal.

55 *People v. Rivera,* 390 N.E.2d 1259, 1268 (Ill. 1979).

56 *State v. Burris,* 643 P.2d 8, 14 (Az 1982).

57 *Id.* (holding that an interpreter's competency may be attacked by direct or cross examination or even by independent testimony).

58 *Kan v. State,* 4 S.W.3d 38, 41 (Tex. 1999).

59 Interestingly, the Federal Court Interpreting Act, 28 U.S.C. § 1827, *et seq.,* requires consecutive interpretation for NES witnesses because it recognizes that when the interpreter is in control of the timing of the source language input, the interpretation in the target language is more accurate. The court, always concerned about time, generally prefers the speed of simultaneous interpretation at the expense of accuracy.

60 *Id.*

61 *United States v. Torres,* 793 F.2d 436, 443 (1st Cir. 1986).

62 Hewitt, W. (1995) p. 208.

63 *Id..*

64 It is not unusual for interpreters in the post-secondary setting to require that they are given the course textbooks during a class. They review the materials prior to each class in order to be able to provide a more effective and consistent interpretation. If a deaf person is taking the lead on an assignment, it is common for the interpreter to meet with the person ahead of time, obtain an outline and discuss the person's

goals for the presentation. These standards have been in place for years in community interpreting. Interpreters have access to far less in legal proceedings, yet it is perplexing that many do not take advantage of what is available.

[65] The author has been a litigator since 1993, and a good portion of her practice in court is with deaf clients. Sadly, she can count on one hand the number of times a court interpreter has asked her for any preparation materials prior to a proceeding.

[66] NAJIT Position Paper on Preparing Interpreters in Rare Languages. Available at www.najit.org (last accessed December 21, 2005). While the paper addresses rare languages, the principles in the preparation section are equally applicable to preparation for all interpreters.

[67] Hewitt, W. (1995) p. 203. *See also Ozuna v. State,* 703 N.E.2d 1093 (Ind. 1998); *People v. Rivera,* 390 N.E.2d 1259 (Ill. 1979) for case in which the interpreter's pretrial interpreting for the parties formed a basis for appeal.

[68] Hewitt, W. (1995) p.17 (Emphasis added).

[69] *Tamayo-Reyes v. Keeney,* 926 F.2d 1492, 1495 (9th Cir. 1991).

[70] *United States v. Anguloa,* 598 F.2d 1182, 1183-84 (9th Cir. 1979); *see also Stubblefield v. Commonwealth,* 392 S.E.2d 197 (Va. 1990).

[71] *Id.* at 1184.

[72] *People v. Starling,* 315 N.E.2d 217 (Ill. 1 Dist. 1974).

[73] *Starling,* 315 N.E.2d at 222.

[74] *Echemendia v. State,* 735 So.2d 555, 555-56 (Fla. 3 Dist. 1999).

[75] *Id.* at 555.

[76] *Ledezma v. State,* 626 N.W.2d 134, 149 (IA 2001).

[77] *Id.*

[78] *Id.* at 149.

[79] The author has experienced the same issue of being unable to judge the accuracy of the interpretation when deaf people call through the **video relay service ("VRS").** It is common for an attorney to give limited legal advice to callers; however, when communicating directly the attorney can gauge the caller's reaction personally and knows for certain what specific advice was given. Through the medium of an interpreter, the attorney has no way to know whether their words were unchanged. If the attorney provides legal advice which is relied upon by the deaf person and it turns out the interpretation was inaccurate, the deaf person can claim they were injured (and they could have been) by relying on the inaccurately interpreted advice. The deaf person's

recourse is against the attorney. The attorney has no recourse against the interpreter.

[80] In *People v. Allen,* 317 N.E.2d 633 (Ill. 1 Dist. 1974), a conviction was reversed because the defendant had complained that the interpreter used was a friend of the complaining witness and was prejudiced against him.

[81] *State In the Interest of R.R,* 398 A.2d 76, 85-86 (N.J. 1979)(mother of a four-year-old victim should not have been permitted to interpret because she had an interest in seeing that the respondent was punished).

[82] *State v. Tamez,* 506 So.2d 531, 533 (La.App. 1 Cir. 1987).

[83] *Commonwealth v. Kozec,* 487 N.E.2d 216, 223 (Mass. App. 1975); *Peoples National Bank v. Manos Brothers,* 84 S.E.2d 857 (S.C. 1954)(permitting a witness to interpret*); Claycomb v. State,* 211 P. 429 (Okla. 1923)(permitting a witness' husband – who was also a witness – to interpret for her).

[84] *United States v. Addonizio,* 451 F.2d 49 (3rd Cir. 1972).

[85] *Renick v. Hayes,* 201 Ky 192 (1923).

[86] *Id.*

[87] *People v. Allen,* 317 N.E.2d 633 (Ill. App. 1974).

[88] Hewitt, W. (1995) p. 202-03, 209.

[89] Hewitt, W. (1995) p. 203.

[90] *Id.*

[91] *Id.*

[92] Russell, D. (2002) p. 131.

[93] *Commonwealth v. Festa,* 341 N.E.2d 276, 283 (Mass. 1979).

[94] *State v. Alvarez,* 797 N.E.2d 1043, 1044-45 (Ohio 2003).

[95] *Prokop v. State,* 28 N.W.2d 200 (Neb. 1947).

[96] *Prokop,* 28 N.W.2d at 202. *See also Santana v. New York Transit Authority,* 505 N.Y.S.2d 775, 779 (Sup. 1986)(stating in any trial where an interpreter's services are required, the party/witness, at the outset, is placed at a disadvantage – Much of the impact and demeanor of the party/witness becomes obscured by the presence of an interpreter).

[97] *People v. Cunningham,* 546 N.W.2d 715 (Mich. 1996).

[98] *Id.* at 716. (Emphasis added).

[99] *Id.*

[100] *Stubblefield v. Commonwealth,* 392 S.E.2d 197 (Va. 1990).

[101] *Commonwealth v. Stubbfield,* 392 S.E.2d 197, 199 (Va. 1990).

[102] Hewitt, W. (1995) p.206.

[103] *See* note 37 and the accompanying text and *see generally* Johnson, R., Liddell S., & Erting C. (1989).

[104] Federal Rule of Evidence 605 states "the judge presiding at the trial may not testify in that trial as a witness. No objection need be made in order to preserve the point." *See also* Harrison, D. (2005).

[105] *State v. Mitjans,* 408 N.W.2d 824, (Minn. 1987)(holding that the court interpreters should have been required to interpret for the police officer's version of the *Miranda* warning in order for the appellate court to have a record to know if the officer's version was correct).

[106] *Hernandez v. State,* 978 S.W.2d 137 (Tex. 1998); *see also Rodriguez v. New York City Housing Authority,* 626 N.Y.S.2d 240, 242 (2 Dept. 1995)(holding it was an error to permit the court interpreter to testify as to the meaning of a Spanish term used in a prior hearing); *State v. Rodriguez,* 169 N.E.2d 444, 450 (Oh. 1959)(holding that interpreters should not be permitted to give their opinions about what they think the NES witness's testimony means).

[107] *People v. Ovalle,* 307 N.W.2d 685 (Mich. 1981). It should be obvious that membership in the bar does not confer any special level of expertise in language assessment.

[108] *State v. Aquino-Cervantes,* 945 P.2d 767 (Wash. App. 1997).

[109] Hewitt, W. (1995) pp. 200-01, 207.

[110] *Ledezma v. State,* 626 N.W.2d 134, 149 (Iowa 2001).

[111] *Id.* at 149.

[112] *Id.* at 149.

Index